D1527186

The Anti-dumping Agreement and Developing Countries

The Anti-dumping Agreement and Developing Countries

An Introduction

Aradhna Aggarwal

OXFORD
UNIVERSITY PRESS

OXFORD
UNIVERSITY PRESS

YMCA Library Building, Jai Singh Road, New Delhi 110 001

Oxford University Press is a department of the University of Oxford. It furthers the
University's objective of excellence in research, scholarship, and education
by publishing worldwide in

Oxford   New York

Auckland   Cape Town   Dar es Salaam   Hong Kong   Karachi
Kuala Lumpur   Madrid   Melbourne   Mexico City   Nairobi
New Delhi   Shanghai   Taipei   Toronto

With offices in

Argentina   Austria   Brazil   Chile   Czech Republic   France   Greece
Guatemala   Hungary   Italy   Japan   Poland   Portugal   Singapore
South Korea   Switzerland   Thailand   Turkey   Ukraine   Vietnam

Oxford is a registered trademark of Oxford University Press
in the UK and in certain other countries

Published in India by Oxford University Press, New Delhi

© Oxford University Press 2007

The moral rights of the author have been asserted
Database right Oxford University Press (maker)

First published in 2007

ISBN 13: 978-0-19-568927-3
ISBN 10: 0-19-568927-5

Typeset in AGaramond 10/12 at Le Studio Graphique, Gurgaon 122 001
Printed in India at DeUnique, New Delhi 110 018
Published by Oxford University Press
YMCA Library Building, Jai Singh Road, New Delhi 110 001

Contents

Tables and Figures

APPENDIX TABLES

FIGURES

Abbreviations

AB	Appellate Body
ADA	Anti-dumping Agreement
ADD	Anti-dumping duty
ADP	Anti-dumping practices
APO	Administrative Protective Order
ASCM	Agreement on Subsidies and Countervailing Measures
ASG	Agreement on Safeguard
CADIC	Comparative Analysis of the Domestic Industry's Condition
CITT	Canadian International Trade Tribunal
CPM	contingent protection measures
CU	Custom Union
CVD	countervailing duty
DEPB	Duty Entitlement Passbook Scheme
DSB	Dispute Settlement Body
DSU	Dispute Settlement Undertaking
EC	European Commission
EEA	European Economic Area
EFTA	European Free Trade Association
EINTAD	EU—India Network on Trade and Development
EU	European Union
FAN	The Friends of Anti-dumping Negotiation
FDI	foreign direct investment
FTA	free trade agreement
GAP	Group on Anti-dumping Policies
GATS	General Agreement on Trade in Services
GATT	General Agreement on Tariffs and Trade
GIMELEC	Groupement des industries de l'équipement électrique, du contrôle-commande et des services associés
	Groupement des industries de l'equipement electrique, du controle-commande et des services associes (French Industry Association for Electrical Equipment, Automation and Related Services)
GSP	Generalized System of Preferences
HFCS	High Fructose Corn Syrup

IP	investigation period
ITA	International Trade Administration
ITC	International Trade Commission
ITO	International Trade Organization
MFA	Multi-fibre Arrangement
MFN	most favoured nation
NAFTA	North American Free Trade Agreement
NME	non-market economies
NTB	non-tariff barriers
OECD	Organisation for Economic Co-operation and Development
PET	Polyethylene terephthalate
PSF	Polyester Staple Fibre
PTY	polyester textured filament yarn
QR	quantitative restrictions
R&D	research and development
S&D	special and differential
SAA	Statement of Administrative Actions
SAIL	Steel Authority of India Limited
SIMA	Special Import Measures Act
SGA	administrative, selling, and general costs
SPS	Sanitary and Phytosanitary Agreement
SSG	Special Safeguards
SWR	Steel Ropes and Cables
TBT	Technical Barriers to Trade
TMB	Textile Monitoring Body
TNC	Trade Negotiations Committee
TRIPS	Trade Related Intellectual Property Rights
UNCTAD	United Nations Conference on Trade and Development
USDOC	United States Department of Commerce
USITC	United States International Trade Commission
WTO	World Trade Organization

Foreword

The surge of antidumping practice in the 1990s in many countries has triggered an intense debate over the contents of the anti-dumping agreement of the WTO and its implementation. This in turn has led to a growing literature studying the legal and economic implications of the agreement. While some have raised questions about the ambiguities in the antidumping regulations and procedures as spelt out in the agreement, others have questioned the economic rationale behind such provisions. Several suggestions have also been made to contain the use of anti-dumping. This book draws on the extensive research in this area and addresses the legal and economic issues raised by the anti-dumping agreement from a developing country perspective.

This volume examines the genesis and evolution of the agreement and reviews the evolution of the legal provisions in the existing agreement. It provides an analytical overview of the agreement from a developing country viewpoint and investigates the use of anti-dumping in the developed and the developing countries in a comparative framework. Reviewing the various economic and non economic justifications of anti-dumping offered in the literature, the study analyses the macro-economic factors which motivate the developed and the developing countries to use anti-dumping. It critically examines the wide ranging proposals for reform of the WTO antidumping code and offers suggestions for the current round of negotiations. The analysis endorses the view that antidumping provisions are anti-competitive and are fraught with serious ambiguities. The legal provisions of the agreement are highly biased against the developing countries, harming them both as users and targets. Developing countries must therefore push hard to achieve meaningful reforms with regard to strengthening the provisions in the current round on S&D treatment (Chapter 15).

The book will be not only useful to students, researchers, academicians, and negotiators but also to non-technical audience in business and politics. It will generate further debate on this very important and topical subject and will help clarify the issues that need urgent attention.

Isher Judge Ahluwalia
Chairperson
Indian Council for Research on
International Economic Relations

Acknowledgements

This study draws on my research carried out at ICRIER during my tenure there first as a senior fellow and then as a consultant. It is a part of the research output on WTO-related issues, which has been funded by the research grant from the Sir Ratan Tata Trust to ICRIER. I owe my deepest gratitude to Isher Judge Ahluwalia who introduced me to the world of WTO when she invited me to work on anti-dumping related issues at ICRIER in 2001. She lent her whole hearted support to this project and arranged valuable guidance whenever sought. She invited P.K.M. Tharakan, University of Antwerp, for a series of lectures on anti-dumping at ICRIER, FICCI, and CII to stimulate initial thoughts on anti-dumping related issues and took deep interest in the progress of the work. I also thank her for writing the foreword for my book. I must express my sincere gratitude to P.K.M. Tharakan for his valuable advice and comments on preliminary drafts of various papers that I published at ICRIER. I am deeply indebted to the DGAD, Ministry of Commerce, for inviting me to attend various seminars it organized and present my papers. My thanks are due to Abhijit Dasgupta, Sharad Bhansali, A.K. Gupta, and Parthasarthy for providing me insight on this highly complex issue. Sharad Bhansali had been extremely patient with me when I held my first interview with him to understand the finer nuances of this law. A part of the study is published in World Development. I must express my sincere thanks to the anonymous referees of the journal whose comments were the source of inspiration for me to extend my work in the form of a book. I would also like to thank Michael Friis, Danish Institute of International Studies, Copenhagen and Hilda, National Board of Trade, Sweden for inviting me to present my research findings to the policy makers there. The question–answer sessions were extremely stimulating and laid the foundation of the book. My special thanks are due to Arvind Virmani for encouraging me to compile my research in the form of a book.

I would also like to express my gratitude to my teachers and mentors K.L. Krishna and N.S. Siddharthan who always encouraged me to do quality research, believed in me, and stood by me. This book is my tribute to their dedicated and selfless devotion to their profession. I wish to emulate them and imbibe their principles in my life. I would like to thank my ICRIER friends

Nisha Taneja, Renu Kohli, Rama Goyal, and Shubhobrota for giving me moral support in my endeavour.

As mentioned above, parts of this study also formed the basis for seminars organized by the Ministry of Commerce, Management Development Institute, Gurgaon, Institute of International Studies, Copenhagen, National Board of Trade, Sweden, ICRIER, New Delhi. I am grateful to the participants at the seminars for their constructive suggestions.

I acknowledge the valuable support given by Radhika Ayengar, Bandita, Karan Singh, and Pragyan Deb in handing and processing the data during various stages of my research. Pragyan who joined me in the last stages of this book was excellent. But for his enthusiasm and dedication, the completion of this manuscript would have taken considerably longer.

Finally, on a personal note, I would like to acknowledge that the greatest debt is due to my son for his patient bearing with my long hours of work. I knew that I was stealing his share of my time and that he was missing my company but he never ever complained. It is with a sense of great gratitude that I dedicate this book to him. My husband had been a source of encouragement as usual. I would like to take this opportunity to express my sincere gratitude to him for his role in my career. I would be failing in my duty if I do not express my gratitude to my parents, my father in particular who taught me to dream and make efforts to fulfill them.

1 Introduction

In this era of globalization, trade and trade policies are becoming critical component of economic strategies of an increasingly large number of developing countries, which are embracing international economic integration (or globalization). But an overwhelming evidence in recent years indicates that trade liberalization has generated benefits that have been much smaller than estimated earlier and are very unevenly distributed across countries (UNCTAD 1999, Easterly 2001, Shafaeddin 2005, Ackerman 2005, Stiglitz and Charlton 2004, DeLong and Dowrick 2003, and Dowrick and Golley 2004 among many others).[1] According to a recent UNCTAD study of 46 developing countries (Shafaeddin 2005), the experience of the majority of the countries, mostly in Africa and Latin America, has not been satisfactory. The study shows that only 40 per cent of the sample countries have experienced rapid expansion of exports of manufactured goods. In fact, half of the sample, most of them low income countries, have faced de-industrialization. Slow growth of exports and de-industrialization has also been accompanied by increased vulnerability of the economy, the manufacturing sector in particular, to external factors. There is, thus, a growing realization that the priorities of the world's developing economies should be made key to the ongoing progress of trade liberalization and that the World Trade Organization (WTO), as the maker and arbiter of international trade rules, should play a supporting role in fulfiling developing countries' development goals and contribute significantly in promoting the beneficial integration of Third World nations into the world economy. Developing countries now form a formidable bloc[2] and the absence of any recognition of their problems would undermine the credibility of the WTO and its advocacy of trade liberalization. There is therefore need to ensure that the system fosters, rather than undermines, development.

The preamble of the WTO itself treats trade liberalization as a means of promoting sustainable broad-based economic growth only if it is designed to ensure that developing countries secure a share in the growth in international trade commensurate with the needs of their economic development. In fact, it refers to the 'special and differential status' of the developing countries as the guiding principle for the WTO. It reads as follows:

The Parties to this Agreement,

Recognising that their relations in the field of trade and economic endeavour should be conducted with a view to raising standards of living, ensuring full employment and large and steadily growing volume of real income and effective demand, and expanding the production of and trade in goods and services, while allowing for the optimal use of the world's resources in accordance with the objective of sustainable development, seeking both to protect and preserve the environment and to enhance the means for doing so in a manner consistent with their respective needs and concerns at different levels of economic development.

Recognising further that there is need for positive efforts designed to ensure that developing countries, especially the least developed among them, secure a share in the growth in international trade commensurate with the needs of their economic development ...

Despite the mandate to link trade with sustainable development and the differentiated needs of member countries, the overall preoccupation of the WTO until recently remained on trade liberalization; the development agenda remained neglected. It was with these considerations in mind that Trade Ministers finally launched the Doha Development Agenda at the Doha Ministerial Conference in November 2001. This agenda has made development issues and the interests of poorer members a central consideration of trade negotiations. Interestingly, even though the WTO preamble indicates that trade liberalization and rule making must support sustainable development and take account of the capacities and constraints of developing countries in all negotiations, the development needs of these countries have been made an explicit objective for negotiations in this Round only. This Round should therefore be considered an important opportunity to address the most fundamental and critical issues from the perspective of developing countries and ensure that these countries are able to take greater advantage of the WTO rules and procedures.

One of the critical challenges faced by developing countries is how to increase market access, particularly to 'developed countries'. This developed country bias exists because these countries offer the most significant markets for the exports of the developing countries (the law of comparative advantage). However there still exists a wide variety of trade barriers in these countries, which are mainly biased against developing countries' exports. These developed country trade barriers include tariff peaks and tariff escalation for agricultural and labour-intensive goods, agricultural subsidies (for exports and domestic production), rules of origin, pyramid trade preferences, anti-dumping rules, and contingent protection measures. Perhaps the most egregious of these barriers (in the non-agricultural goods sector) is anti-dumping duties.[3] There has been a great proliferation in the use of anti-dumping cases for the past twenty-five years and it has emerged as the most widespread trade impediment under the WTO regime.

Anti-dumping is the most important contingent protection measure provided in the General Agreement on Tariffs and Trade (GATT)/WTO framework, with countervailing duties and safeguard protection being the other instruments. Between 1995 and 2005, the number of anti-dumping cases initiated accounted for 89.1 per cent of the total of these three main contingent measures used. The share of countervailing duties and safeguard remained as small as 7.1 per cent and 3.8 per cent respectively over this period. WTO records show that during 1991–2000 there were 2,675 anti-dumping cases, an average of over 267 cases per year, while there were no more than 12 cases per year between 1947 and 1968 (Guasch and Rajapatirana 1998).

Until the late 1980s, the use of anti-dumping remained confined to developed countries, while the developing countries were only on the receiving end. In the late 1980s, developing countries also started employing anti-dumping measures. Although these countries have dramatically increased their use of anti-dumping measures, they nevertheless remain the main victims of such measures. It is believed that without improving the disciplines of the Anti-dumping Agreement (ADA), benefits from further tariff liberalization will be seriously undermined for developing countries (Neufeld 2001). A joint statement issued by the senior officials responsible for trade of several developing countries[4] in Geneva on 5 February 2003 recognized that 'as part of a single undertaking, substantial results in the AD negotiations are a key component of overall market access liberalization, and are essential for the success of the Doha Development Agenda'. Developing countries therefore need to systematically identify their interests, set realistic objectives, and pursue these objectives by formulating technically sound proposals. This requires a deep understanding of the issues relating to the ADA. While reviewing the Doha Negotiations, Panagariya (2002) observes that much of the negotiating power continues to reside with developed countries while developing countries suffer from lack of research capacity and strategic thinking. The message is clear. Developing countries must improve clarity of the issues to negotiate effectively in the multilateral trade rounds.

Against this background, this book analyses the legal and economic issues stemming from the use of anti-dumping law from a developing country perspective. In particular, it analyses the experience of developing countries vis-à-vis the ADA of the GATT/WTO. The objectives of the study are as follows:

- It looks at the genesis and evolution of the Agreement from the perspective of the developing countries.

- It reviews the evolution of the legal provisions in the existing agreement and provides an analytical overview of the current ADA in a non-technical manner from a developing country viewpoint.
- It investigates the use of anti-dumping in developed and developing countries in a comparative framework.
- It delves into various economic and non-economic justifications of anti-dumping use, empirically analyses the macroeconomic factors motivating the developed and developing countries to use anti-dumping.
- It critically examines wide-ranging proposals for the reform of the WTO anti-dumping code.
- Finally, it offers suggestions regarding the proposals that these countries need to focus on in the current round of negotiations.

The study notes that the Agreement and its implementation both are heavily biased against the developing countries. The law was designed by the developed countries, who later shaped the multilateral agreement pertaining to the law to cater to their requirements. There is a fundamental flaw in the basic concept of 'dumping' itself in the agreement from the *developing country perspective*. According to the Agreement, 'a product can be said to be dumped by an exporter if it is being introduced into the commerce of another country at less than its normal value, or more particularly, if the export price of the product exported from one country to another is less than the comparable price, in the ordinary course of trade, for the like product when destined for consumption in the exporting country' (Article 2.1 of the ADA). However, a huge proportion of developing countries' exports is unfair when judged by this criterion. These economies, many of which are high-cost producers, segregate their production structures for domestic and export markets and extend special facilities to the production for export markets to enable the firms to break into these markets, which is not possible otherwise. Their home market prices are therefore likely to be higher than the export prices in most cases, which could easily be condemned as dumping under the Agreement. Even though developing countries voiced their concern over the applicability of the definition in their context, no concession was given to them in this provision.

Furthermore, legal provisions of the Agreement are overlegalized, complex, arcane, and plagued with several conceptual and technical problems and that reforms introduced in these provisions in various rounds of negotiation have been of little value to the developing countries. Implementation of these provisions is highly discretionary and subjective and allow multiple interpretations by domestic administrative authorities. These ambiguities increase the technical and legal complexity of this regime and provide huge room for maneuverability within the rules, which developed countries exploit intensively to realize their objectives. Poor countries on the other hand do not have the wherewithal and legal expertise either to deal with anti-dumping cases directed against them or to exploit the ambiguities in the Agreement in a WTO-consistent manner while conducting the investigations initiated by themselves.

The study also analyses the use of anti-dumping by developed and developing countries in a comparative framework and finds that the use of the tool is also biased against the developing countries. While analysing the international use of anti-dumping most scholars look at the large number of total anti-dumping investigations initiated by the developing countries. This study argues that one must be cautious in drawing ambitious conclusions from this statistics alone. There is evidence that United States and the EU still far outdistance even the most active user among the developing countries. Furthermore, a detailed analysis of the use of anti-dumping tool suggests that it is still not widespread among the developing countries. Very few developing countries have acquired the capability to use it. The number of developing countries targeted in these cases is much larger.

The study reveals that the effects of anti-dumping actions weigh heavily against the developing countries. In most cases, developing countries have a very small share in trade. When they initiates a case, it does not significantly affect the exports in the target country, especially if the target country is a developed country. On the other hand, in cases where a developing country's exports are challenged by a developed country, its effect could be highly destabilizing. This can undermine a developing country's interest in reallocating resources to the affected export sector. An important implication of this asymmetry is that the costs of such actions may be especially severe for developing countries when targeted because anti-dumping actions applied by countries with major markets can have a devastating impact on their emerging competitive industries with serious consequences for the entire economy. Ironically, the use of these actions can also cause huge losses to them. There is evidence[5] that anti-dumping actions involve huge welfare costs for both developed and developing countries; but while the developed countries are in a position to bear high protectionist costs, for developing countries it may mean substantial reversal of gains expected by them from trade liberalization. Clearly, heavy costs are imposed on developing countries both as targets and users of this tool.

While the use of anti-dumping has been surging, it is not clearly known what is the justification of the tool. The agreement is silent on this. This has triggered an intense debate among economists, legal experts, and bureaucrats. Three major approaches have evolved over time due to this debate: the political approach, the economic approach, and the political economy approach. The study critically examines these approaches and econometrically analyses the factors that affect filing patterns in developed and developing countries. It finds that the use of anti-dumping is systematically related with macroeconomic factors in both developed and developing countries. The conclusion supports the view acknowledged among economists that anti-dumping has become the tool of choice for industries seeking protection in both developed and developing countries. However, while developed countries invoked the use of anti-dumping tool to provide protection to the domestic producers from internal business cycles, developing countries made use of the tool on the basis of the balance of payment consideration. Developing countries have recently started opening up their economies. To sustain the process of liberalization in these economies it is important that the national industry has a safety net to protect it from foreign competition during the initial stages and the country does not have balance of payment crisis. The industry should be able to gain a significant market share within the domestic market, before this cover is taken off. The WTO also recognizes this infant industry argument to make concessions in various agreements. Developed countries however have no valid excuses to provide safety valves to protect the industry from internal business cycles.

Furthermore, the study presents evidence to suggest that developing countries sometimes initiate anti-dumping actions primarily to develop the capacity to challenge the cases targeted against them and post some retaliatory threats. In this endeavour, perhaps they target other developing countries first, which obviously are the soft targets. This generates a chain effect resulting in an increasing number of cases involving developing countries both as defendants and complainants. Thus the increasing use of the tool against developing countries itself is partly responsible for the increasing use of the tool by them.

In view of the above findings, the study argues that the use of anti-dumping must be restrained especially against developing countries. It critically examines wide-ranging proposals for reforming the agreement to control its use. These include both hard and soft proposals. While hard proposals call for fundamental reforms in the law, soft reforms seek incremental changes in several substantive and procedural aspects of the agreement, which presently run against the interests of the developing countries. The study finds that from a practical point of view, incorporating 'fundamental reforms' in the law is not a realistic option. Refining the existing provisions of the law is a practical option but it may not be effective in restraining the use of anti-dumping. While negotiating on such proposals developing countries need to be highly selective and should focus on remedying the existing imbalances and attempt to set suitably focused negotiating parameters to safeguard their interests. *The goal of negotiations should be to restrict the use of the tool against them* and not to facilitate the use of anti-dumping. For this they must press hard for expanding the provision of 'special regard' that they are promised under the Agreement. This will allow them significant relief from anti-dumping rules without the need for more contentious changes to the rules.

WTO negotiations on anti-dumping are being undertaken in the Negotiating Group of Rules. Negotiations in the area of 'WTO rules' relate to the following subject matter: the Agreement on Implementation of Article VI of GATT 1994 (better known as the Anti-dumping Agreement); The Agreement on Subsidies and Countervailing measures, and in this context, WTO disciplines on fisheries subsidies; and WTO provisions applying to regional trade agreements. Anti-dumping has been the most active area of the rules negotiations. During the first phase of negotiations, participants pointed to the provisions in the Anti-dumping and Subsidies agreements that they would like to clarify or improve in the subsequent phase. From the 141 submissions tabled, most of them on the ADA, the chairman issued a compilation of issues and proposals (TN/RL/W/143). During the second phase after Cancun, the Group began meeting in informal sessions to consider more detailed and specific 'elaborated proposals'. The detailed exchanges gave the Group a clearer idea of what exactly the proponents were seeking, and at the same time provided the proponents valuable feedback on what proposals may or may not attract broad support. In the spring of 2005, the chairman launched the third phase of negotiations by adding bilateral and plurilateral consultations for rigorous consideration of legal texts of proposed amendments to the relevant agreements. However, the draft ministerial text and the rules annex could not report consensus on any negotiating issue. This shows how hotly this issue is being debated in the current round of negotiations. The Hong Kong Ministerial Declaration merely reaffirmed the members' commitment to the negotiations on rules as mandated in the Doha Ministerial Declaration. It insisted on the need to clarify and improve disciplines with a view to strengthening the due process, transparency, and predictability of such proceedings and measures to facilitate its implementation and to curb the protectionist use of anti-dumping measures. Advancing the Doha negotiations in the post-Hong Kong period, the mini-ministerial held on the sideline of the Davos World Economic Forum in January 2006 set a December-end deadline to conclude the Doha Round. On anti-dumping measures, it was decided that a proposal in the form of a legal draft would be ready by July 2006. However, these deadlines were missed. At the WTO Trade Negotiations

Committee (TNC) on 24 July 2006, the director general of the WTO recommended that the Doha Round negotiations be suspended as a result of the inability of key players to reach agreement on issues related to agriculture and industrial goods. The Doha Round was suspended in July and there had been no meetings, no scheduled negotiating group meetings on the WTO agenda for several months. Since February this year, the WTO has resumed the negotiations on the Doha Development Round. In this context, this study is an attempt to suggest a way forward for developing countries.

We now summarize the issues treated in individual chapters that comprise this book.

Chapter 2 explains the notion of contingent protection within the WTO framework and provides an overview of the various agreements in the WTO relating to contingent protection in a non-technical manner. It discusses the legal provisions of the three trade remedy agreements, namely anti-dumping, countervailing (anti-subsidy), and safeguard measures and explains differences in them. While doing so, it discusses the contents and characteristics of the three trade remedy rules in a comparative framework. It also examines time trends in the use of contingent protection measures. The analysis in this chapter shows that there has been an alarmingly high proportion of anti-dumping measures in total contingent protection investigations and that this had made it an important research topic.

Chapter 3 looks back on the genesis and history of negotiations relating to anti-dumping. In particular, it examines the role and concerns of developing countries in various rounds and the extent to which these were addressed. It reveals that developing countries have historically played only a minor role in the evolution of the law. Uruguay Round was the first major attempt by the developing countries to participate in the negotiations earnestly. The final outcome however was determined by the two powerful players, namely, the United States and the European Union (EU). An early and earnest participation by the developing countries could not turn the outcome in their favour.

Chapter 3 also examines the evolution of the major legal provisions through various rounds and presents a critical examination of the existing provisions particularly from the viewpoint of the developing countries. While a number of studies have discussed the ambiguities in various provisions of the current agreement, there has been little examination of how anti-dumping provisions evolved over time. This chapter examines the changes introduced in major provisions relating to dumping finding, injury finding, and administrative procedures in different rounds and shows how insignificant the reforms have been in addressing the real issues. Refinements added further vagueness and complexities to the agreement. As a result, the current legal provisions relating to anti-dumping remain highly subjective, complex, and ambiguous and that there is enormous potential of their misuse. Such a complex legal regime with huge potential of misuse requires that a country should have access to substantial financial and legal resources to effectively protect its rights. Since developing countries have both a limited 'legal capacity' and familiarity with the complex international legal regimes, this puts them at a disadvantage.

Chapter 4 then presents research concerning the use of anti-dumping in both developed and developing countries. It analyses the trends and patterns of the use of anti-dumping measures broken down by country group and by time period. Much of the existing literature focuses on the number of initiations/measures imposed per year. However, the number of initiations and measures per year do not reflect the rigour with which the tool is used. It is captured by various aspects such as the number of measures in force (actual measures), duration of the duties, duty rates, and trade effects. This chapter presents information on these aspects of anti-dumping use also. The analysis indicates that there is a clear-cut evidence of a bias against developing countries. Even though the number of cases initiated by developing countries has increased, only a few of them are using it actively. A few developed countries are still responsible for a large proportion of the cases initiated and since these countries account for a large chunk of world trade, their actions are also responsible for hitting the world trade originating from developing countries very adversely. Developed countries that are preaching trade liberalization to these countries are themselves turning to anti-dumping to protect their markets against developing countries' exports. This may lead to marginalization of these countries in the process of globalization and defeat the purpose of the multilateral agreement.

Chapter 5 deals with theoretical explanations of the justification of anti-dumping. It identifies three major perspectives of anti-dumping: the political perspective, the economic perspective, and the political economy perspective and describes them. It also examines whether in practice the actual use of anti-dumping measures can be justified from the standpoint of any of the perspectives explained in the chapter. The analysis is based on a comprehensive review of the existing theoretical and empirical literature. It then empirically investigates the macroeconomic determinants of anti-dumping filings in developed and developing countries in a comparative framework using the 'political economy approach'. It draws on the existing literature to identify a number of possible motives of the users of anti-dumping and empirically examines, using a panel data set of ninety-nine countries over the period

1980–2000, which of the motives receive support in the data. The analysis in the study reveals that anti-dumping rules do not necessarily prevent 'unfair' competition in international markets. They are primarily aimed at providing protection. A more important finding of this exercise however is that the political economy factors that motivate anti-dumping use differ across developed and developing country groups and that the use of anti-dumping actions against developing countries itself prompted the use of the tool by them, at least partly.

Chapter 6 critically assesses different policy options advanced by scholars to reform ADA. These proposals that vary widely from eliminating anti-dumping laws to refining their provisions are placed under two categories: hard proposals and soft proposals. While hard proposals seek fundamental reforms in anti-dumping rules, soft proposals centre around refining the existing provisions without changing the basic characteristics of the Agreement. This chapter stresses the need for a fundamental reform of current anti-dumping rules. These rules have enormous potential for protectionist abuse in the current form. This chapter argues that enhancing them in such way as to incorporate the basic principles and objectives within the agreement can minimize this risk. What could be the basic principles? Since consensus is not at any time reached in the economic and legal debate about the merits and necessity of alternative perspectives of anti-dumping, it argues that it does not matter whether such principles are provided by the political perspective, the economic perspective, or the political economy perspective. What is important is that the law must have clear-cut objectives to achieve and the rules should be closely realigned and harmonized with those basic principles and objectives. It argues that such reforms can go a long way in eliminating a number of unwarranted cases. The chapter critically reviews various proposals regarding how the rules can be realigned with the basic objectives within the framework of different perspectives. It also examines whether such reforms have been introduced in the Regional Trade Agreements and if yes, what approaches have been adopted in such cases. It concludes with a pessimistic note that introducing such reforms at the multilateral level is perhaps a distant dream. Countries that matter are not willing to introduce these reforms even at the regional level. It is therefore more realistic to acknowledge that the practical solution lies in refining the existing provisions termed 'soft reform proposals'. This chapter then critically reviews a number of specific proposals offered for reforming the existing ADA. These proposals address the provisions that allow the authorities to use their discretionary powers. Wherever possible, quantitative thresholds are proposed to be added to the key provisions. It is expected that these reforms would only reduce gap between the ADA as they exist and are practiced but would not contain the use of anti-dumping. This chapter concludes that the developing countries need to be very selective and cautious while negotiating on these proposals. There is no justification in harmonizing the standards across countries due to the difference in the level of development. They should focus only on those proposals that directly benefit them without wasting efforts on fine technical details. Besides, they should press for more fundamental reforms within the existing framework. It proposes to consider two such proposals: inclusion of a public interest test and strengthening of the S&D treatment.

Chapter 7 explores, first, the possibility of reforming the agreement by addressing the issue of 'balancing of interests' of producers and consumers. A public-interest test, if properly devised and implemented, can help to reconcile a country's anti-dumping policy with its larger national interests. All concerned stakeholders such as consumer groups, producers, and importers would be involved before a decision to impose anti-dumping measures is taken. The chapter discusses the rationale of mandating the inclusion of a public interest clause in the Anti-dumping Agreement and offers in detail proposals of how inclusion of a public interest test should be applied. It also discusses the possible costs and time implications of the proposal. After weighing pros and cons it argues that it might affect the interests of the developing countries asymmetrically. It, then, reviews the evolution of the S&D treatment from a historical perspective, discusses the relevance of updating them, and provides inputs and possible alternatives for future negotiations. It suggests that operationalizing the 'special and differential treatment' is the key instrument to safeguard the interests of the developing countries in regard to anti-dumping use. Updating the S&D instruments is perhaps the only way to remedy the existing imbalances in the agreement. Tightening of the rules may not go far in restraining the use of anti-dumping and a public welfare test may put heavy administrative burden on the developing countries. In this scenario, developing countries need to focus on how to operationalise the 'special and differential treatment' provision to derive the maximum benefit out of the current round negotiations.

Notes

1 A large body of literature has also examined the impact of financial integration on growth. While reviewing empirical research on (financial) liberalization and growth, a study by the International Monetary Fund, one of the main proponents of liberalization, concludes that there is as yet no clear and robust empirical proof that the effect of financial liberalization on growth is quantitatively significant (Prasad et al. 2003, p. 1).

2 As of today, there are 148 members of the WTO, of which more than 70 per cent are developing countries.

3 Others include: agriculture, services, technical barriers, textiles, and intellectual property rights.

4 These included : Brazil; Chile; Colombia; Costa Rica; Hong Kong, China; Israel; Korea; Mexico; Singapore; the Separate Customs Territory of Taiwan, Penghu, Kinmen, and Matsu; Thailand; and Turkey. Also included the officials from developed countries namely Japan, Norway, and Switzerland.

5 USITC (1995) and Gallaway et al. (1999) examined the net aggregate effects of all US anti-dumping and counter-vailing duties orders for 1991 and 1993, respectively, using a computable general equilibrium model. While the USITC estimated the loss at $1.6 billion, the latter found that the welfare loss ranged from $2 to $4 billion annually.

2 Understanding Contingent Protection

As described in the previous chapter, anti-dumping actions are contingent protection measures permitted under Article VI of GATT/WTO rules. To begin with, therefore, it is crucial to understand what contingent protection is all about. This chapter addresses some basic questions relating to contingent protection. What is contingent protection? What is the rationale of including contingent protection measures in the GATT/WTO framework? What are major legal provisions of different agreements relating to contingent protection measures? Which measures of contingent protection are used more commonly than the others? This chapter begins with explaining the notion of contingent protection and the rationale of their presence within the WTO framework. It also provides an overview of articles embedded in the WTO agreements relating to various contingent protection measures. The next section compares major provisions of various agreements dealing with contingent protections. The third section examines time trends in the use of contingent protection measures. The penultimate section analyses the trends in contingent protection use across countries on the basis of the level of development. The last section concludes the analysis.

CONTINGENT PROTECTION: AN OVERVIEW

GATT 1947, which bound the original twenty-three members to a multilateral free trade agreement, had envisioned an elaborate plan for trade liberalization. Its objective was to eliminate or substantially reduce tariffs and other trade barriers on the basis of reciprocity and mutual advantage. In 1994, GATT 1947 culminated in the Agreement establishing the WTO. Although a great deal of substantive international trade laws have changed, the GATT's cornerstone principles remain the same. WTO agreements are thus based on following three fundamental principles of the GATT:

- the principle of progressive trade liberalization;
- the principle of non-discrimination between trade members; and
- the principle of reciprocity.

    The first principle provides for the reduction and elimination of tariffs and other non-tariff barriers (NTB) to trade through multilateral negotiations.

It prohibits countries from using quantitative restrictions (QR), except in specified cases. Protection can be extended only through tariffs and is kept at low levels. Tariffs are reduced and the tariffs so reduced are listed on a tariff-line basis in each country's schedule of concessions. The rates given in these schedules are known as bound rates. Countries are under an obligation not to increase tariffs above the bound rates shown in their schedules.

The second principle dictates trade to be conducted on the basis of non-discrimination between members of the WTO. This principle is embodied in Article 1 (most favoured nation, MFN) and Article 3 (national treatment) of the WTO Agreement. Article 1 requires that countries can not discriminate between their trading partners (giving them equally MFN status), while Article 3 requires countries not to discriminate between their own and foreign products, services, or nationals.

According to the third principle, a country requesting improved access to the market of other countries, through tariff reductions or the removal of other barriers such as quantitative restrictions, must be ready to make concessions in tariffs and other areas that those countries consider to be advantageous and of reciprocal or equivalent value to the concessions that they are making.

In some circumstances, a country may *temporarily* break these principles and impose higher protection (breaking the first principle) against import of one or more goods from one or more countries (in disregard of the second principle) without being subject to the (third) principle of full reciprocity. These exceptional arrangements, which depart from the fundamental principles of the WTO, are termed 'contingent trade protection provisions'. They are based on the realization that openness might make economies vulnerable to injury due to adverse trade shocks and that any government that maintains an open trade regime must have some sort of flexibility to adjust to these shocks (see Dam 1970, Fischer and Prusa 1999 for formal analysis). Contingent protection measures allow member countries to temporarily protect the domestic industry facing competition either from imports that are artificially under priced, usually as a result of 'foreign subsidies or other unfair trade practices' (Nivola 1993, p. 30) or from a surge of imports that though are fairly traded might have caused serious injury to the domestic industry. These arrangements are thus designed to secure fair conditions of trade. Even though they depart from the fundamental principles of the WTO, the rationale of including them in the Agreement is to 'ensure free and fair trading environment'.

These provisions fall under two categories: (i) measures that ensure remedies against unfair trade and (ii) measures that provide remedies against surge in imports. Within the WTO framework, contingent protection is taken to mean the safeguard measures, which are a remedy against increase in imports, and anti-dumping and countervailing duties, which address the issue of unfair trade.

The Anti-dumping Agreement

The Agreement on Implementation of Article VI of GATT 1994, popularly known as the WTO ADA, allows governments to act against dumping where there is 'material' injury to the competing domestic industry. Typically, anti-dumping action means charging extra import duty on the particular product from the particular exporting country in order to bring its price closer to the 'normal value' to remove the injury to domestic industry in the importing country. In order to do that the government has to show that dumping is taking place, calculate the extent of dumping (how much lower the export price is compared to the exporter's home market price), and show that the dumping is causing injury or threatening to do so. Therefore, a detailed investigation has to be conducted within the specified set of rules. The WTO ADA sets the standards for the conduct of anti-dumping investigations including initiation of cases, calculation of dumping margins, the application of remedial measures, injury determinations, enforcement, reviews, duration of the measure, and dispute settlement. National laws need to be in consonance with the WTO Agreement on anti-dumping.

The first Anti-dumping Code was negotiated during the Kennedy Round and entered into force in 1967. Its disciplines were improved further during the Tokyo Round (Tokyo Code). The current ADA came into force upon the establishment of the WTO on January 1, 1995, and superseded the Tokyo Code. It is divided into three parts and two important annexes. Part I, covering Articles 1 to 15, contains the definitions of dumping (Article 2) and injury (Article 3) as well as all procedural provisions that must be complied with by importing member authorities wishing to take anti-dumping measures. Articles 16 and 17 in Part II establish respectively the WTO Committee on Anti-dumping Practices (ADP) and special rules for WTO dispute settlement relating to anti-dumping matters. Article 18 in Part III contains the final provisions. Annex I provides procedures for conducting on-the-spot investigations while Annex II imposes constraints on the use of best information available in cases where interested parties insufficiently cooperate in the investigation. In what follows we provide a brief overview of the substantive legal provisions of the Agreement.

Principle of using anti-dumping measures (Article 1)

- Under the Agreement 'An anti-dumping measure shall be applied only under the circumstances provided for in Article VI of GATT 1994 and pursuant to investigations initiated and conducted in accordance with the provisions of this Agreement.' (Article 1). GATT 1947 applies only to goods. This implies that dumping of services is not covered.

Determination of dumping margins (Article 2)

- Dumping has been defined as the type of *price discrimination* between national markets. Conceptually, the calculation of dumping is a comparison between the export price and a benchmark domestic price, the normal value of the like product (Article 2.1). Article 2.6 defines the like product. Within the like product, there will invariably be many types or models. To give a simple example, in the case of colour TVs, colour TVs with different screen sizes (14", 20", 24") will constitute different models. For calculation purposes, authorities will then normally compare identical or very similar models or types.

- Three special situations are envisaged in which the authorities can reject the actual data on normal value (Article 2.2). These are: (i) when there are no sales of the like product in the ordinary course of trade in the domestic market of the exporting country; (ii) when volume of sales in the domestic market of the exporting country are low; and (iii) when because of the particular market situation such sales do not permit a proper comparison. Two alternative methods for constructing normal value are provided in such cases: use of 'appropriate' third country export price or the constructed normal value. The constructed value in the country of origin is required to be based upon the sum of the production costs, overhead expenses, and reasonable profits.

- In some cases, the export price may also not be reliable. Thus, where the exporter and the importer are related, the price between them may be unreliable because of transfer pricing reasons. Article 2.3 therefore provides that the export price then may be constructed on the basis of the price at which the imported products are first resold to an independent buyer. In such cases, allowances for costs, duties, and taxes incurred between importation and resale and for profits accruing, should be made.

- Article 2.4 of the Agreement lays down as key principle that a fair comparison shall be made between export price and the normal value. This comparison shall be made at the same level of trade, normally the ex-factory level, and in respect of sales made at as nearly as possible the same time.

- Article 2.4.2 contemplates basic rules for calculating dumping margins. Under the article prices in the two markets shall normally be compared on a weighted average to weighted average basis or on a transaction-to-transaction basis. Under exceptional conditions however weighted average normal value may be compared to prices of individual export transactions.
- Where products are not imported directly from the *country of origin* but are exported from an intermediate country, the export price shall normally be compared with the comparable price in the *country of export*/country of transshipment (Article 2.5).
- Last, Article 2.7 confirms the applicability of the second supplementary provision to paragraph 1 of Article VI in Annex I to GATT 1994, the so-called non-market economy provision. Under this rule, the investigating authority may reject the prices or costs in non-market economies as an appropriate basis for the calculation of normal value and resort to prices or costs in a third market-economy country as the basis for normal value.

Injury analysis (Article 3)

- The determination of injury consists of a determination that the dumped imports have caused material injury/threat of injury/material retardation to the domestic industry; the domestic industry is defined to include the domestic producers as a whole of the like products or those of them whose collective output of the products constitutes a major proportion of the total domestic production. Articles 3.1 and 3.2 provide details on injury determination. The determination of material injury shall involve an objective examination of the volume of the dumped imports, the effect of the dumped imports on prices in the domestic market for like products and the consequent impact of these imports on the domestic producers of such products. A list of 15 injury factors that must be evaluated by the investigating authority is provided in Article 3.4. Articles 3.7 and 3.8 describe special rules for a determination of threat of material injury.
- The practice of cumulation is permitted by Article 3.3, which means that imports from several countries are simultaneously subject to anti-dumping investigations. It specifies the conditions under which their effects may be assessed cumulatively for injury purposes.
- The demonstration of the causal link must be based on an examination of all relevant evidence before the authorities. The injurious effects of all other factors (other than dumped imports) must also be examined and the injury resulting from such factors must not be attributed to dumped imports. This is known as the non-attribution rule.

Procedural provisions (Article 5–15)

- An anti-dumping case normally starts with the official submission of a written complaint (application) by the domestic industry to the importing member authorities that injurious dumping is taking place. Article 5.2 contains the requirements for the contents of this application. It must include *evidence* on dumping, injury, and the causal link between the two; simple assertion is not sufficient. Article 5.3 imposes obligation on the importing member authorities to examine, before initiation, the accuracy and the adequacy of the evidence in the application.
- Under Article 5.4 of ADA, importing member authorities must determine *before* initiation that the application has been made by, or on behalf of, the domestic industry. The underlying requirement is that no investigation shall be initiated when domestic producers expressly supporting the application account for less than 25 per cent of total production of the like product.
- Authorities are required to reject an application and terminate investigations when the margin of dumping is *de minimis* (less than 2 per cent of the export price) *or* when the volume of dumped imports actual or potential from the subject countries, is negligible (less than 3 per cent of imports of the like product in the importing member individually and less than 7 per cent collectively) *or* when injury is negligible (Article 5.8).
- Article 5.10 provides that investigations shall normally be concluded within one year and in no case more than 18 months, after their initiation.
- Throughout the anti-dumping investigation all interested parties (i.e. the domestic producers, foreign producers and exporters, importers, the government of the exporting country, and representative trade associations) shall have a full opportunity for the defence of their interests. Article 6 contains various due process rights of interested parties. Authorities are required to provide timely opportunities for all interested parties to see all non-confidential information. Furthermore, it is envisaged (Article 6.5) that while confidentiality must be protected, summaries of confidential information must be made available to interested parties to facilitate informed debate by interested parties. Article 6.8 (with Annex II) of the Agreement provides that in cases where an interested party refuses access to, or otherwise does not provide, necessary information within a reasonable period or significantly impedes the investigation, preliminary and final determinations, affirmative or negative, may be made on the basis of the facts available.
- Articles 7 through 9 provide rules on provisional measures, price undertakings, and imposition and collection of anti-dumping duties ADD.

- Article 10 stipulates that ADDs may be levied retroactively for the period for which provisional measures, if any, have been applied. This type of retroactivity is often applied by importing members. Under certain conditions a definitive ADD may be levied on products that were entered for consumption not more than 90 days prior to the date of application of provisional measures. This type of retroactivity is seldom applied because the conditions are very stringent.
- Article 12 obliges importing member authorities to publish public notices of initiation, and of preliminary and final determinations.

Reviews

- The ADA recognizes three types of reviews of anti-dumping measures: new shippers' reviews, interim (mid-term) reviews, and expiry (sunset) reviews. Article 9.5 requires importing member authorities to carry out reviews requested by newcomers, that is producers who did not export during the original investigation period. Article 11 contains the provisions for interim and expiry (sunset) reviews. Definitive ADDs normally expire after five years from their imposition (sunset clause), unless the authorities determine in expiry reviews that the expiry of the duty would be likely to lead to continuation or recurrence of dumping and injury. However, during the five-year period also, interested parties may request the authorities to review the decision, hence the interim or mid-term review.

Judicial Reviews

- Article 13 provides that members, who do adopt anti-dumping legislation, must also maintain independent judicial, arbitral, or administrative tribunals or procedures for the purpose of prompt review of administrative final and review determinations.

Special and differential treatment to developing countries

- Article 15 recognizes that special regard must be given by developed country members to the special situation of developing country members when considering the application of anti-dumping measures under this Agreement.

Part II: Committee on Anti-dumping Practices (Articles 16–17)

- Article 16 lays down rules for the establishment and functioning of a Committee on ADP. It requires members to report without delay to the Committee all preliminary or final anti-dumping actions taken.
- Countries are obliged to bring their national laws in line with the Agreement. The Anti-dumping Committee is charged with reviewing

national legislations, and countries are required both to notify the relevant laws to the Committee and to respond to questions from other countries about their systems.

Procedures related to dispute settlement (Article 17)

- Common rule of dispute settlement do not apply to anti-dumping. While Articles XXII and XXIII of the GATT 1994 create a legal basis for claims in disputes relating to provisions of the GATT 1994, Article 17 of the ADA addresses dispute settlement under that Agreement. Article 17.6 provides special provisions in the Agreement relating to settlement of disputes in the anti-dumping area which *inter alia* require panels not to challenge 'the evaluation of facts' made by the investigating authorities, where 'establishment of facts was proper and the evaluation was unbiased and objective'.

- The ADA specifies the types of 'measure' which may be referred as part of a 'matter' to the Dispute Settlement Body (DSB). Three types of anti-dumping measures are specified in Article 17.4: definitive anti-dumping duties, the acceptance of price undertakings, and provisional measures. A 'matter' may be referred to the DSB only if one of the relevant three anti-dumping measures is in place.

Part III: Final provisions (Article 18)

- No specific action against dumping of exports from another member can be taken except in accordance with the provisions of GATT 1994, as interpreted by this Agreement.

Agreement on Subsidies and Countervailing Measures (ASCM)

The ASCM embodied in Article XVI of GATT 1994 aims at the unfair trade practices of governments, allowing the imposition of compensatory duties on imports of products that are benefiting from trade distorting subsidies given by the exporting country governments. Subsidies are of concern to the members of the WTO/GATT system because they can undermine market access commitments by importing nations and tilt the playing field 'in a way that is unfair to the importing country'. A country can use the WTO's dispute settlement mechanism to seek the withdrawal of a subsidy or the removal of its adverse effects (multilateral remedy). Alternatively, it can launch its own investigation and ultimately charge extra duty (known as 'countervailing duty' in short 'CVD') on subsidized imports that are found to be hurting domestic producers. CVD can only be charged after the importing country has conducted a detailed investigation *similar to that required for anti-dumping action.* There are detailed rules for deciding whether a product is being subsidized (not always an easy calculation), criteria for determining whether imports of subsidized products are hurting ('causing injury to') domestic industry, procedures for initiating and conducting investigations, and rules on the implementation and duration (normally five years) of countervailing measures (see also Horlicks and Clarke 1994, Vermulst 2000, Sykes 1989, Marvel and Ray 1995, Andoh 1992). Only a measure which is a 'specific subsidy' (targets for subsidization, a particular company/companies or a particular sector/sectors or specified regions or export goods using domestic inputs) is subject to multilateral remedies can be subject to countervailing measures.

The GATT treatment of subsidies has historically been controversial and the disciplines weak notably because of policy differences between the United States and the EC (UNCTAD 2003). A Subsidies Code was agreed upon in the Tokyo Round, but it skirted around important issues. The Uruguay Round Agreement on Subsidies and Countervailing Measures is a major improvement over previous regimes, because it provides for the first time a definition of 'subsidy', lays down detailed standards for the conduct of countervailing duty investigations, and provides a workable multilateral discipline over subsidies (Schott 1994). The current agreement is divided into eleven parts. These are as follows:

Part I: General (Articles 1–2)

- This part contains a definition of subsidy. It also introduces the concept of a 'specific' subsidy—that is, a trade distorting subsidy available only to an enterprise, industry, group of enterprises, or group of industries in the country (or state, etc.) that gives the subsidy. The disciplines set out in the Agreement apply to only specific subsidies. They can be domestic or export subsidies, prohibited or actionable subsidies.

Part II: Prohibited subsidies (Article 3–4)

- Under the Agreement export subsidies and import substitution subsidies are prohibited (Article 3). Prohibited subsidies are deemed and presumed to be specific.
- A member can seek the withdrawal of the subsidy through the dispute settlement mechanism. Article 4 lays down rules for multilateral remedies against prohibited subsidies. Whenever a member has reason to believe that a prohibited subsidy is being granted or maintained by another member, such member may request consultations with such other member. If no mutually agreed solution has been reached within 30 days of the request for consultations, any member party to such consultations may

refer the matter to the DSB. In the event the recommendation of the DSB is not followed within the time period specified by the panel, which shall commence from the date of adoption of the panel's report or the Appellate Body's (AB) report, the DSB shall grant authorization to the complaining member to take appropriate countermeasures.

Part III: Actionable subsidies (Article 5–7)

- Article 5 provides that no member should cause, through the use of actionable subsidies, adverse effects to the interests of other members, that is, injury to the domestic industry of another member; nullification or impairment of benefits accruing directly or indirectly to other members under GATT 1994, in particular the benefits of concessions bound under Article II of GATT 1994; and serious prejudice to the interests of another member (Article 6).
- Article 7 is the mirror provision of Article 4 in discussing the multilateral remedies against actionable subsidies.

Part IV: Non-actionable subsidies (Articles 8–9)

- Article 8 provides that subsidies, which are not specific, are non-actionable. It furthermore exempts certain environmental, research and development (R&D) and regional subsidies, even though they are specific.
- Article 9 keeps multilateral remedies open even in the case of non-actionable subsidies. If a member has reasons to believe that this programme has resulted in serious adverse effects to its domestic industry, such member may request consultations with the member granting or maintaining the subsidy. If no mutually acceptable solution has been reached in consultations under Paragraph 2 within 60 days of the request for such consultations, the requesting member may refer the matter to the Committee. In the event the recommendation of the Committee is not followed within six months, the Committee shall authorize the requesting member to take appropriate countermeasures.

Part V: Countervailing Duties (Articles 10–23)

- This part largely mirrors procedural and material injury provisions of the ADA. Instead of dumping margin calculations, however, it contains rules on the calculation of the amount of certain subsidy.

Part VI: Institutions (Article 24)

- Establishes the Committee on Subsidies and Countervailing Measures of representatives from each of the members and authorizes the establishment of a Permanent Group of experts.

Part VII: Notification and surveillance (Articles 25–26)

■ Contains important notification and surveillance procedures by the committee on ASCM.

Part VIII: Special and differential treatment (S&DT) to developing countries

■ It grants significant special and differential treatment to developing country members. The Agreement on Subsidies and Countervailing Measures recognizes two broad categories of developing country members:
  • Annex VII countries (the countries that are referred to in Annex VII of the Agreement):
    – the least developed countries and
    – the countries that have GNP per capita less than $1000 per year
  • other developing countries.

■ The lower a member country's level of development, the more favourable treatment it receives. S&DT provisions embodied in this article are as follows:
  • Prohibition on export subsidies does not apply to Annex VII countries. Other developing countries were exempted from it until 31 December 2002.
  • Prohibition on import substitution subsidies did not apply to developing countries until 31 December 1999, and to Annex VII countries until 31 December 2002.
  • A developing country member which has acquired a share of at least 3.25 per cent in world trade of any given product for two consecutive calendar years is required to phase out its export subsidies for such product(s) over a period of two years. In respect of Annex VII countries a longer phase out period of eight years has been specified.
  • In the case of a product originating from a developing country, the de minimis level of subsidy is fixed at 2 per cent rather than 1 per cent, which is applicable for developed member countries.
  • The volume of subsidized imports below which the countervailing duty investigation is required to be terminated in respect of a product originating in a developing country is 4 per cent where imports of a product from more than one country are simultaneously subject to a countervailing duty investigation, the investigating authority is required to terminate the investigation if the targeted countries collectively account for less than 9 per cent of the imports of the like products in the importing country. For developed member countries there are no threshold volume of negligible imports.

Part IX: Transitional arrangements (Article 28–29)
- Deals with accessions and transition economies.

Part X: Dispute settlement
- Article 30 provides that the common Dispute Settlement Understanding (DSU) provisions apply, except as otherwise specified, in the ASCM.

Part XI: Final provisions
- Each member shall inform the committee of any changes in its laws and regulations relevant to this Agreement and in the administration of such laws and regulations. The committee shall review annually the implementation and operation of this Agreement.

Furthermore, the Agreement contains important annexes covering the following:

- the illustrative list of export subsidies (Annex I);
- guidelines on consumption of inputs in the production process (Annex II);
- guidelines in the determination of substitution drawback systems as export subsidies (Annex III);
- calculation of the total ad valorem subsidization for purposes of Article 6.1(a) (Annex IV);
- procedures for developing information concerning serious prejudice (Annex V); procedures for on-the-spot investigations ex Article 12.6 (Annex VI); and
- coverage of developing and least developed country members (Annex VII).

Agreement on Safeguard Measures

Roots of safeguard measures may be traced to the United States–Mexico trade agreement of 1942. Fearing that the lowering of a tariff on some particular good could result in a larger-than-expected import surge that would hurt domestic firms, the US Government insisted that the Agreement include a provision permitting it to re-introduce protection in the face of large import surges (Bown and Crowley 2003). Later, the GATT also incorporated the use of temporary trade restrictions into the agreement in the form of Article XIX then titled 'Emergency Actions on Imports of Particular Products', but often referred to as the escape clause or the safeguard clause. An *Agreement on Safeguards* (ASG) was negotiated during the Uruguay Round. But at the same time, Article XIX of GATT 1947 was also carried forward into GATT 1994. Currently, Article XIX of GATT 1994 and the ASG apply together.

A safeguard measure is a temporary restriction on trade—either a tariff or a quota—that is used by a member country if its domestic industry is injured or threatened with injury caused by an absolute or relative surge in imports. Such measures may be imposed only when imports are found to cause or threaten serious injury to a competing domestic industry. Unlike ADD and CVD that offset what is deemed to be unfair trade practices by foreigners, safeguard measures protect a domestic industry from fair foreign competition and therefore are subject to more stringent requirements. Detailed investigations similar to those anti-dumping and countervailing measures are undertaken before the imposition of any safeguard measure. The guiding principles of safeguard measures are as follows:

- they (generally) be applied on a non-selective (i.e. most-favoured-nation, or 'MFN') basis;
- they be progressively liberalized while in effect;
- member imposing them (generally) must pay compensation to the members whose trade is affected; and
- they must strictly be temporary.

The Uruguay Round Safeguards Agreement has relaxed the standards of safeguard measures. Earlier, these measures could not be targeted at imports from a particular country. However, the current Agreement allows explicit discrimination among exporters in the following specified circumstances (Bown and Mc Culloch 2003).

- First, if a quantitative restriction is used by a member, and assuming no prior agreement has been reached among all interested parties concerning the allocation of market shares, the ASG specifies that market-share allocations during the safeguard period should be based on the average market shares in a previous representative period, usually the three years prior to the investigation of the safeguard.
- Second, the WTO safeguard provisions explicitly allow an importing country to place a larger share of the safeguard burden on any exporter whose share in the affected market has recently shown a 'disproportionate' increase. Clearly, safeguard measures discriminate against faster growing exporters and new entrants in import markets.
- Third, the ASG also explicitly requires safeguard-imposing countries to discriminate *in favour of* developing-country exporters by exempting them from safeguard measures, thus providing 'special and differential treatment'.
- Fourth, other suppliers, especially partners in a preferential trading arrangement (PTA), may also be exempted.

Furthermore, the requirement of compensation is diluted by incorporating a provision that such action is not allowed for the first three years of the safeguard measure.[1] A number of procedural reforms were also introduced in the Uruguay Round ASG. These include, defining the injury requirement, establishing a surveillance monitoring body, and specifying the maximum length that a safeguard measure can be in place. These reforms aimed at making it easier for the member countries to use safeguard measures. Due to stringent requirements, safeguard measures were used only rarely in the past. Member countries often resorted to measures that were often designated with the term 'grey area' measures (see for instance, UNCTAD 2003, Finger et al. 2001) and included the so-called Voluntary Export Restraints (VERs), also known as Voluntary Restraint Arrangements (VRAs).[2] The Uruguay Round negotiations prohibited these highly discriminatory measures to encourage the use of WTO-consistent safeguard measures (see also, Hochman 2006, NBT 2004, Lee 2003, Hochman 2004, Bown 2002, Finger 1998, Sykes 1991, Bronckers 1985).

The current ASG covers the following areas.

Substantive requirements for safeguard measure (Article 2)

- Together with Article XIX:1 of GATT 1994, Article 2 lays down three conditions for applying safeguard measures: (i) increased imports, absolute or relative to domestic production, (ii) serious injury/threat of serious injury to the domestic industry that produces like or directly competitive products, and (iii) causal relationship between increased imports and serious injury.
- Safeguard measures shall be applied to a product being imported irrespective of its source.

Procedural requirements (Article 3)

- Initiation of safeguard investigations must be the subject of public notice (Article 3.1).
- Detailed report setting forth the domestic authorities' findings and reasoned conclusions on all pertinent issues of fact and law must be published at the end of the safeguard investigation (Article 3.1).
- During the investigation interested parties must be given an opportunity to present evidence and arguments and to respond to the evidence and arguments presented by other parties; if, in the course of an investigation, the competent authorities receive information, which is confidential by its nature or is provided on a confidential basis, they cannot disclose it without permission of the party submitting it, provided certain conditions are met (Article 3.2); parties providing confidential information may be requested to furnish non-confidential summaries thereof.

Serious injury (Article 4)

- Article 4.1 provides the definitions of 'serious injury' and of 'threat of serious injury', as well as elements to identify the 'domestic industry'. Article 4.1(a) defines 'serious injury' as '...a significant overall impairment in the position of a domestic industry'.
- The injury assessment must be based on the valuation of all relevant factors of an objective and quantifiable nature having a bearing on the domestic industry situation (the so-called 'injury factors'). It then lists a series of such factors, all of which must at a minimum be evaluated by domestic authorities (Article 4.2a).
- Article 4.2(b) lays down the causation requirement. The non-attribution rule, which is applicable in the ADA and ASCM is applied here also.

Conditions relating to safeguard measures (Articles 5–9)

- All safeguard measures can be applied 'only to the extent necessary to prevent or remedy serious injury and to facilitate adjustment of the domestic industry' (Article 5.1a). In case of quantitative restrictions, the quantity of import must not fall below the previous three years' average unless clear justification is given that a different level is necessary to prevent or remedy serious injury.
- Article 5.2(a) also lays down specific rules applicable to the allocation of quotas between supplying countries. Normally, allocation of shares would be on the basis of proportion of total quantity or value of the imported product over a previous representative period.
- Article 5.2(c) sets the conditions in which the countries can depart from the rules stipulated in 5.2(a) and discriminate amongst exporters (as described above).
- Article 6 covers duration and the type of provisional measures. Under this article, duration of the provisional measure shall not exceed 200 days. Such measures should take the form of only tariff increases (not quantitative restrictions) to be promptly refunded if the subsequent investigation does not determine that increased imports have caused or threatened to cause serious injury to a domestic industry.
- Article 7.1 of the ASG only allows safeguards 'for such period of time as may be necessary to prevent or remedy serious injury and to facilitate adjustment'. More specifically, the initial period of application of definitive safeguard measures must not exceed four years, including the duration of provisional measures. In the case of extension, the total period of application, including provisional measures, must in any event not exceed

eight years (Article 7.3 of the ASG). Any measure imposed for a period greater than one year should be progressively liberalized.

- Paragraph 5 of Article 7.1 does not allow the application of safeguard measure to the import of a product, which has been subject to such a measure for a period of time equal to that during which such measure had been previously applied, provided that the period of non-application is at least two years.
- Notwithstanding the provisions of Paragraph 5 of Article 7.1, a safeguard measure with a duration of 180 days or less may be applied again to the import of a product if: (i) at least one year has elapsed since the date of introduction of a safeguard measure on the import of that product; and (ii) such a safeguard measure has not been applied on the same product more than twice in the five-year period immediately preceding the date of introduction of the measure.

Compensation and concessions (Article 8)

Article 8 provides for mutually agreed trade compensation by the WTO member taking the measure to those affected by the measure. The right of suspension referred to in Paragraph 2 shall not be exercised for the first three years that a safeguard measure is in effect.

Special and differential treatment to developing countries (Article 9)

Article 9 sets the following special and differential treatment for the developing countries.

- Article 9.1 requires that a safeguard-imposing country exclude developing country suppliers if their share in affected imports is less than 3 per cent and cumulatively it is less than 9 per cent.
- A developing country has the right to extend the period of application of a safeguard measure for a period upto two years beyond the maximum period.
- Notwithstanding the provisions of Paragraph 5 of Article 7, a developing country may apply safeguard measures again to the import of a product that has been subject to such a measure, provided that the period of non-application is at least two years.

Prohibition of grey area measures (Article 11)

- Article 11 prohibits all the grey area measures.

Committee and surveillance (Article 12)

- Article 12 provides that the investigations have to be conducted in accordance with procedures previously established and published. These must also be notified to the Committee on Safeguards (Article 12.6), the body established to oversee the functioning of the ASG [infra, Section 6.3].

- Article 13 establishes multilateral surveillance over the implementation of the agreement by setting up a Committee on Safeguards under the authority of the Council for Trade in Goods.

Dispute settlement (Article 14)

- The provisions of Articles XXII and XXIII of GATT 1994 as elaborated and applied by the DSU shall apply to consultations and the settlement of disputes arising under this Agreement.

In sum, the objective of contingent protection measures is to protect the domestic industry injured due to import competition. This injury can be attributed either to unfair trade practices of foreigners (anti-dumping and countervailing measures) or to unforeseen developments (safeguards). WTO members may apply any measure of contingent protection if after conducting investigations they establish that the conditions set out in the related agreement are satisfied. Thus the flexibility provided to the governments by the rules enshrined in these agreements is critical in determining their relative attractiveness. Let us now examine the key features of the three agreements in a comparative framework.

A Comparative Analysis of the Three Agreements Related to Contingent Protection

Appendix Table A1 illustrates major features of the three Agreements that relate to contingent protection in a comparative framework. In what follows we describe major differences in the provisions of the three agreements.

Anti-dumping Agreement vs Agreement on Subsidies and Countervailing Measures

While both the ASCM and the ADA address unfairly traded imports, there are fundamental and conceptual differences between the two.

- ASCM addresses subsidy while ADA addresses dumping. Dumping is an action by a company while subsidy is the action of another government or a government agency. Contrary to an anti-dumping proceeding, the exporting country government also will have to complete a questionnaire response, which is subsequently be verified by the importing country member. Anti-subsidy investigations are therefore politically more sensitive.
- While ASCM is based on the premise that such measures are needed to offset artificial advantages created by market-distorting government subsidies,

the ADA promises to punish international price discrimination if it causes injury to the importing country. It does not have basic principles defining the conditions under which price discrimination could be punishable as 'unfair trade practice'. As a result, it punishes price discrimination even when it is a perfectly normal commercial practice.

- The ASCM involves establishment of subsidy while anti-dumping investigations focus on difference between the export price and normal value. ADA allows the use of constructed normal value and constructed export prices against actual company data to establish dumping. It also allows importing countries to use 'best available facts' in the estimation of dumping under certain conditions. In both the cases, there is a high probability of overstated and questionable dumping. Countervailing measures however are based on establishing subsidization. The ASCM provides that the national legislation or implementing regulations of member countries should specify the methods to be used by the investigating authorities in determining per unit subsidy. In addition, to ensure transparency, it imposes an obligation on the investigating authorities to explain in their decision how the per unit subsidization was arrived at by using the method specified in the legislation. Subsidy calculation methodologies are more complex and less manipulative[3] than dumping calculations.

In addition to fundamental differences, there have also been other asymmetries in the two agreements, which indicate that anti-dumping involves softer standards than the ASCM. These are as follows.

- Prior consultation: The ASCM imposes an obligation on the investigating country to enter into consultations with the government of the exporting country after the petition is accepted but before the investigations begin. Such consultations provide the government of the investigating country an opportunity to ascertain whether, taking into account the information presented in the application on the alleged injurious effects of subsidies on the industry, the exporting country is prepared to modify its subsidy practices so as to reach mutually acceptable solutions. In the United States and the EC, such consultations may be an important tool to limit the harassment aspect of a CVD investigation (UNCTAD 2003). No such provision of pre-initiation consultations is provided in the ADA.
- Provisional measures: Article 17 of the ASCM and Article 7 of the ADA, both deal with provisional measures. While Article 17.4 of the ASCM only establishes that the application of provisional measures shall be limited to as short a period as possible, not exceeding 4 months, Article 7.4 of the

ADA allows that the period may be extended to 6 months. Furthermore, while Article 17.2 of the ASCM establishes that provisional duties cannot be collected but only guaranteed by a security, Article 7.2 of the ADA fails to provide such limitation.

- Injury Margin: Article 6.5 of the ASCM defines injury margin. It reads 'Price undercutting shall include any case in which such price undercutting has been demonstrated through a comparison of prices of the subsidized product with prices of a non-subsidized like product supplied to the same market. The comparison shall be made at the same level of trade and at comparable times, due account being taken of any other factor affecting price comparability. However, if such a direct comparison is not possible, the existence of price undercutting may be demonstrated on the basis of export unit values'. The ADA does not give any guidance on such calculation and arguably leaves its members substantial discretion.

- Price undertaking: Article 18.1 of the ASCM envisages two types of undertakings: (i) an *undertaking by the exporting country government* to eliminate or limit the subsidy or to take other measures concerning its effects or (ii) an *undertaking by an exporter* to revise its prices to eliminate the injurious effect of the subsidy or the amount if the subsidy itself, whichever is lower. Furthermore, under the agreement price undertakings from exporters cannot be accepted unless the authorities of the importing member have obtained the consent of the exporting member also. Anti-dumping Agreement on the other hand allows investigating authorities of the importing countries to suspend/terminate proceedings without the imposition of provisional measures or anti-dumping duties upon receipt of satisfactory voluntary undertakings *from any exporter* to revise its prices or to cease exports to the area in question at dumped prices.

- Special and differential treatment: There are provisions of special and differential treatment for the developing countries in the ASCM (Article 27). However, there are no such provisions in the ADA. Article 15 in the ADA, which deals with special and differential treatment. It merely requires the authorities to explore the possibilities of constructive remedies before applying ADDs where they would affect the essential interests of developing country members. No specific provisions have been made to guide as to how this could be done. In contrast, the ASCM has well-defined provisions for extending special and differential treatment to developing countries in Article 27 (as described above). For a product originating in a developing country, *de minimis* subsidy is 2 per cent rather than 1 per cent, which is applicable to other countries and the Agreement requires the authorities to terminate the investigation if import volumes are below threshold level. The Agreement also contains preferential measures for developing countries concerning prohibited subsidies.

■ Dispute Settlement: Article 30 of the ASCM stipulates that 'The provisions of Articles XXII and XXIII of GATT 1994 as elaborated and applied by the DSU shall apply to consultations and the settlement of disputes under this Agreement, except as otherwise specifically provided herein'. However, the role of panels is considerably weakened by Article 17.6 in the ADA. It allows more than one interpretation of the legal provisions of the Agreement and stipulates that 'the panel shall find the authorities' measure to be in conformity with the Agreement if it rests upon one of those permissible interpretations'.[4]

Even if substantive provisions of the agreement of subsidies and anti-dumping are similar, they do not belong to the same analytical category. The Uruguay Round ASCM provides broad proscriptions against trade subsidies. Within the GATT/WTO system a valid economic rationale for countervailing measures is that they provide additional disincentive for exporting countries to apply trade subsidies. Anti-dumping on the other hand has no economic rationale. Furthermore, the subsidies and countervailing measures agreement also specifies when and how a member can apply a countervailing measure. These standards are higher than the ones specified in the ADA. The result is that these measures are used much less frequently than the anti-dumping measures.

Anti-dumping Agreement/ASCM vs Agreement on Safeguards

The requirements for safeguard measures are more stringent compared with both anti-dumping and countervailing measures. Such differences have been introduced in the agreements due to the recognition that safeguard measures punish fair trade whereas anti-dumping/countervailing measures deal with unfair trade. The fundamental differences are as follows.

■ Anti-dumping (and even countervailing) measures are based on the premise that foreign players are adopting unfair trade practices, while safeguard measures are based on the recognition that the domestic industry is facing structural problems and requires structural adjustments. The aim of safeguard measures is clearly indicated in the preamble to the ASG, which recognizes the importance of structural adjustment and the need to enhance, rather than limit, competition in international markets. Safeguard measures provide a grace period to domestic industries, which have lost their competitive advantage, enabling capital and facilities to be shifted into industries, which retain this advantage, and the labour force to be retrained. There are no such basic objectives of the ADA. It has an emotional appeal and is often used in a blunt and highly discriminatory way.

- While anti-dumping and countervailing measures are applied to imports from only the named countries, thus allowing for the substantial differential and discriminatory treatment across trading partners, the safeguard law is supposed to result in protection being applied through non-discriminatory tariffs on imports, irrespective of the source country.[5] This increases the political visibility of the measure.
- The member applying safeguard measures must also give something in return for safeguarding its domestic interests. Safeguard measures thus involve compensation. In case no agreement on compensation is reached, countries affected by safeguard measures have the right to retaliate subject to certain conditions. These measures are therefore considered risky due to the possibility of retaliation. Anti-dumping/ASCM does not give the affected country a right to demand compensation or to retaliate.

Thus, unlike anti-dumping and countervailing measures both of which involve explicit deviation from the three basic principles of the WTO described above, allowing the member countries to charge extra import duty (violating the first principle of tariff binding) on the particular product from the particular exporting country (deviating from the principle of non-discrimination) without any compensation (against the principle of reciprocity), safeguard measures *in principle* are consistent with the principles of non-discrimination and reciprocity even though the current Agreement does provide conditions to deviate from these principles.

There are other procedural differences as well. Some of these differences are as under.

- For initiating an anti-dumping/CVD case, there is need for the evidence of dumping/subsidy, injury, and causal relationship between the two. However for a safeguard investigation to initiate there must also be evidence that it is in public interest to initiate such investigation.
- Safeguard investigations need to focus only on the domestic industry whereas both ADA and ASCM require an investigation of the behaviour of companies in the exporting country.
- While the ADA and the ASCM require the authorities to implement provisional measures, in the case of safeguard measures such measures are implemented in critical circumstances where delay may cause damage that is difficult to repair. In the case of special safeguard no provisional measures are applicable.

- The injury test for anti-dumping action/CVD tends to be softer than the injury test for action under the ASG and Article XIX. For safeguard measures to be applied the industry need to suffer or run the risk of suffering 'serious injury' causing a significant overall impairment in the position of a domestic industry. For an anti-dumping/countervailing measure 'material injury' or 'threat thereof' is sufficient. Serious injury is a higher standard of injury than material injury. The general consensus amongst many trade policy experts has been that the 'serious injury' hurdle in safeguard investigations (as opposed to material injury in anti-dumping) is a tough requirement to meet and therefore it was never anticipated that safeguards would become a commonly used trade protection instrument.

- While the ADA/ASCM requires the duty to be less than the dumping margin/subsidy (it is not mandatory), a safeguard measure should be applied only to the extent necessary to prevent or remedy serious injury and to help the industry concerned to adjust.

- A safeguard measure must be progressively liberalized while in effect. If it is extended beyond the initial period of application, it can be no more restrictive during this period than it was at the end of the initial period, and it should continue to be liberalized. No similar requirement exists either for anti-dumping measures or for countervailing measures. In both these cases, there are periodic reviews, which may affect the measure depending on the outcome.

- Even though anti-dumping and countervailing measures have five years' duration, in theory they continue as long as the injurious dumping/subsidy continues. These actions can thus be extended without any upper time limit if the authorities find that the removal can result into dumping/subsidy again. Safeguard measures on the other hand are initially applicable for four years, extendable for another four years provided the industry can show that structural adjustment is being implemented with an extension for another two years for developing countries.

- The ADA requires an application to impose anti-dumping measures to be supported by a certain portion of the domestic industry, whereas there is no such requirement in the ASG. Different countries may have different rules in this regard. For instance, in the EU only member states may request the commission to investigate the imposition of a safeguard. Anti-dumping/CVD investigations on the other hand are initiated on the request of the domestic industry.

- Final decision of whether a safeguard action should be imposed has an important political implication and in the United States it is the President who takes the final decision to impose a safeguard measure, taking into account the national economic interest. The International Trade Commission conducts both anti-dumping and safeguard investigations. For anti-dumping/CVD measures to be taken the President plays no formal role. Instead the Department of Commerce is involved in the determination of unfair trade practices. These procedural differences are likely to have important implications for the relative use of the two instruments.

Our analysis suggests that anti-dumping has the lowest standards with the least political visibility. The ASCM has striking similarities with the ADA but there indeed are differences in the basic concepts, prerequisites and procedures, which make the former more stringent in use than the latter. ASG standards are much higher than the ADA or even the ASCM. Thus legal features make anti-dumping more attractive than safeguard or CVD mechanism. Even though safeguard investigations are easier to conduct from the investigators point of view, particularly in developing countries, anti-dumping remains the most preferred trade policy.

USE OF CONTINGENT PROTECTION MEASURES

In GATT's early years, the use of contingent protection measures was not very common. Pressure valve actions used by the countries opening their economies to international competition through the GATT negotiations were mainly renegotiations under Article XXVIII. This article permitted the member countries to reintroduce protective trade policies by permanently raising tariffs. According to Finger et al. (2001) during GATT's first fifteen years (1947–62), countries opening their economies to international competition availed of such measures in large proportion. By 1963, every one of the twenty-nine GATT member countries who had bound tariff reductions under the GATT had undertaken at least one renegotiation. In total, 110 renegotiations were undertaken which amounted to almost four per member country.

The use of renegotiations began to decline from 1963 onwards. These were replaced by VERs. VERs were bilateral negotiations outside GATT' auspices through which exporting countries were persuaded to restrain exports voluntarily. They were GATT-illegal and were known as 'grey-area measure'. The Long Term Cotton Textile Arrangement negotiated in 1962 had brought GATT sanction to industrial economies' VERs on cotton textiles and apparels. The Multi-fibre Arrangement (MFA) negotiated in 1972 extended the GATT sanction for such restrictions to virtually all textiles and clothing products. The industrial countries used VERs in several other sectors like steel, footwear, motor vehicle, machine tools, and electronic products.

While the focus had been on VERs and the use of contingent protection measures had been limited during this period, the countries did not forget about anti-dumping. Though there has been no reliable database for the period prior to 1980, information collected by Irwing (2005) for the United States indicates that there was a steady and substantial use of anti-dumping from the mid-1950s until the mid-1960s. It was interrupted in the late 1960s only to rise rapidly again in the 1970s (Irwing 2005).

TABLE 2.1:   Number of anti-dumping initiations in the US: 1951–80

Years	Anti-dumping initiations (no.)
1951–5	49
1956–60	150
1961–5	139
1966–70	82
1971–5	112
1976–80	163

Source: Irwing (2005).

Thus several anti-dumping petitions had been filed in the United States, particularly in the late 1950s and early 1960s and again in the 1970s. In a recently published paper, Zanardi (2006) reports 421 anti-dumping initiations worldwide during 1948–58 with an average of 42 cases per year. The total number of initiations increased to 926 over 1969–80 with an average of 77 cases per year. The US remained the heaviest user followed by Australia.[6] Unlike today, however, most of these petitions did not result in the imposition of anti-dumping duties. Of the 1347 cases initiated during 1948–80, as reported by Zanardi (2006), only 381 cases resulted in the imposition of duties with the success rate of only 28 per cent. The proportion of successful cases in the US was higher at 34 per cent. The use of other contingent protection measures were very rare. For instance, under the GATT 1947, only 101 safeguard measures had been adopted from the inception of GATT to 1979 (Bown and Crowley 2003).

The post-Tokyo Round period witnessed a relative decline in VERs due to a tremendous rise in the use of 'GATT-consistent' contingent protection measures. But, it was primarily because of anti-dumping measures that surged sharply, the use of safeguard measures did not change noticeably. A study by National Board of Trade, Sweden (NBT 2004) shows that EC and the US had been the largest users of grey-area measures until 1970s. They became the largest anti-dumping users since 1980. Clearly, the grey area measures were replaced by the use of anti-dumping measures. Table 2.2 documents the popularity of anti-dumping as a contingent protection tool during the 1980s.

TABLE 2.2:   Use of contingent protection measures: 1980–8

	Anti-dumping	Safeguard	CVD
1. Total	1764	39	388
2. By four countries*	1689	39	388
3. 2 as a proportion of 1 (%)	96	100	100

Note: * These are: the United States, EU, Australia, and Canada.
Source: Krishna (2002).

It reveals that anti-dumping became immensely popular followed by countervailing measures. Safeguard measures were on the other hand used only rarely. Since application of the safeguards clause required compensation, countries often found it quite difficult to find tariffs in other areas that are high enough that by lowering them can provide adequate compensation to the affected parties. If many parties are involved, compensating each of them could require quite a number of concessions. In addition, safeguard measures prior to the Uruguay Round could not be targeted at imports from a particular country.

The use of contingent protection measures (CPMs) continued to increase in the post-WTO period. Table 2.3 shows that the number of CPM initiations increased significantly from 169 in 1995 to 411 in 1999. It fluctuated during the next two years around this level but dropped after 2001. Although the decline in the number of CPM initiations appears to be significant, it has not resulted in abysmally low use of such measures. Furthermore, the number of safeguard measures provided in the table is somewhat downward biased due to the counting methodology adopted here (NBT 2004). There are two ways of looking at the statistics of safeguard measures. One is to look at the number of notifications of initiated safeguard investigations. The other is based on the number of product categories included in each notification. Until 2000, each notification carried only one product. Since 2001 however an increasingly large number of products are being included in each notification most notably by the United States and the EU. While only thirteen notifications were received by the WTO in 2001, the number of product wise safeguard was fifty-three. In 2002, the corresponding numbers were 33 and 132. If we include the number of products the number, then the number of contingent protection measures will be much higher than what is shown in Table 2.3.

TABLE 2.3:   Use of contingent protection measures (initiations):1995–2005

Year	Anti-dumping	CVD	Safeguard measures*	Total CPM
1995	157	10	2	169
1996	225	7	5	237
1997	243	16	3	262
1998	257	25	10	292
1999	354	41	15	410
2000	292	18	25	335
2001	364	27	13	403
2002	312	9	33	355
2003	232	15	15	262
2004	213	8	14	235
2005	191	6	7	204
Total	2840	182	142	3164

Note: * based on notifications.

Source: Collected from various WTO websites.

Another important observation that can be made is that anti-dumping remains the most widely used measure of contingent protection. Until 1998, the share of anti-dumping in total CPMs used had been above 90 per cent. Thereafter, it declined but remained only slightly below 90 per cent. The share of countervailing measures on the other hand ranged between 5 and 6 per cent. During 1995–2003, only eighteen countries initiated the investigations under ASCM and affected forty countries. In contrast, forty-one countries actually initiated investigations under the ADA, which affected ninety-eight countries. Finally, the use of safeguard measures remained insignificantly small despite the fact that negotiators adopted softer standards for safeguards during the Uruguay Round to encourage the member countries to substitute the grey measures by safeguard measures, as discussed above. The table shows that there was a dramatic increase in the use of safeguards during 2001 and 2002 (by the number of products included in the initiations). However, the spectacular jump of 2001 was largely due to the safeguard investigations on steel launched by the United States. The number of safeguard initiations exploded once again in 2002, mostly driven by the steel-related cases initiated by other countries in response to the United States safeguards of the previous year. The top three users in 2002 (Chile, the EC, and Hungary) a counted for almost half of the total number of initiations; in comparison, the United States alone had been responsible for more than 55 per cent of the initiations in 2001. This demonstrates both the exceptional status of the US steel-related safeguard action in 2001 and the fast response of other members in following the US example in 2002. Since 2003, the United States has not been initiating any case and therefore the number of safeguard measure declined sharply. It was expected that the introduction of the ASG would make safeguards relatively more attractive in comparison with alternative means of obtaining relief from injurious imports, especially anti-dumping. However, safeguard has not yet become an attractive trade policy instrument or an alternative to anti-dumping. Anti-dumping remains hugely popular.

The number of both CVD and safeguard measures declined sharply in 2005. The number of anti-dumping initiations also fell but the decline was not sharp and therefore the share of anti-dumping measures in CPM increased to around 94 per cent. As Prusa and Skeath (2002) put it 'to say that antidumping is now the most popular form of international trade protection is an understatement. In terms of the quantity of trade litigation, antidumping has lapped the field—several times over'.

One pertinent question is what might be the factors, which could have shaped the overriding use of anti-dumping. Could it be that there has been a spurt in unfair trade practices following the process of globalization that attempt to dump in order to dominate the foreign markets? Or is it perhaps that globalization has induced much greater competition and thus caused import competing domestic producers to revert to contingent protection in general? If latter is the case then the obvious reason for preferring anti-dumping to other CPMs could be that it is easier to use/manipulate than countervailing or safeguard measures to provide protection.[7] Several scholars endorse this viewpoint. As Low (1993) stated, 'virtually any industry that considers itself adversely affected by foreign competition and presents a completely assembled application to anti-dumping authorities stands a good chance demonstrating that it is under attack' (p. 86). This view will further be explored in the following chapters.

CONTINGENT PROTECTION AND DEVELOPING COUNTRIES

Prior to 1985, the most frequent users of the contingent protection were developed countries (Table 2.2). From 1980 through 1985 developed countries accounted for 100 per cent of anti-dumping cases. Four users namely the United States, the EU, Australia, and Canada were responsible for more than 99 per cent of all filings. Countervailing and safeguard actions were also used mainly by the developed countries. According to an estimate, 903 anti-dumping measures and 159 countervailing measures were in force in 1995.

Around 62 per cent of the anti-dumping measures were in force in three industrialized countries namely the United States, the EU, and Canada while 85 per cent of the CVD cases were in force in the United States, Canada, and Australia (CITT 1996). By the late 1980s, new users had also started filing these cases. However their share in total cases remained small. We have some estimates of the use of safeguard measures during GATT 1947 prior to 1995. It shows that between 1947 and 1994, 150 safeguard measures resulted in protection, of which 113 (75 per cent) were adopted by only four industrialized countries namely the United States, the EU, Australia, and Canada. Very few developing countries used the measure.[8] Prior to 1995 therefore, developed countries in particular the United States, the EU, Canada, and Australia were the major users of contingent protection.

This scenario changed in the post-Uruguay Round period when there was a sharp increase in the use of CPMs by developing countries (Table 2.4). By the turn of the century these countries were using well over half of anti-dumping and safeguard complaints though their share in countervailing measures remained small. During the period 1995 to June 2004, 2,643 anti-dumping cases were filed. Of these, 1,598 were initiated by the developing countries. During 1995 to September 2003 there were 118 safeguard investigations[9] initiated by thirty-one different countries. Of these, seventeen were developing countries, together accounting for seventy initiations. The most frequent initiators of the safeguard instrument over 1995–2003 have been India (14 initiations), the United States (10)[10]; Chile, the Czech Republic, and Jordan (9 each); and Bulgaria, the Philippines, and Venezuela (6 each). In 2003, fifteen safeguard initiations were reported. Of these, fourteen were initiated by developing countries. The only developed country to have initiated a lone case was the EU. Since 2003, thirty-six safeguard cases have been initiated. Of them, only five are initiated by two developed countries namely Canada and the EU; thirty-one cases are initiated by developing countries. Apparently, safeguards are becoming an attractive trade policy option for developing countries seeking protection for their domestic industries. This could be because a safeguard investigation is relatively easier to conduct, as no evidence from across the border is required. The use of safeguard in terms of number however is still abysmally low. Despite the fact that safeguard measures could have a greater protection, anti-dumping measures are more frequently used. While looking at the patterns of CVD use one finds that these measures are still in the domain of the developed countries. They have been used scarcely by developing countries. It could be due to the complex issue of identification and establishment of subsidization. Of the total 174 initiations during 1995–2004, only thirty-four cases were initiated by

TABLE 2.4:   Use of contingent protection measures—Initiations and targets (by level of development): 1995–2004

	Cases reported by		Cases targeted against	
	Developed countries	Developing countries	Developed countries	Developing countries
Anti-dumping	1045	1598	965	1678
	(39.5)	(60.4)	(36.5)	(63.5)
CVD	140	34	66	108
	(80.5)	(19.5)	(38.0)	(62)
Safeguard	70*	48	–	–
	(59.3)	(40.7)		

Note: Parentheses show percentages.
*: September 2003.
Source: Author's calculations based on the WTO websites.

developing countries that accounted for almost one-fifth of the total initiations. The use of contingent protection measures has been increasing in developing countries. However, this is largely due to the increasing use of anti-dumping measures. Although the share of developing countries in the global use of safeguard measures has also increased, the overall number of safeguard measures itself remains low.

On the receiving end, the number of anti-dumping cases in which developing countries were targeted also increased sharply. Over 68 per cent of the CVD cases were also directed against these countries but the absolute number of CVD measures still remains very small. While 108 countervailing investigations were targeted against developing countries during 1995 to 2004, the number of anti-dumping investigations that were directed against these countries was well above 1500. This is perhaps one reason why ASCM has not attracted the kind of attention that ADA has.

A surge in the number of cases initiated by developing countries and those initiated against them has catapulted anti-dumping as the forerunner of the most controversial topics of international trade for developing countries. It has now become essentially a concern of developing countries. There is an urgent need for having a deeper understanding of how fair is this agreement in dealing with unfair trade practices from the perspective of the developing countries if this problem is to be addressed effectively in the WTO trade rounds.

Appendix

TABLE A2.1:   WTO agreements on contingent protection measures—
A comparative analysis

The Agreement

WTO Anti-dumping Agreement (GATT Article VI)	WTO Agreement on Subsidies and Countervailing Measures (GATT Article XVI)	WTO Agreement on Safeguards sets forth the rules for application of Article XIX of GATT 1994

Nature

Addresses unfairly traded imports	Addresses unfairly traded imports	Addresses fairly traded imports

Objective

Protects the domestic industries against the unfair trade practices of dumping and levels the playing field	Protects the domestic industries against the unfair trade practices of subsidization and levels the playing field	General safeguards will remove injury and facilitate structural adjustments for the industry to be competitive. Special safeguards will assist farmers whose products were previously protected by quantitative restrictions (QRs) that have been tariffied.

Types of action

Investigation by the designated authority.	Multilateral remedies at the WTO. Investigation by the designated authority.	Investigation by the designated authority.

Conditions for use

Evidence of dumping which causes material injury (dumping means that export price is lower than the normal value)	Subsidized production or exportation of the foreign merchandise causing injury More specifically, existence of specific subsidy, which causes material injury.	General safeguard: Increased level of imports absolute or relative to production Special safeguard: Volume of imports

Contd

Table A2.1 Contd

		exceed a base trigger level or price falls below a trigger price level
Coverage		
1. Limited to 'like' products	1. Limited to Like product	1. All 'like' or 'directly competitive' products
2. Exporter specific	2. Country specific	2. All countries
		3. General safeguards apply to industrial and non-tariffed goods
		4. Special safeguards apply to tariffed agricultural products denominated with the acronym 'SSG' in the GATT Schedule of Concessions
Standing for initiation		
A domestic industry which is supported by domestic producers whose collective output constitutes more than 50% of the total production of the like product produced by domestic producers that are expressing either support for or opposition to the application. However, no investigation shall be initiated when	A domestic industry which is supported by domestic producers whose collective output constitutes more than 50% of the total production of the like product produced by other domestic producers that are expressing either support for or opposition to the application. However, no investigation shall be initiated when domestic producers expressly supporting the	General safeguards: Industry filing the case should be a producer of the like or directly competitive product whose collective output constitutes a major proportion of the total domestic production. Special safeguards: Department of Agriculture (*motu proprio*).

Contd

Table A2.1 Contd

domestic producers account for less than 25% of the production of the like product produced by the domestic industry.	application account for less than 25% of the production of the like product produced by the domestic industry.	

Evidence needed for initiation

Satisfactory evidence of dumping, injury, and causal relationship.	Satisfactory evidence of subsidy, injury, and causal relationship.	The evidence must include arguments on whether a measure is in the public interest.

Pre-initiation consulation

None	Provisions of pre-initiation consultation	None

Investigation procedure

Establishing	Establishing	General safeguard: Establishing
1. Product comparability (like products)	1. Product comparability ('like' product)	1. Product comparability ('like' or 'directly competitive' product)
2. Price difference	2. Subsidy	2. Increased imports
3. Material injury or threat of material injury or material retardation	3. Material injury or threat of material injury or material retardation	3. Serious injury or threat of serious injury
4. Causal link	4. Causal link	4. Causal link
		Special safeguards:
		1. Product comparability ('like product')
		2. Volume of imports exceed a base trigger level, or
		3. Price falls below a trigger price level

Contd

Table A2.1 Contd

Form of measures		

1. Provisional anti-dumping duty: Requires the conduct of a preliminary investigation (affirmative preliminary determination) prior to imposition of a dumping or countervailing bond for a duration of 4 months extendable upto 6 months.
2. Definitive anti-dumping duty.
	1. Provisional countervailing duty: Requires the conduct of a preliminary investigation (affirmative preliminary determination) prior to imposition of a duty or countervailing bond for a duration of 4 months.
	2. Definitive countervailing duty.
		General safeguards:
		1. Provisional measure—tariff increase
		2. Definitive safeguard measure:
		  - tariff increase
		  - quantitative restrictions (e.g., import quota; import licensing)
		Special safeguards:
		1. Additional duty not exceeding one-third of the level of the ordinary customs duty in effect during the year in which the action is taken.

Provisional measures		
Requires the conduct of a preliminary investigation.	Requires the conduct of a preliminary investigation.	General: Preliminary determination special; not provisionally applied.

Duration of the measure		
Five years, subject to sunset review to determine whether or not to extend the duration of the dumping duty. Can be extended for any number of terms.	Five years, subject to sunset review to determine whether or not to extend the duration of the countervailing duty. Can be extended for any number of terms.	General: Four years, extendable for another 4 years provided the industry can show that structural adjustment is being implemented with an extension for another two (2) years for developing countries.

Contd

Table A2.1 Contd

		Special safeguards: Shall only be maintained until the end of the year in which it has been imposed
Extent of measure		
Preferably less than full dumping margin	Preferably less than the subsidy	Should be applied only to the extent necessary to prevent or remedy serious injury and to help the industry concerned to adjust. Where quantitative restrictions (quotas) are imposed, they normally should not reduce the quantities of imports below the annual average for the last three representative years for which statistics are available, unless clear justification is given that a different level is necessary to prevent or remedy serious injury.
Strength of the measure		
Periodic review may affect the measure depending on the outcome.	Periodic review may affect the measure depending on the outcome.	The measure must be progressively liberalized while in effect. If a safeguard measure is extended beyond the initial period of application, it can be

Contd

Table A2.1 Contd

		no more restrictive during this period than it was at the end of the initial period, and it should continue to be liberalized.
Compensation		
No compensation	No compensation	Members applying safeguard measures must generally 'pay' for them through compensation. Any adequate means of trade compensation may be agreed among the affected members through consultation. Absent such agreement on compensation within 30 days, the affected exporting members may retaliate. However, this right to retaliate may not be exercised for the first three years that a safeguard is in effect, provided that the measure has been taken as a result of an absolute increase in imports.
Special and differential treatment		
No concrete S&DT provisions	Well-defined provisions in Article 27	Well-defined provisions in Article 9

Source: Based on the WTO.

Notes

1 On the other hand, the WTO Agreement on Agriculture allows for the application of special transitional safeguards (additional duty not exceeding one-third of the level of the effective tariff) against importations of agricultural products whose quantitative import restrictions (QRs) were converted ('tariffied') into ordinary customs duties and agricultural products designated with the symbol 'SSG' (Special Safeguard Measures) in the GATT Schedule of Concessions. Special safeguard measures may be invoked, if: (i) the volume of imports exceeds a trigger level; or (but not concurrently) (ii) the price of imports falls below a trigger price. In either case, injury to the domestic industry need not be established.

2 Under VERs, exporting countries were asked to voluntarily accept a quantitative restriction on exports. More details are provided later in the chapter.

3 This issue of how manipulative are the anti-dumping practices will be dealt with in detail in Chapter 3.

4 This will be discussed in detail in Chapter 3.

5 However, as mentioned earlier, the Safeguard Agreement does allow some form of explicit discrimination.

6 During 1948–58, however, South Africa reported the highest number of cases. Of 421 cases reported by Zanardi (2006), 211 were initiated by South Africa alone. However, it appears from the available information that the tool remained out of use in the country for a long time. Its use was resumed during the 1990s.

7 The rationale of anti-dumping use will be examined in detail later in the study,

8 Developing countries who used the tool included Chile, Brazil, South Africa, India, Egypt, and Argentina.

9 By number of filings (not by product).

10 The number is significantly higher in terms of the number of products.

3 Genesis and Evolution of the Agreement

The world's first anti-dumping law was adopted by Canada in 1904. It was soon followed by similar legislation in major developed countries including Australia, New Zealand, and Britain. Anti-dumping provisions were later incorporated into the GATT 1947. It has since evolved into an important trade policy tool for both developed and developing countries. A large number of countries have adopted anti-dumping legislation. According to an estimate, 90 per cent of the world trade is now subject to potential use of anti-dumping measures (Zanardi 2004).

This chapter provides an overview of the evolution of the ADA. The first section deals with the genesis of the *anti-dumping law* and its accession to GATT 1947, while the section following it discusses the evolution, through various GATT/WTO Rounds, of the multilateral agreement on this law. The next section examines the reforms introduced in its legal provisions of the agreements in successive Rounds of negotiations and finally the last section assesses their relevance from the developing country perspective.

GENESIS OF THE ANTI-DUMPING AGREEMENT

Emergence and Spread of the Anti-dumping Laws

Anti-dumping rules started to develop in the early part of the twentieth century with the adoption of anti-dumping provisions by Canada in 1904. The provisions adopted in1904 were a part of the amendments to the Custom Tariff Act 1897 (Ciuriak 2005). While the proposed amendments were concerned mainly with the tariff schedules of wide-ranging items, Section 19 of the Act introduced a 'special duty on undervalued products' with the following salient features.

- The special duty was set at the difference between the selling price in Canada and the fair market value (the price at which the products were sold in the country of production).
- The application of the duty was limited to such goods as were also produced in Canada.

- Goods were exempted from the special duty if domestic supply conditions were inadequate.
- Maximum protection offered by the special duty was capped at 50 per cent of the regular duty.
- No provision was made for injury test.

There was little parliamentary discussion on the provision of this special duty and the first anti-dumping law in the world came into existence 'with rather sparing comments' (Ciuriak 2005). This law introduced anti-dumping measure as a 'special duty' that could be levied administratively rather than being enacted. The real impetus for introducing this law was the Canadian manufacturing's concern about low import prices of steel and its primary objective was to protect Canadian firms from steel dumped in Canada by the US firms (Finger 1993).

New Zealand (1905) and Australia (1906) soon followed Canada. In Australia, the threat came from the International Harvester Trust, which was preparing to introduce US and Canadian agricultural machinery into the Australian market. It was feared that this would wipe out the emerging Australian manufacturing sector, which at that time was centered around agricultural machinery (Plowman 1993). In New Zealand also the immediate cause that prompted that country's legislation was the pressure from the International Harvester Trust on both local and British suppliers (Ciuriak 2005).

The United States introduced the first anti-dumping legislation in 1916. The legislation was enacted against the backdrop of the Sherman Antitrust Act of 1890, which declared illegal any effort to combine or conspire to monopolize a particular market and the Clayton Act of 1914, which made price discrimination an illegal practice if it reduced competition or tended to create a monopoly. The anti-dumping legislation was an extension of these laws to international trade and aimed at predatory dumping by foreign exporters (Irwing 2005, Sykes 1998, Hufbauer 1999). It was a criminal statute with criminal punishments. It required the complainant to prove before the judiciary that the foreign supplier resorted to predatory dumping.[1] The remedy was not import duties but fines and possible imprisonment for those found guilty.[2] However, the law could rarely be invoked due to the stringent conditions for its use.

In 1921, the United States enacted the 'Anti-dumping Act of 1921'. It empowered the Secretary of the Treasury to impose duties on dumped goods without regard to the dumper's intent. It was this act that set the stage for the US anti-dumping law as it stands today. It closely resembled Canada's anti-dumping law but differed substantially from the 1916 law. While the

1916 law focused on the intent of the exporter, the 1921 law hinged on a finding of price discrimination and injury. Furthermore, the 1916 law was a criminal law whereas the 1921 law was a civil statute to assess penalty duties to compensate for price differentials. Finally, the 1916 law specified fines and imprisonment to the dumper while 1921 law specified imposing ADD. Higher import duties were considered to be the appropriate remedy for dumping.

According to the Anti-dumping Act of 1921 (Title II of the Emergency Tariff Act of 1921):

Whenever the Secretary of the Treasure finds that an industry in the US is being or is likely to be injured or is prevented from being established, by reasons of importation into the US of foreign merchandise and that merchandise of such class is being sold or is likely to be sold in the US at less than its fair value, he shall make such finding public. If the purchase price or the exporter's sale price is less than the foreign market value (or in the absence of such value, than the cost of production) there shall be levied, collected and paid a special duty in an amount equal to such difference.

The salient features of the act were as follows.

- Duties could be imposed if the exporter's price was less than the foreign market value.
- Foreign cost of production might be calculated if the foreign market value was not ascertainable.
- Dumping must be related to injury suffered by the domestic industry.

It is noteworthy that it laid the basis for the use of 'constructed value' when few or no foreign prices existed. It also introduced the idea that the dumping must be related to injury suffered by the domestic industry. In a way, the Anti-dumping Act of 1921 contained all the key elements of the anti-dumping law as we recognize today. This act thus set the stage for the evolution of this law in its current form.

In 1921, Britain also adopted its first anti-dumping legislation whilst Canada, New Zealand, and Australia substantially amended their acts. Subsequently more European countries passed anti-dumping laws between 1920–2. Some scholars attribute this spate of anti-dumping laws to a fear that Germany had amassed huge stockpiles of goods during the war to dump on the world market 'to win on the economic battlefield through predatory pricing'. There were a number of industries where Germany had scientific superiority, a cartel structure, and a protective tariff, all factors which could make dumping more likely (Stewart, Markel, and Kerwin 1993, p. 1391). It is suggested (CBO 1994) that the United States also feared that surplus stockpiles of goods in Europe caused due to cessation of trade during the war would be dumped on it, damaging its industries. According to many scholars however this surge in anti-dumping laws had its genesis in the post-World War I efforts of the European countries to rebuild their economies. Many of the war-devastated European countries found competitive devaluation as an important device for securing employment and political stabilization. The US and Britain among others responded to this 'exchange dumping', as it came to be known, by enacting anti-dumping legislation (Eichengreen and James 2001). Another important reason cited (CBO 1994) for growing number of countries adopting this legislation was the increased political pressures from uncompetitive firms. The war had disrupted international trade, which had resulted in the growth of import substituting domestic industries in these countries. With the end of the war the goods could once again be imported and this threatened the new emerging domestic industries. Countries sought solution in anti-dumping legislation. In the historical context thus providing protection was the driving force of the concurrent evolution of the anti-dumping laws in several (now industrialized) countries. Ciuriak (2005) calls it an era that was a high season of globalization[3] that was marked by an awakening of economic nationalism in the then newly industrializing countries and growing anxiety over the power of large corporations that were emerging to exploit economies of scale. It was however surrounded by anti-monopoly/anti-predatory dumping rhetoric. In the budget speech in which the first anti-dumping legislation was proposed in 1904, the then Canadian Finance Minister W.S. Fielding expressed a concern for predatory pricing and did not suggest any other reason for his concern over dumping (Sykes 1998). Later, in all those countries that introduced this legislation it was promoted as anti-monopoly legislation. It was insisted that the anti-dumping law was the best line of defence against companies and countries that resorted to predatory and mercantilist tactics to make trade gains.

After various countries individually adopted the legislation on anti-dumping, multilateral initiatives were also commenced. In 1922, the League of Nations undertook a study on dumping and differential pricing. No agreement could however be reached on a collective basis. A collective agreement was finally achieved with the GATT 1947.

Formation of the GATT: A Turning Point

In 1947, formation of the GATT marked the birth of the multilateral trading system. The GATT had its genesis in the International Conference on Trade and Employment that was called by the Economic and Social Council of the United Nations for the purpose of promoting the expansion of the production, exchange, and consumption of goods in 1947 (Waincymer 2001). One of the purposes of this UN Conference on Trade and Employment was to set up an International Trade Organization (ITO) as a third world economic pillar alongside the World Bank and International Monetary Fund. The Conference, which met at Havana on 21 November 1947 and ended on 24 March 1948, drew up the Havana Charter for an ITO, which was meant to establish a multilateral trade organization. For various reasons, the charter never came into force. However, tariff negotiations had resulted in 450,000 tariff concessions affecting $10 billion of trade, which formed about one-fifth of the world's total trade (WTO website). Pending the talks on the Havana Charter, the twenty-three negotiating countries decided to accept some of the trade rules of the draft ITO Charter and combine them with tariff concessions that were already negotiated. The combined package of trade rules and tariff concessions became known as the GATT. It entered into force in January 1948. Although the ITO Charter was finally agreed at a UN Conference on Trade and Employment in Havana in March 1948, ratification in national legislatures proved impossible in some cases. When the United States' Government announced in 1950 that it would not seek Congressional approval of the Havana Charter, the ITO was effectively dead. Therefore, despite its provisional nature, the GATT remained the only multilateral instrument governing international trade from 1948 until the establishment of the WTO (see Mavroidis 2005 for an excellent commentary).

In the course of negotiating the GATT 1947, the contracting parties envisaged an elaborate plan for trade liberalization and undertook to facilitate further reduction of trade-distorting practices in future negotiating Rounds. The United States was keen to include trade remedies in the agreement as some response to allegedly unfair trade in the form of dumping or subsidized goods. It argued that the application of trade remedies is important to ensure that neither government subsidy practices nor dumping upset the balance struck at the negotiating table. At the insistence of the United States, GATT 1947 incorporated the basic conditions for adopting anti-dumping measures and it became an international law. The 1921 US legislation formed the textual basis for Article VI of the GATT 1947 (Irwing 2005).

As originally drafted, Article VI contained no details on administration or calculation methodology. It was left for each individual signatory to devise its own regime. Article VI controlled anti-subsidy activity also although more comprehensive amendments occurred with the introduction of a revised Article XVI during the Kennedy Round.

Article VI of GATT 1947 set out the following basic principles.

- A product would be considered as dumped if it was being introduced into the commerce of an importing country at less than its normal value, that is, if the price of the product exported from one country to another

- was less than the comparable price, in the ordinary course of trade, for the like product when destined for consumption in the exporting country, or,
- in the absence of such domestic price, was less than either
    - the highest comparable price for the like product for export to any third country in the ordinary course of trade, or
    - the cost of production of the product in the country of origin plus a reasonable addition for selling cost and profit.

- Dumping needs to be condemned and offset by imposing an ADD if it caused or threatened material injury to an established industry in the territory of a contracting party or materially retarded the establishment of a domestic industry.
- Due allowance would be made in each case for differences in conditions and terms of sale, for differences in taxation, and for other differences affecting price comparability.
- A contracting party might levy on any dumped product an ADD not greater in amount than the margin of dumping in respect of such product.
- No contracting party would levy any ADD unless it determined that the effect of the dumping as the case might be, was such as to cause or threaten material injury to an established domestic industry, or was such as to retard materially the establishment of a domestic industry.

In short, the anti-dumping law was designed by developed countries to protect their nascent industries and was incorporated in the GATT at their insistence. Developing countries had no role in its origin.

ORIGIN AND EVOLUTION OF THE ADA AND THE DEVELOPING COUNTRIES: THE SUCCESSIVE GATT ROUNDS

Early GATT Rounds: 1947–61

Negotiations in the early GATT rounds remained concentrated on further tariff reductions (Table 3.1). Even though ADAs started surging in the mid-1950s, it remained a minor trade instrument in the GATT framework.

In the 1950s, Italy challenged a dumping finding by Sweden against Italian nylon stockings. The challenge was against the use of a minimum price system, delays in administration, and reversal of burden of proof. In the absence of any detailed rules on anti-dumping, the panel made very broad recommendations without a formal ruling. After this early experience of an anti-dumping dispute at the GATT level some further studies were undertaken on anti-dumping. In 1958, contracting parties asked the Secretariat to undertake a comparative study of anti-dumping laws. Following this study of

TABLE 3.1:   GATT/WTO trade rounds

Year	Place/name	Subjects covered	Number of countries
1947	Geneva	Tariffs	23
1949	Annecy	Tariffs	13
1951	Torquay	Tariffs	38
1956	Geneva	Tariffs	26
1960–1	Geneva (Dillon Round	Tariffs	26
1964–7	Geneva (Kennedy Round)	Tariffs and antidumping measures	62
1973–9	Geneva (Tokyo Round)	Tariffs, non-tariff measures, anti-dumping, 'Framework' agreements	102
1986–94	Geneva (Uruguay Round)	Tariffs, non-tariff measures, anti-dumping, subsidies, and safeguard measures, rules, anti-dumping services, intellectual property, dispute settlement, textiles, agriculture, creation of WTO	123
2002– (till date)	Doha Round	All goods and services, tariffs, non-tariff measures, anti-dumping and subsidies, regional trade agreements, IPR, environment, dispute settlement	144

Source: WTO website.

national anti-dumping laws, a Group of Experts was established that in 1960 agreed on certain common interpretations of ambiguous terms of Article VI. Discussions concerning the development of comprehensive anti-dumping rules were also held by GATT Working Parties. However, developing countries did not make any significant proposal on any aspect of the rules relating to anti-dumping during these discussions (Hoda 1987). This is not surprising in view of the fact that the GATT had a 'rich men's club' image. The general feeling among developing countries was that they were second-class members in this exclusive club and that it had failed to address their concerns.[4]

During this period the primary focus of developing countries had been on getting concessions within the GATT framework. Essentially comprising a facility to negotiate reciprocal tariff cut GATT was not geared to respond to the needs of developing countries (WTO 1999, p. 11). The first attempt to accommodate developing countries' concerns was made in 1954 through Article 18 (Whalley 1999, Grant 2006). It was revised to provide greater flexibility to developing countries. Article 18A allowed for developing countries to renegotiate tariff bindings in order to promote the establishment of particular industries. Article 18B included a specific provision to allow countries at 'an early stage of their development' to adopt quantitative restrictions on imports whenever monetary reserves were deemed to be inadequate in terms of the country's long term development strategy. Article 18C allowed developing countries to impose trade restrictions (both tariffs and quantitative restrictions) to support infant industries (GATT 1954). Developing countries however felt that the inclusion of these articles did not effectively address their trade concerns. While Articles 18a and 18c were subject to compensation and retaliation,[5] application of Article 18B had a limited implication (see Whalley 1999 for more discussion).

In 1957 an expert panel, known as the Haberler panel, was set up to consider the failure of less-developed countries to develop as rapidly as industrial countries (WTO 1999, p. 12). The result of the Haberler report was a number of changes made in favour of developing countries, including a Declaration on the Promotion of Trade of Less-Developed Countries adopted in 1961 (Grant 2006).

Part IV was incorporated into GATT articles in 1965. Part IV introduced a development dimension into GATT. It introduced the notion of non-reciprocity in tariff negotiations for developing countries and thus made it possible to grant preferential treatment to developing countries in international trade rules. Part IV has the title Trade and Development, and it has three articles. Article 36 recognizes the development needs of developing countries. It contains a statement of the principle of non-reciprocity, that is, developing countries need not reciprocate trade concessions made to them by developed countries in negotiation. Article 37 represents a best efforts commitment (with no obligation for action) to the prioritization of products of interest to developing countries in any trade liberalization. Article 38 provides for joint developed–developing country actions, citing possibilities for actions in the commodities field, inter-agency cooperation, possibilities of studying the export potential of developing countries, and other related issues.

During the negotiations, which led to the addition of Part IV to GATT, one proposal made was that the industrialized countries should refrain from applying such measures as anti-dumping if they affect the essential interests of developing countries. The proposal was turned down by developed countries.

Instead, in the final agreement, Paragraph 3c was added in Article 37, which required the developed countries

To have special regard to the trade interest of less developed countries when considering the application of other measures permitted under this Agreement to meet particular problems and explore all possibilities of constructive remedies before applying such measures where they would affect essential interests of the these countries.

It did not make any specific mention of anti-dumping (Hoda 1987) and did not make any concrete suggestion to provide remedy for the developing countries from such measures.

The Kennedy Round: 1964–7

In the Kennedy Round (1963–7), regulation of anti-dumping rules was taken up in earnest. Negotiations during this Round produced a code on multilateral rules for anti-dumping. It was the first major attempt to negotiate an ADA. The code set out the conditions for the initiation of investigations and provided details regarding the calculation of dumping margin and establishing injury and causal relationship between the two. It also laid down the provisions for the administrative guidance for conducting investigations and for imposition and collection of duties and specified provisions and principles of accepting Price-Undertaking.

Some of the key features of the code were as follows.

- Provisional duties could only be imposed following a preliminary finding of dumping and injury.
- Duties could be less than the dumping margin where that lesser duty would remove the injury.
- Where causation was concerned, the dumped imports had to be *demonstrably the principal cause* of material injury or of threat of material injury to a domestic industry or the principal cause of material retardation of the establishment of such an industry. The code required the authorities to weigh, on one hand, the effect of the dumping and, on the other hand, all other factors taken together that may be adversely affecting the industry.
- In the case of retarding the establishment of a new industry in the country of importation, investigating authorities were required to have convincing evidence of the forthcoming establishment of an industry, for example that the plans for a new industry had reached a fairly advanced stage, a factory was being constructed or machinery had been ordered.

The United States was not a signatory of this code. Since the Kennedy Round negotiations in the 1960s arrived at an anti-dumping code with a much more stringent test of 'causality' than in US law, the US Congress objected to the higher standard and passed a law stipulating that the United States would abide by the code only so long as it did not conflict with existing US law (Irwing 2005). The US Congress had thus been highly sensitive to weakening of the US anti-dumping policy in multilateral negotiations right since the beginning and made it clear that it would not be a party to any such attempt.

Negotiations during this Round were the responsibility of a Group on Anti-dumping Policies (GAP), which was dominated by OECD countries. Even though by this time the number of developing country members had increased they did not participate in the negotiations in the initial phases. In the closing phases, however, they did voice their concerns over the definition of dumping which considered a product as being dumped if the export price of the product exported from one country to another, was less than the comparable price in the ordinary course of trade, for the like product when destined for consumption in the exporting country.[6] They questioned the relevance of the concept of dumping for developing countries as adopted by GATT 1947. They enjoined the developed countries to give them a special treatment in the provision of anti-dumping. They argued that a central problem for the developing countries in respect of possible anti-dumping measures against their exports was that their home market prices for domestically manufactured products were in most cases higher than those in their export markets. The main reasoning was based on fact that inefficient cost structures which resulted primarily from the high cost of capital, labour market conditions, labour laws, poor infrastructural facilities and bad governance and lack of economies of scale distorted domestic market prices. For breaking into the export markets therefore these firms had to sell at a price below their domestic price. It was, therefore, not a sound policy to rely on home market prices/production costs as normal values in dumping investigations against developing countries. The normal value of all exports should be based on international prices for the goods concerned and not on home market prices/production costs. The developing countries proposed a footnote to Article 2 (d) of the 1967 Code that would have allowed for reference to a third country export prices instead of prices in their home country whenever they were alleged to be dumping. The proposal was however rejected due to strong objections by the developed countries (Kufuor 1998).

The first international code on anti-dumping procedures, which entered into force in 1968, was thus tailored by the developed countries to suit their requirements. Despite the concerns expressed by the developing countries, the identification of exports below the normal prices of the like product in the ordinary course of trade remained the key elements of dumping with no special treatment provided for developing countries.

In 1970, a GATT Working Party was established to examine the special problem of the developing countries under the 1967 Code. Developing countries again raised the basic problem in adhering to the 1967 Code. The Working Party admitted that a solution to the problem would have to be based on the recognition that in the case of the developing countries it was not reasonable to use home market prices/production costs as normal values in anti-dumping investigation. At one stage it appeared that an agreement could be reached to adopt the norm of comparison of export price with third country export price as a preferred criterion in the case of the developing countries (Hoda 1987). However, a compromise on the matter could not be made and the Working Party reported to the Council that it had not been possible to reach an agreement on a text that was acceptable to all members and the basic concept of dumping remained unchanged.

The Tokyo Round

In the Tokyo Round (1973–9), developing countries succeeded in getting 'Enabling Clause' (1979) incorporated in the GATT. This clause provided for a GATT Article 1 exception (MFN) for developing country trade preferences and established the principle of differential and more favourable treatment to developing countries.[7] It provided for: (i) the preferential market access of developing countries to developed country markets on a non-reciprocal, non-discriminatory basis; (ii) 'more favourable' treatment for developing countries in other GATT rules dealing with non-tariff barriers; (iii) the introduction of preferential trade regimes between developing countries; and (iv) the special treatment (see Krishna 1997 for details). Besides, a number of codes that were negotiated in the Tokyo Round contained 'Special and Differential Treatment' provisions. In this context, a clause for developing countries was added to the anti-dumping code also in the form of Article 13. Interestingly, the wordings of Article 13 were the same as those of Article 37(c) of Part IV of the GATT. Developing countries expressed their concerns over the usefulness of this article. Since the developing countries were not satisfied with the provision, discussions were held again in 1979 in which these countries pressed hard to get it recognized that comparisons with domestic prices cannot be relied upon to determine dumping charges against their exports. There were also proposals for providing technical assistance to the developing countries in implementing the provisions of anti-dumping. However no concrete achievements could be made in this direction.

Negotiations on ADA during this Round were also conducted by developed countries to cater to their concerns. Tokyo Round negotiations resulted in an average one-third cut in custom duties in the world's nine major industrial markets, bringing the average tariff in industrial products down to 4.7 per cent. The Tokyo Round was also the first attempt to reform the non-tariff barrier system. Clearly, the developed world wanted an easy-to-use safety valve to protect their industries from import competition. Major amendments introduced in the Tokyo Round therefore aimed at making the dumping allegations easier to prove. One of the most important changes introduced in the Tokyo Round was the removal of the principal cause test. Article 3(a) of the Kennedy Round read

A determination of injury shall be made only when the authorities concerned are satisfied that the dumped imports are demonstrably the principal cause of material injury or of threat of material injury to a domestic industry or the principal cause of material retardation of the establishment of such an industry.

On the contrary Article 3(4) of the Tokyo Code merely indicated that

There may be 'other factors', which at the same time are injuring the industry, and the injuries caused by other factors must not be attributed to the dumped imports.

The agreement did not even require the authorities to examine these factors and establish the injury caused by them. Furthermore, the list of 'other factors', which was provided in the main text in the First Code, was reduced to a footnote. Thus the standards of the causal test were lowered to facilitate the use of the anti-dumping measures in the post-Tokyo Round.

Standards of the injury test were also eased. The Kennedy Round Anti-dumping Code included export performance and restrictive trade practices in the list of injury indicators. These indicators were deleted during the Tokyo Round negotiations softening the rigour of the test. In addition, improvements were introduced in the procedural aspects of injury finding to set clear guidelines for the authorities to proceed while establishing injury. The Kennedy Round combined the causes and effects of injury on the domestic industry. It required the authorities to evaluate injury on the basis of examination of all factors having a bearing on the state of the industry in question. A list of these factors was provided in the code. The Tokyo Round distinguished between the factors indicating the cause and the effects of injury. A more methodical treatment was to facilitate the procedures of establishing injury and not to raise the standards. Another important reform introduced during this Round was that investigation period was fixed to one year to avoid delays in final determination.

There were some minor reforms also, which aimed at improving transparency in the system. For instance, Article 8(5) was incorporated requiring public notices to be given of all decisions whether negative or affirmative, the role of anti-dumping committee was extended and Article 15 was inserted for the consultation, and dispute mechanism. Article 15(2) required each party to afford sympathetic consideration to any request from another party for consultation. Article 15(3) provided that if consultations failed to achieve a mutually agreed solution the matter could be referred to the committee for conciliation, which would encourage the parties involved to develop a mutually acceptable solution. If no mutually agreed solution could be reached the committee would establish a panel to examine the matter, based upon a written statement of the party or the facts made available. But the incorporation of a dispute mechanism in this Round did not encourage greater recourse to panels. Only six cases were brought forward under the Tokyo Round Anti-dumping Code (Ciuriak 2005).

There were no significant improvements made in the dumping-related provisions. The major features of the Tokyo Round negotiations were: softening the standards for injury test and causal link between injury and dumping and improvements in the procedural aspects of injury finding. These measures facilitated the use of this tool. This is evident from the surge of anti-dumping activity in the post-Tokyo Round negotiations. One can therefore conclude that there was no improvement in the position of the developing countries at the end of the Round.

The Uruguay Round

The Ministerial Declaration adopted in Punta Del Este on 20 September 1986 to launch the Uruguay Round did not have an express reference to anti-dumping. Developing countries pushed to have it included (Leebron 1997). The number of developing countries involved in the negotiations had increased substantially in this Round compared to previous rounds.[8] Since many developing countries had begun to reevaluate their own import substitution trade policies, and to unilaterally liberalize their own trade policies by the time the Round started, their main concern was that ADP were obstacle in their attempts to have market access especially in industrialized countries. They criticized the developed countries, the United States in particular, for the extensive use of anti-dumping and submitted many more proposals and participated more actively in negotiating groups in this Round than in the previous Rounds. Another important development during the Round was that while in the 1960s and 1970s, developing countries developed a joint call for a differential treatment in the system as discussed above, in the Uruguay Round they weakened their call and submitted a large number of submissions that were primarily aimed at fine-tuning the agreement. They also made some important suggestions. These included: insertion of a public interest clause, exclusion of imports that were below some threshold level from the provision of cumulation, inclusion of a provision on anti-circumvention and sunset reviews, and strengthening of the dispute settlement system to prevent misuse of anti-dumping by domestic protectionist groups. However, negotiations remained focused on specific changes neglecting almost all the major suggestions made by the developing countries.

This was the period when the debate on the role of competition laws in relation to anti-dumping had intensified in the developed world. This debate was driven by the growing sentiments that anti-dumping was becoming a back-door protectionism and that competition policy was the appropriate answer for its reform (Messerlin 1986). A suggestion was made that anti-dumping be scrapped and replaced by competition laws. Though the proposal was turned down, some soft reforms were introduced to address the concern of the pro-competition lobbyists (Bekker 2004). Incorporation of a suggestion that consumers and industrial users should be allowed to make their views known during the investigations, an instruction to the authorities to examine all known factors other than the dumped imports and procedural reforms to enhance transparency in the agreement could be traced back to this new development that was taking place in the developed countries. Several reforms were introduced during the Uruguay Round, which were focused on the procedural aspects of the anti-dumping investigations to improve transparency. In particular, more detailed rules were incorporated in relation to the procedures to be followed in initiating and conducting anti-dumping investigations and the implementation of anti-dumping measures. Provisions on the application of provisional measures and the use of price undertakings in anti-dumping cases were strengthened. A new provision was added, which requires the immediate termination of an anti-dumping investigation in cases where the authorities determine that the margin of dumping is *de minimis* (which is defined as less than 2 per cent, expressed as a percentage of the export price of the product) or that the volume of dumped imports is negligible (generally when the volume of dumped imports from an individual country accounts for less than 3 per cent of the imports of the product in question into the importing country). Besides, the agreement calls for prompt and detailed notification of all preliminary or final anti-dumping actions to a committee on ADP.

Some of the changes such as inclusion of the provision of cumulation and cost-based test for ascertaining ordinary course of trade were aimed at legalizing the ADP prevailing in the United States and the EU. Unfortunately, developing countries also without realizing the implications remained focused only on such technical changes.

Major suggestions made by the developing countries except the one on Sunset clause were rejected. Insertion of the Sunset Review clause was considered a major victory for the developing countries. However, developing countries gained little because the anti-dumping measures under the agreement can be extended for successive new terms of five years if the authorities determine that the expiry of the duty would lead to recurrence of dumping and injury. One of the important proposals made by developing countries was to strengthen the dispute settlement mechanism. However, the developed countries desperately required less interference with domestic decisions during the Uruguay Round. At their insistence, Article 17.6(ii) was added into anti-dumping agreement in the Uruguay Round. This has strictly limited the panels' role in the ADA as compared with normal Dispute Settlement Procedure. Finally, no efforts were made to elaborate and operationalize the 'Special and Differential' provisions for the developing countries (Article 13 in the Tokyo Round and Article 15 in the Uruguay Round).

It is evident that participation by the developing countries in the Uruguay Round did not yield substantial gains to these countries. The outcome was largely determined by the United States and the EU. Major concerns of the developing countries were not addressed. Some changes were introduced, which addressed areas in which the Tokyo Round Agreement lacked precision and detail. Many of these changes were motivated by the debate on the competition-oriented approach to anti-dumping, which was building up in particular in the United States while some others were to legalize anti-dumping practices in the United States and EU. Thus, despite the early and active participation by developing countries in the negotiations, they had little influence on the final outcome.

Doha Round Negotiations

The Doha Ministerial Conference of the WTO set the stage for launching a New Post-Uruguay Round of Multilateral Trade Negotiations. Getting immediate negotiations on Singaporean issues: investment, competition policy, government procurement, and trade facilitation was at the top of the agenda of the developed countries during the run up to the Ministerial. Developing countries on the other hand, pushed hard for including several issues of their concerns including reform of the use of anti-dumping on the Doha agenda. The United States strongly opposed the move to include the ADA on the agenda of the Doha Round. In the run-up to the launching of the Round in November 2001, on the eve of the Doha Ministerial Conference, both houses of Congress passed strongly worded resolutions advising the President not to agree to major revisions in the current regime. The House of Representatives resolution passed by 410 to 4. In May 2001, sixty-two senators had signed a letter to the President warning him not to agree to any trade deals that would weaken the anti-dumping laws (Lindsey and Ikenson 2002b). Defenders of US trade laws wanted the administration to veto any discussion of these issues in the upcoming negotiations. However, the US Government ultimately had to bow to the international pressure due to an overwhelming support for the inclusion of anti-dumping on the agenda of the Doha Round. It agreed to include the agreement on the agenda but sought to limit the scope of such negotiations. The declaration (Paragraph 28) therefore provides:

In the light of experience and of the increasing application of these instrument by Members we agree to negotiations aimed at clarifying and improving disciplines under the Agreements on Implementation of Article VI of the GATT 1994 and on Subsidies and Countervailing measures, while preserving the basic concepts, principles and effectiveness of these agreement their instruments and objectives and taking into account the needs of developing and least developing countries....

The decision of the Ministerial Conference of the WTO at Doha thus emphasized the preservation of the basic concepts, principles, and effectiveness of this agreement, its instruments and its objectives. It mandates members to enter into 'negotiations aimed at clarifying and improving disciplines' under the ADA. Several proposals have been submitted by the developing countries. Most of them are guided by their own experience in the use of anti-dumping and are seeking clarifications and technical details of current provisions with little analysis of the issues that are important from their perspective (WTO 2003). The US agenda on the other hand is clear. It wants to improve transparency and adherence to the law to impact on the ability of other countries (in particular the developing countries) to initiate the investigations and impose duties against its firms. It is also keen to ensure that Article 17.6 that sets the role of the panels in the DSU is properly applied (WTO 2003). In this scenario, negotiations are expected to remain exclusively focused on specific clarifications in the provision or stricter procedural requirement. Though developing countries succeeded in including anti-dumping reform amongst the topics of immediate negotiation, it may not ultimately turn out to be a major victory for them unless there is an understanding of the objectives that they need to pursue. A number of developing countries along with a few developed countries have joined together in a group called 'The Friends of Anti-dumping' (FANs). This group comprises Brazil; Chile; Colombia; Costa Rica; Hong Kong, China; Israel; Japan; Rep. of Korea; Mexico; Norway; Singapore; Switzerland; the Separate Customs Territory of Taiwan, Penghu, Kinmen, and Matsu; Thailand; and Turkey. They are becoming important players in these negotiations. Their goal is to restrict the use of anti-dumping and to provide clarity to substantive rules for dumping and injury. In a joint statement (TN/RL/W/171), senior officials of these countries reported a that nearly 100 proposals had been tabled for the current Round negotiations. Of them, around thirty have been from the FANs. Other developing countries that have submitted their proposals and have been actively participating in the debate are: India, Egypt, Venezuela, China, and Argentina. All other countries have been playing rather passive role.

EVOLUTION OF THE SUBSTANTIVE LEGAL PROVISIONS: FEW GAINS FOR DEVELOPING COUNTRIES

This section reviews the evolution of the substantive legal provisions of the Agreement in order to demonstrate how ineffectively the reforms introduced in anti-dumping provisions in successive Rounds have addressed the ambiguities present in them and how little the developing countries gained from such elaborations and clarifications. While doing so it draws on the existing literature (Tharakan 1991, 1994, 1995, 1999; Tharakan and Waelbroeck 1994; Murray and Rousslang 1989; Lindsey 2000; Araujo et al. 2001; Jackson and Vermulst 1989; Vermulst 1997; Didier 2001; Hsu 1998; Almstedt and Norton 2000 among others) and several submissions submitted by the Members to GATT/WTO during the previous Rounds and the current Round. For illustrating the ADA's serious methodological flaws it uses actual case records from different dumping investigations carried out against Indian exporters in the United States and the EU and from dispute settlement cases on anti-dumping, in general. Thus, the focus has largely been on the Indian experience. This is because this data was more accessible to us than the data for any other developing country.

Dumping Determination

Like product

A proper identification of 'like product' based on economic considerations is the first step in calculating the normal value. The concept of like product is vital in determining the presence of a domestic industry and also in determining the existence of injury. The Kennedy Round defined the like product as

product which is identical, i.e. alike in all respects to the product under consideration, or in the absence of such a product, another product which, although not alike in all respects, has characteristics closely resembling those of the product under consideration

The code provided no guidance for interpreting the term 'closely resembling'. Despite the vagueness in the definition of the 'like product', however no efforts were made in the subsequent rounds to refine it.[9] In the absence of models of like products that are 'identical' to a particular model of the exported products, authorities are free to decide which models for the normal value 'closely resemble' the exported model and thus may be used in the calculation of dumping margins. This leaves much to the discretion of the authorities. There is both the incentive and the opportunity to manipulate the category of like products in order to achieve specific goals. If 'like product' is defined in too strict a manner then it becomes easier to prove injury. If, on the contrary, the relevant market is defined too broadly it may lead to imposition of duties in cases where it should not (Hoekman and Mavroidis 1996).

What is generally not discussed is the fact that this problem is more serious for the developing countries as the domestic industries in developed countries generally produce more specialized product while developing country exporters export mainly standardized products. The products under consideration are therefore not interchangeable and not comparable as such with the developed country produced goods. However, due to vagueness in the definition the authorities may use their discretion in establishing similarities in the products/ models. Several instances may be cited where the authorities manipulated the category to achieve the specific goals. In the Hot-Rolled Flat Steel Products (1758/2000) case against India for instance, exporting producers claimed that the product concerned that they produced and sold was not interchangeable and not comparable as such with the community produced product. They claimed that the production process of the community producers was more advanced and even used different technology thus producing a higher quality product. They further pointed out that users sometimes had to re-roll the imported products before they could be processed further and thus claimed that their product was not a like product to that of the complaining community producers. The Commission admitted that the products were not *identical* but it argued that 'this cannot lead to the conclusion that hot-rolled coil imported from the countries concerned were not a *like product* [emphasis added] to that produced by the community industry'. In the Steel Ropes and Cables (SWR) case Indian exporters argued that the community was producing more specialized SWR while exporters were exporting mainly commodity SWR. The community suggested that while SWR in the top end and in the bottom end are clearly not interchangeable, SWR in the adjoining groups are interchangeable. Given this overlap between groups, no clear dividing line could be established and therefore all SWR were considered to be one product. These examples illustrate how ambiguous it is, in the absence of a rational and disciplined framework, to establish whether or not the allegedly dumped products are like products to those produced by the domestic industry.

Normal value: Conditions for the use of constructed normal value

Article 2(a) of the Kennedy Round Anti-dumping Code established the framework within which an investigating authority was to determine the normal value to be compared with the export price. It established a presumption that normal value would be the representative market price in the exporter's country. It recognized that it might not always be possible to use the actual information on normal price and that the investigating authorities might have to construct normal price. Comparison of export prices with constructed value is however highly ambiguous. It results not only in artificial dumping findings but also inflates dumping margins. Unfortunately, various Rounds of the GATT increased the scope of the use of constructed values and failed to address the concerns of the developing countries in this regard.

Article 2(d) of the Kennedy Round listed two situations in which the investigating authorities might reject the use of sales in the domestic market of the exporter in the calculation of normal value: (i) when there were no sales of the like product in the ordinary course of trade in the domestic market of the exporting country and (ii) when because of the particular market situation, such sales did not permit a proper comparison. The law provided no guidance in interpreting 'ordinary course of trade', or in determining the 'particular situation' when home market sales did not permit a proper comparison. No further elaborations were made in the provisions during the Tokyo Round either. Uruguay Round negotiations also left the term 'particular market situation' unexplained.[10] However, the term 'ordinary course of trade' (Article 2.2.1) was clarified and one more situation in which the authorities could disregard the actual selling prices in the target country was added. It read 'when because of the particular market situation or *low volume of the sales in the domestic market of the exporting country* [emphasis added], such comparisons were not proper...'. In what follows, we examine how these two situations are defined now and how they affect the dumping findings in particular against the developing countries.

Ordinary course of trade   Under the current agreement, sales of the like products in the domestic markets of the exporting country at prices below per unit cost (plus administrative and selling costs) may be treated as not being in the 'ordinary course of trade' and may be disregarded in determining normal value 'only if such sales are made within an extended period of normally one year (but not less than six months) in substantial quantities (i.e. they represent not less than 20 per cent of the total transaction volume) and are at prices which do not provide for the recovery of all costs within a reasonable period of time'.

This 'cost test' was based on the US practice. The 1974 US Trade Act included a provision that allowed sales at below cost to be disregarded from the determination of the normal value. Gradually, other developed countries such as the EU, Canada, and Australia also adopted this practice and used it extensively. WTO ADA adopted this test during the Uruguay Round to define the term 'ordinary course of trade'. Under the cost test, home-market sales found to be below the cost of production are excluded from the calculation of normal value. In other words, *all* export prices are compared to those of *only the* above-cost home-market sales. This asymmetric comparison skews the calculation in favour of finding dumping. Lindsey and Ikenson (2002a, 2002b) have argued that the use of the 'cost test' is probably the single most egregious methodological distortion in contemporary ADP. They examined dumping margin determination in seventeen cases investigated in the United States against the market economies. In two cases, the calculated dumping margin would have been zero had the cost test not been administered while most of the remaining fifteen cases would have had margins at least 50 per cent lower than the rate ultimately calculated. Many scholars have argued that it is normal business practice to sell at below cost in times of recession and that the exclusion of such sales distorts the normal value (Kuofor 1998, Vermulst 1987, Bierwagen 1990). It has however become a common practice to exclude such sales. Lindsey and Ikenson (2002a) examined thirty-seven determinations and found that in thirty-three of them the Department of Commerce excluded some or all home market sales through use of the cost test.

What compounds the problem is that the agreement has nothing to suggest that only the transactions not in the ordinary course of trade be rejected. As a result, countries may tend to reject the entire sale if the condition is not met. The EC for instance discards price data and uses the constructed normal value where per product type the volume of sales above unit cost represented less than 10 per cent of the total sales.

This problem is particularly acute in the sectors producing perishable goods, which are cyclical in nature or in the case of the growing manufacturing sector. Since these sectors predominate mainly in developing countries, these countries are particularly vulnerable to this provision and hence dumping finding.

Low volume of sales   The Uruguay Round negotiations permitted the authorities to construct the normal value 'when there is a low volume of sales in the domestic markets of the exporting country'. The law clarifies that home market sales will normally be considered a sufficient quantity for the determination of the normal value when the similar product destined for the home market of the exporting country constitutes 5 per cent or more of the sales of the product under consideration destined for sale in the importing country. This check may be performed at the following two different levels:

- total domestic sales of like product vs total exports of like products;
- domestic sales of each particular model/type/category vs exports of that particular model/type.

The agreement does not specify which of the above two is preferable or is referred to. In the EC, the rule of 5 per cent is applied at both these levels. Didier (2001) observed that in most cases the requirement fails to meet at the model/type level and this provides the authorities an opportunity to use constructed value. Moreover, though the agreement is not rigid about the 5 per cent viability test, it leaves it entirely to the discretion of the authorities to decide when and under what conditions a lower ratio could be used.

These loopholes in the agreement have significant implications from the developing country perspective. This is because domestic markets are very small for many export-oriented products in these countries. Furthermore, due to segregation of the domestic and export markets, there may not be domestic sales of many models. This gives an easy opportunity to the authorities to establish low volume of sales and construct the normal value. Apparently, the agreement is highly asymmetrical and make developing countries in particular, vulnerable to the use of constructed normal value by the investigating authorities.

Construction of the normal value

Two alternative methods for constructing normal value were provided in the Kennedy Round Code: (i) the 'cost of production method' and (ii) the 'export price to the third country method'. In addition to these two methods, the agreement also permitted to use the 'best fact available' to calculate the normal value. Finally, there are separate provisions for non-market economies. In what follows, evolution and ambiguities of each of these methods is reviewed in detail.

Cost of production method   The agreement permits the authorities to construct the normal value by adding a reasonable amount for administrative, selling, and general costs and for profits to the cost of production in the country of origin. This has come to be known as the 'cost of production method'. The Kennedy Round Code provided little guidance in using the methodology where the data on the reasonable amount of administrative, selling, and general costs and profit was either not available or it was not reliable. It merely indicated that 'the addition for profit shall not exceed the profit normally realized on sales of products of the same general category in the domestic market of the country of origin'. Furthermore, there was no guidance on cost allocation for making adjustments for the non-recurring items or start up operations.

The Tokyo Round did not add any further elaborations to the existing provisions. Uruguay Round however added Article 2.2.1.1, which introduced certain clarifying reforms to these provisions. First of all, the authorities are instructed to use the cost data that was maintained in accordance with the 'generally accepted accounting principles' (GAAP) only. It clarifies that 'costs shall be calculated on the basis of records kept by exporters under investigation if they are in accordance with the GAAP of the exporting countries'. But it also added that costs data thus maintained should 'reasonably reflect' the cost associated with production and sale of the product under consideration. This means that the authorities can reject the GAAP data also if it does not 'reasonably reflect the costs...'. This provision however does not clarify the circumstances in which the authorities can reject or adjust the data maintained in the producer's records (WTO 2002). This ambiguity allows the authorities to reconstruct a producer's costs arbitrarily claiming that the particular cost accounting method does not 'reasonably reflect' costs for anti-dumping investigations. The reconstruction of costs then results into artificial dumping margins.

Second, the Uruguay Round also clarifies that when the amounts for administrative, selling, and general costs and for profits cannot be determined on the basis of actual information, investigating authorities have a complete discretion to choose between profits and costs either (i) of the exporter in question in respect of production and sales in the same general category of product, or (ii) of any other exporter/producer subject to investigation in respect of production and sales of the like product in the domestic market of the country of origin, or (iii) any other reasonable method.

The options provided in the article have no preferential significance. Clearly, if the authorities prefer (iii), this may lead to substantial bias in the calculation of normal values. Moreover, this approach is often unfair as different producers of a like product often incur significantly different administrative, selling, and general costs and profits from each other either because they are selling different types of like products or because they have different cost efficiency. Lindsey (2000) has observed that the profit rates used by the US Department of Commerce (USDOC) in constructed value are frequently much higher than any conceivable norm. Comparing the profit rates actually used by the USDOC for some products to the average profit rates of the equivalent US industries during the year the respective initiations were made, he found that the difference between them ranged from 6.57 per cent to as large as 20.7 per cent. Thus, unrealistic normal profits and/or administrative, selling, or general costs may introduce serious ambiguities in the calculation of constructed normal value. The famous cotton bed linen case investigated by the EC against India elucidates this ambiguity further. In this case, the EC had constructed normal value for most exporters, using for all of them a profit margin of 18.65 per cent found to have been obtained by an Indian producer on his domestic sales for a limited volume of the product concerned. This led to a sharp increase in the normal value and in turn resulted in a very high dumping margin.

TABLE 3.2:   Comparison of USDOC profit rates and US industry profit rates—
             Some illustrations (in per cent)

Investigation	USDOC rate	US industry rate
Dinnerware from Taiwan	25.77	5.23
Brake drums and rotors from China	12.50	5.93
Cut-to-length steel plate from China	10.14	3.43
Dinnerware from Indonesia	22.61	5.23
Collated roofing nails from China	20.50	7.20

Source: Lindsey (2000).

Last, the Uruguay Round also added a provision about cost allocation (Article 2.2.1.1). The article requires the national authorities to adjust costs appropriately for those non-recurring items of cost that benefit future and/or current production or for circumstances in which costs during the period of investigation are affected by start-up operations. The provision is subject to different interpretations with regard to the treatment of the non-recurring costs, treatment in case of start-up operations, and the length of a start-up operation. The agreement directs authorities to ignore, when computing normal values, abnormally high costs and/or losses in domestic prices where production is in a start-up phase. It provides that in case of start-up operations, the cost at the end of the start-up period will be taken into account, which generally would be the time when the cost of production in the new line would have stabilized. However, if the start-up period extends beyond the investigation period, the most recent cost will be taken into account. No limit is made in the text with respect to the types of costs or the types of operations or the types of adjustments. It is thus not clear whether this applies to start-up losses due only to the new production facilities or whether the launching of new products within old facilities is also to be taken into account. It is also not clear what costs are included in this special regime? The EC allows respondents to claim for adjustments for new production facilities only.

Furthermore, it does not allow for R&D expenditures or start-up sales expenses. The US legislation, on the other hand, allows adjustments for start-up operations where a producer is using new production facilities or producing a new product for which substantial investments are required and where production levels are limited by technical factors associated with the initial phase of production. Though these provisions appear to be elaborate, they are somewhat generalized and may allow for any number of start-up scenarios. In several instances (such as Stainless Wires case investigated by the EC, Preserved Mushroom case, Administrative Review by the USDOC) Indian exporting producers who sustained losses throughout the investigation period claimed that these losses had occurred during the start-up phase and that this should be taken into account. However, the investing authorities rejected their claim on one or the other ground.

Thus the technical details incorporated during the Uruguay Round for constructing normal value ultimately resulted in legal justifications for misusing the law.

Export price to the third country method   The first anti-dumping code allowed the authorities to use the price when exported to any third country. It clarified that 'the export price used should be the highest price subject to the condition that it should be reasonable' but there was no guidance in determining the reasonableness of the export price. The Tokyo Round introduced no change. The Uruguay Round softened the requirement. It stipulates that 'the authorities may use the price of goods when exported to an 'appropriate third country'. But there is no well-defined criteria for choosing 'appropriate third country'. It is usually the 'third country' suggested by the complainants that is retained by the investigating authorities for the calculations. In many cases, therefore, that finding dumping is a foregone conclusion.

Best available information   Article 6(i) of the Kennedy Round Code permitted the authorities to make a final finding on basis of the 'facts available' in cases in which any interested party withholds the necessary information. The authorities thus enjoyed an unlimited discretion of demanding unnecessary information and rejecting the information furnished by the exporters. Article 6(8) of the Tokyo Code allowed additional powers of manipulations to the authorities by adding 'within a reasonable period'. It stated

In cases in which any interested party refuses access to, or otherwise does not provide, necessary information *within a reasonable period* [emphasis added] or significantly impedes the investigation, preliminary and final findings, affirmative or negative, may be made on the basis of the facts available.

The term 'reasonable period of time' was not elucidated. Authorities could thus reject the information simply on the plea that the information was not provided within a reasonable period of time. The Uruguay Round added Annex II to specify various rules in that respect. The objective was to limit the wide discretion the national authorities had hitherto enjoyed of rejecting the information furnished by the exporters. It has stipulates that

all information which is verifiable, which is appropriately submitted so that it can be used in the investigation without undue difficulties, which is supplied in timely fashion and wherever applicable ... should be taken into account when determinations are made. Even though the information provided may not be ideal in all respects, this should not justify the authorities from disregarding it, provided the interested party has acted to the best of its ability.

It also stipulates that if the explanations are considered by the authorities as not being satisfactory, the reasons for the rejection of such evidence or information should be given....

The above 'guidelines' leave many questions unanswered with regard to the application of the 'facts available' rules (Dutta 2004). Can the information that is 'deficient' only in some respects submitted by a party to the best of its ability be rejected or is the investigating authority bound to use it? Can the 'satisfaction' of the investigating authority be measured by any objective analysis of the information submitted? How does the investigating authority discharge its onus to '*examine* those elements of information with which it is *not* satisfied'? How does one determine whether there are any 'undue difficulties' in using the information as submitted? How to construe what is 'within a reasonable period' or 'in a timely fashion' in any given case? To what extent does rejection of any particular element of information justify the rejection of other related information submitted?

The Uruguay Round reforms have not resulted in a reduction in either the use of this methodology or the average dumping margins based on this methodology. Lindsey (2000) examined all USDOC anti-dumping investigations from 1995 through 1998 (see Table 3.3). Of the 141 total determinations, 36 (one-third) were based on 'facts available'. He found that the USDOC made affirmative findings for 107 of the 141 companies investigated over this period. What is more interesting to note is that in all the cases based on facts available, the USDOC made affirmative dumping findings. The success rate was 50 per cent for those companies for which the USDOC used actual home market price.

He has also shown that the average dumping margin in the cases based on facts available had been as high as 95.58 per cent against an average of 58.79 per cent in all the affirmative findings. In contrast, in the four cases

TABLE 3.3:   Summary of dumping margin calculation methodologies used in anti-dumping investigations: 1995–8

Calculation methodology	Determination (affirmative only)	Average dumping margin for affirmative findings (%)
Best information	36 (36)	95.58
Constructed value	20 (14)	35.70
Third country price	1 (0)	0
Non-market economy	47 (28)	67.05
Home market price	4 (2)	7.36
Mixed	33 (27)	17.20
Total	141 (107)	58.79

Source: Lindsey (2000).

that were based on the actual price data, the average margin was just 7.36 per cent. While analysing the effect of the Uruguay Round reforms on the use of the 'fact available' methodology in the United States, Moore (2006) reveals that during the pre-WTO period of 1980–94, 681 investigations were made by the Department of Commerce. Of them, 279 (29 per cent) were based on the 'best fact available' methodology. During 1995–2002, the proportion of investigations based on 'fact available' increased to over 44 per cent (224 of 501 investigations). Furthermore, the average dumping margin in cases based on fact available was 70 per cent (as against 22 per cent for the other cases) during 1980–94;[11] it increased to 74 per cent (against 32 per cent for other cases) during 1995–2002.

Developing countries are particularly vulnerable to the use of best facts available. This is because firms in these countries do not generally have well-developed data maintenance systems. Any failure of the domestic firm to respond to the authorities' onerous questionnaires allows the authority to disregard all its data and instead use the best information available, which typically means data reported in the domestic firm's petition. How the authorities (ab)use this provisions may very well be illustrated by the Steel Plate case against India investigated by the USDOC. The USDOC had problems with the originally submitted electronic databases that were found to be incorrectly formatted and incomplete. The USDOC issued several supplemental questionnaires. The subject firm (SAIL) responded to all of them. On product specific costs, it admitted that the company did not maintain costs on the product specific basis as required by the questionnaire but it did report different costs for different products using certain cost allocation. The USDOC, however, expressed its doubts over the reliability of these figures and finally, discarded all information provided by the exporter and instead used the information provided by the petitioners.[12]

Use of surrogate country data: The non-market economies   These are the economies where due to strict government controls, prices are not determined by the market forces. They reflect various other social and political considerations. The interpretive note[13] to Article VI of GATT allowed the authorities to use any method to determine a normal value in such cases. Its wordings are as follows:

It is recognized that, in the case of imports from a country which has a complete or substantially complete monopoly of its trade and where all domestic prices are fixed by the State, special difficulties may exist in determining price comparability for the purposes of paragraph 1, and in such cases importing contracting parties may find it necessary to take into account the possibility that a strict comparison with domestic prices in such a country may not always be appropriate.

It merely states that the domestic prices are not strictly comparable with export prices in such cases. It does not forbid the use of the constructed normal value. However, unreliable cost information, it is argued, makes it impossible to use the cost of production method while the export price to a third country is as suspect as any other price and hence cannot be used for determining normal value. In practice therefore, anti-dumping legislation in most countries allows the investigating authorities to ignore the nominal prices or costs in the non-market economies (NME) and base the normal value estimated on the price or cost of a producer of the like product in an surrogate market economy 'which may be regarded as a substitute for the purposes of the investigation'. The constructed cost depends on the choice of the surrogate country, its competitiveness, and market structures. If the cost of production in the selected country is higher, it may result into higher normal value (Krishna 1997, Wang 1999). What compounds the problem is the fact that this is the applicant who usually suggests the 'surrogate country', which makes the favourable dumping finding a foregone conclusion. Furthermore, there is no limit on the choice of the surrogate economy. It could be the investigating country itself!! The United States uses a method known as the 'factor of production method'. Under this method, the United States uses the input quantities of the product used in the targeted NME and values them at prices prevailing in a surrogate country (Vermulst 1987, Horlics and Oliver 1989, Messerlin 1991). Although this method allows the authorities to take into account the technical factors while calculating a normal value, it does not do away with the basic problem inherent in the calculations. The 'surrogate method' makes NMEs particularly vulnerable to dumping finding. Miranda et al. (1998) revealed that the proportion of investigations resulting in final imposition in all the completed cases is the highest for the NMEs. Although these economies are no more completely centrally controlled, they are continued to be treated in the same way.

Article 2, Paragraph 2.2 explicitly mentions the 'particular market situation' as a condition for using the constructed cost method or the export to the third country method. However, following the Note 2 of Article VI, almost all the countries use the surrogate method, which facilitates positive dumping finding against these countries.

Use of constructed normal value and developing countries

The above discussion suggests that developing countries are highly vulnerable to the use of constructed normal values and that there is a huge potential for manipulation inherent in the methodologies used for constructing these value. Evidence also suggests that developing countries became particularly vulnerable to the use of these methodologies. Blonigen (2003a) provides detailed data on all anti-dumping cases investigated between 1980 and 1995 by the USDOC. The data reveal that affirmative findings were made for 631 companies in all over this period (Table 3.4). Of these over 54 per cent were

TABLE 3.4:   Summary of methodologies adopted for constructing normal value by USDOC: 1980–95

	Best information		CP	Export	NME	Total
	Complete	Partial				
Cases (company-wise) with affirmative findings	195	6	33	19	84	337 (54)
Cases against developed countries	120	4	10	7	2	349 (41)
Developing	75	2	23	12	82	281 (70)

Note: CP: cost of production method; export: third country export data; NME: non-market economy. Parentheses show per cent of total affirmative findings.

Source: Based on author's calculations using Blonigen (2003a).

based on constructed normal value. What was more serious was the fact that around 69 per cent of the affirmative cases investigated against developing countries were based on the constructed normal value. For the developed countries the proportion was only 41 per cent.

The situation did not improve even after the Uruguay Round Agreement came into force. Lindsey (2000) reported data on the dumping methodologies adopted by the USDOC in the anti-dumping investigation of 141 companies during the post WTO period of 1995 to 1998. This information is summarized in Table 3.5 below. It revealed that the cases involving developing countries are much more likely to be based on constructed normal value than those involving developed countries. The only exception is Japan against which there appears to be a direct bias.

TABLE 3.5:   Summary of methodologies adopted for constructing normal value by USDOC: 1995–8

Companies from	Home market price based normal value (Col 2)	Constructed normal value (Col 3)	Total number of cases (Col 4)	Col 3 as % of Col 4
Developing countries other than China	10	23	33	70
China	0	41	41	100
Transition economies other than China	0	6	6	100
Taiwan	8	11	19	58
Japan	2	13	15	87
OECD other than Japan	16	11	27	41

Source: Author's calculations based on Lindsey (2000).

Estimation of export prices

Ex-factory export prices are arrived at after making numerous adjustments. In cases where there is no export price or where it appears to the authorities concerned that the export price is unreliable because of association or a compensatory arrangement between the exporter and the importer or a third party, the export price has to be constructed on the basis of the price at which the imported products are first resold to an independent buyer, or if the products are not resold to an independent buyer, or not resold in the condition as imported, on such reasonable basis as the authorities may determine (Article 2e of the Kennedy Round Code). The agreement stipulates that in such cases allowances for costs (including duties and taxes) incurred between importation and resale and for profits accruing should be made. When a manufacturer performs all export functions (for instance, administration of exports and networking, etc.) in-house, his export price reflects these costs and is comparatively high. On the contrary, when he sells to a related importer who performs all these functions on his behalf then the price does not reflect this cost and is comparatively low. Adjustments made in the price in these cases therefore result in anomaly, penalizing exports via related importers (Didier 2001). Despite this anamoly no further refinement was introduced in this article in the subsequent Rounds.

Fair comparison

Article 2(f) of the Kennedy Round demanded that fair comparison be made between export price and normal value. It stipulated that

Comparison between normal value and export price shall be made at the same level of trade, normally at ex-factory level, and in respect of sales made at nearly the same time. It specified that due allowance is made for differences that affect price comparability including, differences in conditions and terms of sale, taxation, levels of trade, quantities and physical characteristics.

The language of the code was very general and lacked specific disciplines. Little guidance was provided to make allowances for the differences that affected price comparability. Despite the vagueness of the article no significant change was introduced in this provision in the Tokyo Round. The Uruguay Round negotiations also failed to address the basic issues effectively. One of the major issues in fair comparison was that Article 2(e) of the Kennedy Round [Article 2(5) of the Tokyo Round] directed investigating authorities to construct export prices at ex-factory level when exports take place via related importers but the agreement had no provision for adjustments in normal value when sales are made through affiliates (as discussed above). As a result, export prices constructed at the ex-factory level were generally compared with domestic sales prices to the first unrelated buyer without effective adjustments. To address this problem, the Uruguay Round added that 'if in the cases where export prices are constructed, price comparability has been affected the authorities shall establish the normal value at a level of trade equivalent to the level of trade of constructed export price or shall make due allowances to ensure a fair comparison' (Article 2.4). This did not resolve the matter. The authorities continued to use discretion. In the Certain Hot-rolled Steel Products from Japan case (investigated by the United States), Japan raised this issue at the WTO level. The Panel and the AB gave different rulings. The Panel noted that downstream sales made by affiliates of exporters/producers though in the ordinary course of trade has no relevance because they are not sales of the exporters for whom normal value is calculated. The Panel found support for this view in Articles 2.2 and 2.3 of the ADA, which provide alternative methods of calculating, respectively, normal value and export price. While Article 2.3 expressly allows the use of downstream sales where the 'export price is unreliable because of association', Article 2.2 is silent as to whether the use of downstream sales is a permitted alternative method of calculating 'normal value'. The Panel could 'see no basis' for concluding that because Article 2.3 allows the use of downstream sales to construct export price, it must also be possible to use a similar method to 'construct' normal value. In other words, the Panel ruled to exclude sales to related parties as not being made in the ordinary course of trade. The AB, however, reversed the Panel judgement. In its view, the identity of the seller is no ground for precluding downstream transactions and the authorities may make allowances under Article 2.4 to arrive at a price that is comparable with the export price. It ruled that in the case of sales to a related party, domestic prices may be adjusted at the same level of trade as export prices. The authorities however are highly restrictive in granting level of trade allowances in the absence of clear guidance.

Furthermore, current provisions of Article 2.4 are not specific enough to ensure symmetrical adjustments between the two. As a result, authorities make unjustifiable comparisons between export price and normal value (Lindsey and Ikenson 2002a, 2002b; Bhansali 2004a). While export prices are adjusted for selling (indirect and indirect) expenses and profits authorities fail to make such adjustments in the normal value giving an upward bias to the latter. Similarly, while the rules require the authorities to disregard sales not in ordinary course for calculating the normal value, there are no specific rules with regard to the exclusion of sales 'not in ordinary course of trade (sales of samples, sales to employees, barter sales, sales of the like products to a toller or subcontractor for further manufacture upon the condition that the further-manufactured products will be returned to the responding party, and certain sales to affiliated parties') from the calculation of export price and constructed export price (Bhansali 2004a). These practices result in asymmetrical adjustments in exports and normal value.

Finally, if any interested party demands price adjustments because of a difference in physical characteristics or quantity and condition of sales, he/she has to establish the fact that the difference directly affected the market price or the manufacturing costs and that the difference is quantifiable. However the investigating authorities at times do not permit the required allowances on unreasonable grounds. One such allowance is duty drawback claims. This problem is particularly serious for developing countries where import duties are higher than in developed countries. In the Synthetic Fibre Polyester (from India) case (1992) where the provisional dumping margins exceeded 100 per cent as a result of the EC not taking into account duty drawback, the final margins were reduced significantly when such allowances were made. However, in most cases the authorities reject the claims for duty drawback adjustments. Detailed guidelines are laid down in Annexes II and III of the ASCM for investigating authorities to examine whether inputs are consumed in the production of the exported product. But the problem is that such procedures are not adopted by authorities in investigating anti-dumping cases. They insist upon the producers positively establishing that domestically purchased raw materials have at no times been used in exported finished goods. The EC, for instance, insists that a duty adjustment is only granted provided two conditions are satisfied: first, it must be shown that import charges are borne by the like product and by materials physically incorporated therein, and second, these import charges are refunded/not collected when the product is exported to the community. The USDOC practice is to evaluate duty drawback adjustment claims with a 'two-part test' to determine (i) whether the import duty and rebate are directly linked to, and dependent upon, one another and (ii) whether the company claiming the adjustment can show that there are sufficient imports of raw materials to account for the duty drawback received on exports of the manufactured product. Exporters find it extremely difficult to conclusively provide evidence with regard to the these requirements. Thus, in many cases authorities compare an artificially high normal value (excluding low-priced sales) with an export price that includes all sales.

In the Polyester Staple Fibre case against India, the EC rejected the claim at the provisional stage due to lack of evidence. One exporter before the final determination submitted new information to support the duty drawback claim but the EC did not consider this claim on the ground that it was not submitted in time. In the Certain Polyethylene Terephthalate case, the EC rejected the claim made by Indian companies on the import duties refund. The companies argued that the findings of the anti-dumping investigations were in contradiction with the findings in the parallel anti-subsidy proceedings in which the Duty Entitlement Passbook Scheme (DEPB) scheme was considered as an export subsidy that benefited the companies. The Commission, however, changed its stance and argued that since countervailing duty will be deducted from ADD, any adjustment made in the normal value would amount to double adjustment. There are several other cases in which importers' claims on duty drawback were rejected. These are, for instance, Steel Fasteners, Polyethylene Terephthalate Film, and Sulphanic Acid cases. In the Polyester textured filament yarn (PTY) case against India, all the three investigated companies claimed a duty drawback adjustment. However, the Commission rejected the duty drawback adjustment claim made by all Indian exporters on the ground that there was no evidence that any import charge was borne by the like product when destined for domestic consumption. Two Indian exporters argued that in the context of the parallel anti-subsidy investigation the Commission had accepted the scheme as non-countervailable. Therefore, in order to remedy this contradiction between the two proceedings the said allowance should have been granted. However, the Commission argued that each anti-dumping case is examined on the basis of its own factual circumstances, which may differ from all other proceedings. In the Stainless Steel Wire Rod from India case, the USDOC rebutted the Indian company's duty drawback claim stating categorically that relying on the Indian government's predetermined import content for exported merchandise is an inadequate means of calculating and reporting duty drawbacks.

Determining dumping margin

It is generally claimed that a significant improvement was made during the Uruguay Round in the methodology for comparing the domestic sale price and the export price to determine the margin of dumping. The earlier Rounds had not addressed this issue. Prior to the conclusion of the Uruguay Round, it was a standard practice of some members to compare the weighted normal value with individual export prices (Kim 1996 for the EU, Palmeter 1996 for United States). After much criticism this issue was discussed during the Uruguay Round. Finally, Article 2.4.2 was added to provide three alternative methods for comparing export prices with normal value:

- weighted average-by-weighted average method (weighted average normal value to weighted average of prices of all comparable export transactions);
- transaction-to-transaction method; or
- weighted average to transaction method (weighted average normal value to individual export transactions, for so-called 'targeted dumping' cases).

The new provision specified that 'margins of dumping' could be established by comparing a weighted average normal value with a weighted average export price. This method was considered fair. However, ironically, the agreement allowed the authorities to use the weighted average-to-transaction method also, which was being (mis)used by the authorities prior to the Uruguay Round. This method has no empirical or theoretical basis. Authorities are allowed to use this methodology where prices differ among purchasers (due to different bargaining power, different quantities, etc.), different periods (fluctuations in market price), and even sometimes among different regions, that is, dumping is targeted to certain regions, purchasers, or periods. But such differences exist in most cases (Bhansali 2004a). Furthermore, when a normal value established on a weighted average basis is compared to prices of individual export transactions, the probability of finding dumping increases. In the following example, the weighted average normal value is $10 [(15 + 10 + 5)/3].

TABLE 3.6:   Comparison of weighted normal value with individual export prices—An illustration

Date of sale	Domestic price	Normal value	Export price	Dumping margin
1 August	15	10	16	0
10 September	10	10	12	0
22 December	5	10	8	2

Thus, 22 December exports though above the domestic price are nevertheless dumped because the export price happens to be less than the weighted average normal value. The transaction-to-transaction methodology also suffers from weaknesses. It permits authorities broad discretion to choose the individual home-market transactions that are to be compared to individual export sales (Bhansali 2004a). In addition, both these methodologies provide the authorities scope for adopting zeroing practice. When the export price is substantially higher than the normal value, that is dumping margin is negative, the authorities treat such sales as having zero dumping margin. By doing so, the authorities skew their calculations in favour of higher dumping margins.

Loopholes remain even in the weighted average method. While using this methodology, some WTO members apply inter-model zeroing. If, for example, model A was dumped while model B was not dumped, the members would not allow the negative dumping of model B to offset the positive dumping of model A, inflating the weighted dumping margin ascertained for the like product as a whole. In the US–Stainless Steel from Korea Case, the USDOC adopted a new type of zeroing. It divided the investigation period for the purpose of calculating the overall margin of dumping into two averaging periods to take into account the devaluation of the Republic of Korea's won in November–December 1997, corresponding to the pre- and post-devaluation periods. It then calculated a margin of dumping for each sub-period. When combining the margins of dumping calculated for the sub-periods to determine an overall margin of dumping for the entire investigation period, the USDOC treated the period November–December, where the average export price was higher than the average normal value, as a sub-period of zero dumping— where in fact there was *negative dumping* in that sub-period. The matter was taken to the DSB. There the Panel concluded that this was not allowed under Article 2.4.2.

Addition of Article 2.4.2 during the Uruguay Round thus could not address effectively the issue of a highly damaging practice of zeroing. In the Bed Linen case against India, the Panel stated

> We recognise that Article 2.4.2 does not in many words prohibit zeroing. However this does not mean that the practice is permitted, if it produces results inconsistent with the obligations set forth in that Article as we believe it does.

The AB supported this ruling. Dumping margins reduced significantly once the practice of zeroing was dropped and the EC had to withdraw ADD on cotton bed linen originated in India. Even if the EC no longer practices 'zeroing' in other cases following the decision of the Appellate Body in EC–Bed Linen, the problem is not effectively addressed. Highly skilled legal experts found loopholes in the decision. The Appellate Body concluded that zeroing is WTO-inconsistent because it prevents true average-to-average comparisons as called for by Article 2.4.2 of the ADA. This means that zeroing is permitted when dumping is calculated using other methods. Since the agreement explicitly allows individual-to-average comparisons, zeroing remains WTO-consistent. Authorities therefore continue to use the this practice in 'targeted dumping' cases (weighted average to transaction method). One may conclude that although the Uruguay Round Agreement provides the average-to-average method, it nevertheless allows the authorities to use the average-to-transaction method and the transaction-to-transaction methods as well. This has not really changed the situation.

Determination of Injury

In order to levy an ADD, it is not enough to prove that dumping has occurred; the law requires that injury to the domestic industry also has to be proved.

The Kennedy Round specified injury to cover material injury to a domestic industry, threat of material injury, or material retardation of the establishment of such an industry. Though the term 'material injury' was not defined either in the Kennedy Round or in any subsequent Round, it can be taken to mean injury, that is not insignificant. However, in the absence of any specified standards, it is in practice, interpreted as 'any injury'.

The first step in determining injury is to identify the domestic industry that is followed by an injury analysis. In what follows, we have discussed the evolution of the agreement in regard to these two stages of injury determination.

Domestic industry

The support criterion   The anti-dumping authorities must identify the domestic industry before addressing the injury issues. The Kennedy Round provided

The term 'domestic industry' shall be interpreted as referring to the domestic producers as a whole of the like products or to those of them whose collective output of the products constitutes a major proportion of the total domestic production of those products except that *when producers are importers* [emphasis added] of the allegedly dumped product the industry may be interpreted as referring to the rest of the producers ... Article 4 (i)

The Tokyo Round negotiations did not refine the definition by defining the term 'major proportion' but narrowed the scope of the domestic industry facilitating injury finding. It excluded not only the producers who themselves were importers as was done in the Kennedy Round but also the producers who were related to the exporters or importers [Article 4(1)]. The term 'related' was left to the contracting parties to develop. The Uruguay Round also failed to specify quantitative threshold for the 'major proportion' but added 'Footnote 11' to define 'affiliation' in the context of determining the domestic industry. According to this footnote, the concept of related producers in the agreement depends on control. While defining 'control' the agreement stipulates that 'one shall be deemed to control another when the former is *legally or operationally* [emphasis added] in a position to exercise restraint or direction over the latter'. Legally, this means that one of them holds 50 per cent or more (majority share) of the outstanding voting stock of the other. In practice, however, investigating authorities interpret this concept using their discretion. For instance, the EC continues to deem the existence of control even in the case of minimal shareholding of 1–5 per cent. Thus instead of strengthening the discipline it made it easier for the authorities to manipulate the scope of the industry. In countries with substantial presence of foreign direct investment (FDI), a number of producers are likely to be excluded from the definition of domestic producers.

Furthermore, important issues such as the treatment of captive production and exports were left unaddressed and to the discretion of the authorities. This has resulted in a number of disputes.

Captive production   The US statute has 'captive production' provision while most other countries do not have any such provision. Under this provision the US International Trade Commission (USITC) *must* focus its injury analysis on the free (merchant) market and potentially may find injury in the merchant market even if the industry as a whole is not experiencing injury. The EC law has no captive production provision but in practice the EC also excludes captive production from injury assessment. In the Hot-rolled Steel Product Originating in India case, around 70 per cent of the hot-rolled coils manufactured by EC producers was used in a captive market, that is, they were further transformed by the producers in an integrated process. The complainant claimed that two separate markets should be distinguished and that only the hot-rolled coils sold on the free market should be subject to the complaint. Exporting producers, however, suggested that the assessment of the market should include the captive market and the free market taken together. In support of this claim, reference was made to the GIMELEC judgement of the European Court of Justice (case no. C-315-90 of 27 November 1991).[14] However, the Commission considered that the separation between the free and the captive market is in line with the requirement of the past practice. Consequently, it examined the situation of the community industry with respect to the free market.

Japan, however, decided to challenge this practice of ignoring captive production in injury analysis. In the US anti-dumping measures on Hot Rolled Steel Plates from Japan dispute case, Japan argued that the captive production provision of the US law violates Articles 3 and 4 of the ADA. The EC supported the US practice as a third party and argued that where a significant proportion of domestic production is for captive consumption, it is not inconsistent with the ADA to focus the analysis on the merchant market since it is there that the immediate injurious effect of the dumped imports takes place. Developing countries like Chile, Brazil, and Korea, on the other hand, supported the argument given by Japan. The Panel concluded that neither the provision itself nor the manner in which it was applied in the hot-rolled steel case was inconsistent with the ADA's requirement. The AB however disagreed. It ruled that Article 3.1 does not entitle investigating authorities to conduct a selective examination of a domestic industry. Rather, where one part of an industry is the subject of separate examination, other parts of the industry should also be examined in like manner. It thus ruled that the authorities need to examine both the captive and the free market and argued that the United States acted inconsistently with the ADA by not analysing the data for the captive market. The ruling however did not clarify whether the captive market analysis should actually be factored into the injury analysis.

Exports vs domestic sales The law is silent on whether exports be taken into account in the injury analysis. The EC does not think so. In one of the cases investigated by the Commission against Indian exports, exporters argued that limiting the analysis of the Commission's sales to the domestic sales in terms of volumes and prices does not comply with the provision of Article 3(4) of the ADA on the ground that the Agreement refers to total sales, thus including exports. The Commission, however, argued that Article 3(4) in conjunction with Articles 3(1) and 3(2) of the ADA clearly refers to the evaluation of the impact of dumped imports on prices in the domestic market and on the situation of the domestic industry. Injury of the EC industry must be found to exist on the domestic market only and the situation with respect to exports is therefore irrelevant.

There are other several instances where the vagueness of the term 'domestic industry' is exploited to prove injury. For illustrating this point, we cite here a US safeguard case, which has an implication for anti-dumping provisions also. In the 'US safeguard case of imports of fresh, chilled or frozen lamb meat' from New Zealand, the United States included in the domestic industry growers and feeders of live lambs also. The argument was that the term 'producer' must be construed in terms of how the competent authorities will conduct their injury analysis and since the agreement requires an authority to evaluate 'all relevant factors' bearing on the situation of the industry, an authority has to analyse all aspects of the industry, which in some industries may include factors affecting the product in its raw stage. The case was brought to the DSB where the AB ruled against the United States. However, it reveals how skillfully the developed countries can exploit the provisions of trade remedy measures to manipulate the findings.

Injury analysis

There is no mathematical formula for determining the existence of injury. To prove the existence of material injury, the Kennedy Round Code specified certain factors, which could be considered as indicators of injury. The Tokyo Round negotiations did not introduce any substantive change in the methodology. It merely introduced procedural improvement in the analysis of injury finding (as discussed above). The Uruguay Round also failed to make any progress in refining the injury related concepts. It merely added Article 3.7 for making a determination regarding the existence of a threat of material injury.

Thus, the decision about whether the standard of material injury has been satisfied is essentially a matter of judgement about which few general principles can be stated. In a pioneer study Finger et al. (1982) observed that the injury decisions are primarily motivated by political factors. Their findings were supported by a number of studies (see among others Anderson 1993; Moore 1992; Tharakan and Waelbroeck 1994; Hansen and Prusa 1996, 1997). These studies suggest that political pressures matter a lot. Evidence suggests that industries with production facilities in the districts of the oversight members of two key House and Senate Subcommittees that control the USITC's budget fare better at the Commission. Political pressures can also take the form of bias against certain trading partners. For instance, empirical studies suggest that cases against Japan and NMEs are far more likely to result in duties. Strong lobbies also affect the decisions. For instance, the steel industry in the United States fares remarkably well in the anti-dumping investigations due to strong producers' lobby. Among economic factors, the larger is the volume of imports and the larger the profit loss the greater is the chance of an affirmative decision.

We analysed the movement of eleven economic indicators as examined by the EC in twelve anti-dumping investigations against India. These are tabulated in Table 3.7. In almost all the cases, production, productivity, investment, and capacity have gone up. Profits and employment are the two indicators that have shown downward trends in most cases. Apparently, injury assessment means confirming that employment and profits are down. There is no formal economic analysis. In the PET film case, Indian exporters pointed out that the EC industry's situation improved dramatically since the investigation period and that the EC was no longer suffering material injury. The EC argued that Article 6(1) of the basic rule provides that information relating to a period after the investigation period should not normally be taken into account. On the basis of the jurisprudence of the Court, the Commission examined developments in the PET markets during the nine month-period following the investigation period. It was found that prices increased continuously. Market share and sales also increased. However, it was concluded that if the ongoing proceeding was terminated, it was likely that dumped imports would rapidly regain market share and thus the case was made for the injury. No evidence was given to support the argument. Apparently, the authorities enjoy a wide discretion in deciding on whether injury has occurred.

Furthermore, the agreement requires that the examination of the impact of the dumped imports on the domestic industry shall include an evaluation of all relevant economic factors and indices having a bearing on the state of the industry producing the like product in the importing country (Article 3.4). It mentions fifteen specific factors in this context.[15] The scope of this obligation has been examined in various Panel proceedings. In all the rulings, it has been held that the evaluation of the fifteen factors is mandatory in each case and must be clear from the published documents. Notwithstanding the importance attached to these factors, the wordings of the provision suggest that these are merely illustrative factors. The agreement states:

The examination of the impact of dumped products ... shall include an evaluation of all economic factors *including*.... The list is not exhaustive ...

TABLE 3.7: Case-wise summary of injury-assessment—EC investigations against Indian exporters

Case	I	II	III	IV	V	VI	VII	VIII	IX	X	XI
Synthetic fibre ropes	Up	N.C.	Down		Up	Up	Up	Down	Down	Up	Up
Steel fasteners	Up	Up	Down	Up			Down	Down	Up	Up	Up
Potassium permanganate	Down		Up		Up	Up	Up	Down	Down		Up
Stainless steel wires					Up	Up		Down			Up
Steel ropes	Up	Up	Down	Up	Down	N.C.		Down	Down	Up	Up
Flat rolled steel products	Up		Down	Up	Down	Down	Up	Up	Down		Up
Certain PET			N.C.		Up			Down		Up	
Cathode ray colour TV	Down		N.C.		Down	Up			Down		
PSF			Down						Down		
PET Film	Down	Up	Down	Up	Up	Up		Down		Up	N.C.
Sulphanic Acid	Up	Up	Up	N.C.		Up	Up	Down	N.C.	Up	N.C.
PTY	Up	Up	N.C.	Up	Down	Down	Down	Down	Down	N.C.	Down

Note: I = prices; II = stocks; III = market share; IV = capacity; V = sale; VI = production; VII = capacity utilization; VIII = profit; IX = employment; X = productivity; XI = investment; N.C.: no change.

Source: Official Journal of the European Communities, various issues.

Furthermore, in the light of the Panel rulings, it is important not only to review these factors but also to evaluate them carefully. In the US anti-dumping measures on Certain Hot-rolled Steel Products from Japan Dispute case, the Panel ruled that

... it would not be sufficient if the investigating authorities merely mentioned data for Article 3.4 factors without undertaking an evaluation of that factor....

But an evaluation requires context and a well-defined framework. The agreement describes a wide array of economic factors without giving a proper framework as to how the authorities need to evaluate them. Many factors are systematically related. For instance, productivity may have a negative relationship with employment. Similarly, the economic theory suggests that increased competition in the market results in a fall in profits. This may not, therefore, be a sign of injury. Apparently, analysing fifteen factors in a single framework is not practical. Furthermore, many of the Article 3.4 factors are applicable to the business enterprise as a whole and cannot be examined product-wise in multi-product corporations (Bhansali 2002). These are, for instance, employment, wages, growth, ability to raise capital, and investment. Since dumping margin is calculated on product basis, injury should also be product-specific.

Finally, the agreement permits the application of anti-dumping measures in cases where a domestic industry alleges that though it is not yet suffering material injury, it is threatened with material injury, which will develop into material injury unless anti-dumping measures are taken. One of the amendments introduced in the Uruguay Round was to provide elaborate provisions relating to the threat of injury to prevent its misuse. Article 3.7 was incorporated for this purpose. Furthermore, the provision was strengthened by the panel ruling in the Mexico–Corn Syrup case. The Panel was of the view that

While an examination of the Article 3.7 factors is required in a threat of injury case, that analysis alone is not a sufficient basis for a determination of threat of injury, because the Article 3.7 factors do not relate to the consideration of the impact of the dumped imports on the domestic industry.... In our view, consideration of the Article 3.4 factors in examining the consequent impact of imports is required in a case involving threat of injury in order to make a determination consistent with the requirements of Articles 3.1 and 3.7.

An important question that merits attention here is whether initiating anti-dumping investigations on the basis of threat of injury alone should be permissible. Any investigation based on threat of material injury will necessarily be speculative because it involves analysis of events that have not yet happened. Even though the discipline is strengthened, it does not represent any overreaching effect on the use of anti-dumping tool.

Cumulation

The practice of cumulation was not legitimate under the GATT anti-dumping code. This meant that the countries had to make injury analysis on a country-by-country basis even if multiple countries were named in the investigation. In practice this meant that the authorities found it difficult to prove 'injury by reason of dumped imports' unless the import volume was substantial. In 1984, due to aggressive lobbying by domestic industries, the US Congress amended the anti-dumping and CVD laws, making it mandatory to cumulate imports across countries when determining injury. Rather than being rare, cumulation became the norm. This provision allowed the authorities to aggregate all like imports from all countries under investigation and assess the combined effect on domestic industry. Evidence suggests that in the post-1984 period, there was a dramatic increase in the use of cumulation provision in the United States. Between 1985 and 1994, 75 per cent of the USITC decisions involved cumulation (Prusa 1998). The practice was soon adopted by the EU as well due to its usefulness in establishing injury (see Tharakan et al. 1998). To legitimatize this practice, these countries pushed hard to include this provision in the agreement during the Uruguay Round and they succeeded. This was despite the fact that the competition policy had emerged as an important area of interest during the later stages of Uruguay Round negotiations and that anti-dumping is highly anti-competitive (Prusa 1998).

Table 3.8 shows that in the pre-WTO years multiple countries were named in around 25 per cent of the cases initiated in the United States while in the post-WTO period 39 per cent cases had multiple countries. Further-more, naming patterns also changed with an increasing number of cases having more than three named countries. These patterns appear to be more pronounced in the EC where multiple countries were named in 58 per cent of the cases and almost the same proportion of cases involved more than three countries. Some cases even involved 10–12 countries.

Why multiple naming? This is because cumulation increases the likelihood of affirmative findings. If the imports from individual countries are aggregated, the market share of investigated firms will rise and the impact of foreign imports will become more significant. This in turn will result in greater likelihood of affirmative findings. Evidence suggests that over the period from 1985 through 1994, affirmative findings were made in 51 per cent of cases with cumulation while only 40 per cent of the cases without cumulation were successful (Prusa 1998). Hansen and Prusa (1996) found that cumulated cases were about 30 per cent more likely to result in duties than non-cumulated cases. Their findings suggest that more than 50 per cent of USITC affirmative

TABLE 3.8:   Summary of naming patterns in the EC* and US** cases in force

No. of named countries	US		EC
	AD cases dating pre WTO years	Initiated in post 1995 period	
2	11	7	8
3	4	5	6
4–7	4	9	14
8–12	2	3	5
Total cases naming multiple countries	21	24	33
Duties in effect (product-wise)	86	62	58

Note: * as of 29 November 2002. ** as of 14 August 2002.

Source: Author's computations based on data provided on USITC website *http://usitc.gov/7ops/ad_cvd_orders.htm* and EC website *http://europa.eu.int/comm/trade/policy/dumping/stats.htm*

determinations from 1985 through 1988 would have been negative without cumulation.

Aside from this, cumulation also has what Hansen and Prusa (1996) has called the 'super-additivity effect'. They observed that even if the market share effect is controlled by holding the market share of defendant firms constant, aggregating over the exports of several countries itself increases the probability of an affirmative injury determination. Thus the greater is the number of small defendant firms (holding the market share constant), the higher is the probability of a positive finding by the USITC. According to an example considered in Hansen and Prusa (1996), when 40 per cent of imports are under investigation and a single country is involved, the probability of an affirmative injury finding is 0.60. But when the petition is filed against two countries with a cumulated market share of 40 per cent, divided equally between them, the probability rises to 0.72. This change represents a 20 per cent increase in the probability of affirmative action. Extending the example to five countries, holding constant the market share of imports, the probability rises to 0.78 or by 30 per cent. Tharakan et al. (1998) confirmed this finding for the EC injury determination as well. Their estimates for the EC suggest that the probability of an affirmative finding rises from 0.92 for two countries to 0.98 for three countries, holding constant the market share of imports under investigation. Gupta and Panagariya (2006) explained this empirical finding using a theoretical framework. They suggest that the presence of a large number of exporters exacerbates the free rider problem, which leads every firm to invest less on defence and results in the super additivity effect. Thus, cumulation has played a significant role in yielding a positive injury determination not only by increasing the market share of defendant firms but also due to super additivity effect of cumulation. Naming a multitude of small countries with very small import market share raises the probability of gaining protection because it results in super additivity effect.

This practice is likely to be primarily harmful for those developing countries that constitute small fractions of the import market. It is quite likely that their exports would not have caused injury but for having been cumulated with exports of other exporters. They are thus more vulnerable to this practice. For instance, all the ten cases in force against India (as of 14 November 2002) in the United States involved multiple countries. Of the thirteen cases in force against India in the EC, as of 29 November 2002, cumulation was applied in ten of them. Naming more countries has thus become a profitable strategy, particularly against developing countries

Though the Agreement permits cumulation only if the authorities determine that a cumulative assessment of the effects of the imports is appropriate in light of the conditions of competition between the imported products and the conditions of competition between the imported products and the like domestic product, yet there is no provision of specific factors for consideration to justify the presence of these conditions. The USITC does consider four factors when deciding whether to cumulate: (i) interchange ability between imports from different countries and between imports and domestic product; (ii) overlap between the domestic product and the imported product in four geographical markets of the United States; (iii) similar distribution channels; and (iv) simultaneous presence of imports. However, these conditions are rather easy to meet and regardless of whether one country's imports actually harm domestic producers or not, it can be lumped together with big exporters.

Causation

Besides injury, it must also be demonstrated under the agreement that the dumped or subsidised imports are causing injury through the effects of dumping. Disentangling various causes of injury to domestic industry and finding out that part of injury which could be ascribed to dumping is a complicated task. The Kennedy Round (Article 3a) set stringent standards for proving causal link. It required the authorities to prove that dumped imports were demonstrably the principal cause of material injury or of threat of material injury to a domestic industry or the principal cause of material retardation of the establishment of such an industry. The Tokyo Round however lowered these standards. It required authorities to demonstrate that the dumped imports were through the effects of dumping, causing injury within the meaning of this Code. While that indicated that other factors must not be attributed to injury, it did not provide for an express obligation on authorities to examine those other factors. The standards for establishing causation were not raised in the Uruguay Round but it added Article 3.5 that included a non-attribution test. It provides that authorities shall also examine any known factors other than the dumped imports, which at the same time are injuring the domestic industry. The injuries caused by these other factors must not be attributed to the dumped imports. In the United States anti-dumping measures on Certain Hot-rolled Steel Production from Japan, the AB reinforced this provision by ruling that investigating authorities must make an appropriate assessment of the injury caused to the domestic industry by the other known factors. They must separate and distinguish the injurious effects of the dumped imports from the injurious effects of those other factors. Theoretically, this is a significant change from Article 3.4 of the Tokyo Round Anti-dumping Code. In practice however, there has not been much improvement. The agreement does not specify any methodology to do so. In the absence of any quantitative method for doing so, it is based on the subjective analysis and it entirely at the discretion of the authorities. No serious attempt to disentangle the injurious effects of dumped imports from other sources is therefore possible.

Investigation and Administrative Procedures

Procedures for initiation

Conditions for initiation   The Kennedy Round Anti-dumping Code did not clearly set forth the conditions necessary to initiate anti-dumping proceedings. It stipulated that an investigation to determine the existence, degree, and effect of any alleged dumping would normally be initiated upon a written request by or on behalf of the industry (accounting for a major proportion of domestic production) affected. Though the wordings of the provision were general, no change was made in the Tokyo Round. The Uruguay Round however introduced quantitative criteria for initiating proceedings (Article 5.4). It added that the 'petition will be considered to be made "by or on behalf of the domestic industry" if it is supported by 50 per cent of the industry expressing opinion and 25 per cent of the total domestic production'. In practice, however, the authorities examine the share of the petitioners in the total domestic production and if it is established that the petitioners constitute 25 per cent of the domestic production, the case is initiated. There is no procedure whereby it is ascertained at the time of initiation whether there is dissemination of information regarding the petition among all the producers in the industry. No provision is made to determine support/opposition of producers in the industry before the case is initiated. Thus, a mere 25 per cent of domestic producers can trigger protection affecting 100 per cent of producers and consumers.

Content of application   The Uruguay Round provides far more detailed rules than its predecessors, the Kennedy Round and the Tokyo Round, as to the content of application for initiating the investigation. Information to be provided in the application relates to: (i) the identity of applicant, volume and value of domestic production of like product by the applicant. If the application is made on behalf of the industry, applicant shall provide pertinent information relating to other producers; (ii) complete description of dumped product, names of exporting countries, identity of known exporters or foreign producers, list of known importers of the product; (iii) information on prices, inter alia, for which the product is sold in exporter's domestic market; and (iv) information on evolution of volume of imports, effect of these imports in prices in domestic market, and consequent impact of imports on domestic industry.

However, the agreement does not provide any provision for the verification of the information made available by the domestic industry and thus to discourage frivolous cases. As a result, there are cases in which investigating authorities have initiated investigations based on false information supplied by the domestic industry.[16] Since anti-dumping initiations can have serious trade disruptive effects, such cases can seriously damage the exporting countries' trade.

Furthermore, there are no limitations on the initiations of the investigation. As a result, countries have been initiating repeated/back-to-back anti-dumping investigations on the same product originating in the same countries. As an illustration we may cite the Synthetic Fibre Ropes case investigated in the EC. In June 1997 an anti-dumping proceeding related to imports of synthetic fibre ropes originating in India was terminated without the imposition of measures on the ground that a causal relationship between dumping and injury was not sufficiently established to justify such an imposition. In the month of July of the same year, the EC announced the initiation of a new anti-dumping proceeding against this product on the ground that information made subsequently available to the Commission contained sufficient *prima facie* evidence that the situation of the Community industry had further deteriorated as a result of continued dumped imports from India. Indian exporters raised objections to the opening of the proceeding.

They argued that compared with the negative finding on causation made in the previous proceeding concerning imports of synthetic fibre ropes originating in India there were no changed circumstances to explain a different finding in the present case on the causal link between dumping and injury. However, the Commission was convinced that it had reliable information to establish a causal link between injury and dumping in the present case.

Procedures for investigation

Questionnaires   Replying to questionnaires, some of which extend to hundreds of pages, constitutes a major burden, particularly for small and medium-sized exporters from developing countries. Exporters find the questionnaires too time-consuming and complicated. Furthermore, each country develops its own questionnaire based on legal requirements of its own anti-dumping law. There is no standard questionnaire. It has been observed that in traditional user-countries the questionnaires have become more and more complicated over time. Long and detailed questionnaires have harassment value, in particular for the developing countries. This is one possible reason why firms primarily from developing countries choose not to participate in the anti-dumping investigations against them and instead allow the case to proceed using 'facts available', which always means affirmative findings and much punitive duties.

Evidence   Article 6 of the Kennedy Round required the authorities to provide opportunity to interested parties to present all evidence that they consider useful and to defend their interests. Interested parties were defined to include exporters, importers and governments of the exporting countries. Article 6 of the Agreement during the Uruguay Round added further clarifications. Article 6.1 of the current ADA requires the authorities to give all interested parties notice of the information that the authorities require. Evidence given by one interested party is required to be made available to other interested parties (Article 6.1.2). Furthermore, the Agreement also requires national authorities to provide opportunities for industrial users of the good subject to investigation and representative consumer organizations to provide relevant information during investigations. But it does not make any provision that places an obligation on the national investigating authority to give weight to the information provided by other interested parties in actually making determinations or assessing duties. Clearly, the adversely affected parties (including importers, downstream and upstream industrial users, and consumers) have no rights but merely privileges and investigating authorities conducting an anti-dumping action are not obliged to take their views seriously. Furthermore, participation of consumer organization and downstream producers is limited to the cases where the product is commonly sold at the retail level. Obviously, the changes did not represent any overreaching.

Disclosure of information   The Kennedy Round allowed the access of non-confidential information to interested parties, though it did not place any obligation on the parties to furnish non-confidential summary of confidential information. The Tokyo Round plugged this loophole. Uruguay Round did not make any substantial change. Thus, only non-confidential summaries of confidential information are available to the parties concerned. In principle this is to protect the companies' interest. However, this may be of little value to the defendants and complainants.

Public notice   It is generally indicated that one of the most noticeable improvements in the Uruguay Round is the addition of Article 12, which requires the authorities to give public notice of initiation, preliminary and final findings, and termination. Elaborate provisions are added explaining the contents of the notices. Though the intention was to improve the transparency in the system, it has increased the administrative burden on the investigating authorities in developing countries, which are already understaffed and fund starved. Furthermore, this does not indicate that there is an interface between the objectives of import-competing interests and the interests of wider society. It is not clear therefore how it improves the creditability of the mechanism.

Termination of anti-dumping investigations

The Kennedy Round Code provided that there should be immediate termination of cases where the dumping margin and volume of imports actual or potential or the injury is negligible. The levels of *de minimis* dumping margin and import volumes and injury levels were not specified. No refinement in this provision was introduced in the Tokyo Round negotiations. The Uruguay Round however refined this provision by specifying the *de minimis* dumping margins and import shares. Article 5.8 provides

The margin of dumping shall be considered to be de minimis if this margin is less than 2 per cent, expressed as a percentage of the export price. The volume of dumped imports shall normally be regarded as negligible if the volume of dumped imports from a particular country is found to account for less that 3 per cent of imports of the like product in the importing Member, unless countries which individually account for less than 3 per cent of the imports of the like product in the importing country collectively account for more than 7 per cent of imports of the like product in the importing country. (Anti-dumping Agreement, Art. 5.8)

Experts however dismiss these reforms as marginal. Most criticize them for insignificantly low standards of *de minimis*. Summary information on dumping margins in the EU and United States against Indian companies (Table 3.9) suggests that in a majority of cases the dumping margin was above 25 per cent. The threshold for the import share is also much lower than those used by the competition authorities for defining 'dominant position' (30 per cent or 40 per cent in general). Most economists argue that if dominance is defined in a specific way for domestic competition, the same criterion should be applied to foreign competition as well (Hoekman and Mavroidis 1996). One must also observe that no special or differential treatment is accorded to developing countries in regard to this provision while ASCM and ASG both have special provisions for developing countries in this regard.

TABLE 3.9:   Summary of dumping margins calculated by USDOC and EC in anti-dumping investigations against Indian companies

Dumping margins (per cent)	EC (as of 4 June 2003)	US (as of 23 October 2003)
2–5	0	0
5–10	4	1
10–25	14	7
Above 25	28	7
Total	46	15

Source: Author's computation based on *Official Journal of the European Communities*, various issues and USITC website *http://www.usitc.gov/7ops/ad_cvd_orders.htm*

Provisional measures

Article 10(a) of the Kennedy Round stipulated that once a preliminary affirmative decision had been made as to dumping and injury provisional anti-dumping measures might be taken. To this, the Tokyo Round added that 'the provisional measures shall not be applied unless the authorities concerned judge that it is necessary to prevent injury during the investigation period'. These provisions created the impression that the requirements for the initiation of an investigation are sufficient to justify the imposition of provisional duties, in other words, that a provisional duty may be imposed based solely on the evidence set out in the complaint. The provisions were regarded neither fair nor equitable. The Uruguay Round Agreement introduced two improvements. One, it requires that provisional measures may be applied if an investigation has been initiated in accordance with the provisions of Article 5, a public notice has been given to that effect and interested parties have been given adequate opportunities to submit information and make comments. Two, it also specifies time limit before which the measures can not be imposed.[17] These reforms aimed at dampening the ardor of protectionist interests who advocate imposition of provisional duties as early as possible. Apparently, the standards of provisional measures are raised in the Uruguay Round to make it look fairer. However, evidence suggests that initiation of ADD itself has trade de-stabilizing impact. For instance, Staiger and Wolak (1994) find substantial investigative effects with a drop in subject imports of approximately 50 per cent in the period after the case is filed. Prusa (2001) also finds evidence of a harassment effect. His findings reveal that settled cases are about as restrictive as cases that result in duties. In either event the value of imports from named countries falls by 50–70 per cent over the first three years of protection. And, even if the case is rejected imports fall by 15–20 per cent. Reforms introduced in provisional measures may not therefore have desirable effects on the incentives to use the anti-dumping tool.

It is instructive to note that the Uruguay Round Agreement also raised the time limit for which the provisional measures may remain in force to six months extendable to nine months from four months extendable to six months in the Tokyo Round Code and only three months in the Kennedy Round Code. This provision itself is an incentive to use the tool to get at short term relief from imports.

Imposition and collection of ADD

Price undertakings   An alternative to anti-dumping duty that the Kennedy Round allowed was the voluntary undertakings from the exporter. Article 7(b) of the first code provided

If the exporters concerned undertake during the examination of a case, to revise prices or to cease to export the product in question, and the authorities concerned accept the undertaking, the investigation of injury shall nevertheless be completed if the exporters so desire or the authorities concerned so decide.

The Tokyo Round incorporated a provision (Article 7.2) that price undertakings shall not be sought unless the authorities have initiated an investigation. The Uruguay Round however required the authorities not to seek/accept price undertaking before preliminary affirmative determination of dumping and injury. In addition, under the current agreement, the investigation of both dumping and injury need to be completed even after an undertaking has been accepted. Though these changes did eliminate some of the uncompetitive practices, they are not adequate. The criteria for accepting or rejecting the offer of undertaking have been left vague. As a result, authorities can use considerable discretionary powers in accepting price undertaking. Evidence suggests that the acceptance of price undertaking is influenced by a number of non-economic factors in the EU, a frequent user of this mechanism (Tharakan 1991). These include the number of exporters involved, bilateral trade deficit, and the country block. For instance, the Newly Industrializing Country group is not preferred as far as acceptance of price undertaking is concerned. Some scholars argue that undertakings are similar to VERs (Tharakan 1991). They can have even more damaging effects than VERs (Moore 2005) and should therefore be prohibited like VERs.

Anti-dumping duty: The lesser duty law   The lesser duty rule implies that dumping duties should be less than the dumping margin and only high enough to remove injury. The first Anti-dumping Code expressed preference for a lesser duty; however, it did not make it mandatory. No amendments were introduced in the subsequent Rounds. Member countries therefore use wide discretion in this matter as well.[18] Furthermore, WTO members, who apply a lesser duty rule in accordance with Articles 8.1 and 9.1, have to calculate injury margins for which the ADA does not give any guidance. Therefore, different members have evolved different methodologies and practices over a period of time. Normally, injury margin is calculated as the difference between the fair selling price due to the domestic industry and the landed cost of the product under consideration. Two methodologies commonly used for this are: price undercutting and price underselling (Bhansali 2004b, Vermulst and Waer 1991). Price undercutting involves comparing the net sales realization of the domestic industry with the price of the dumped imported products. The price underselling method is used where the prices are depressed or suppressed and the price undercutting method is not likely to protect the domestic industry adequately against injurious dumping. Essentially, this method involves a comparison of what the domestic industry ought to get and the prices at which the dumped goods are offered to the buyers in the domestic market of the importing member.

These methods are subject to several ambiguities (Bhansali 2004b). Both for price undercutting as well as the price underselling methods, it would be necessary to take the non-injurious price of the domestic industry and the comparable import prices at the same level. It may not always be possible. Furthermore, the calculations are based on the information provided by the domestic producers that may be systematically biased. In many cases, the industry has highly inefficient cost structure due to wrong location, smaller size, obsolete technology, high cost of electricity, and waste of raw materials. No account is taken of the fact that the price difference can be caused by a host of factors other than dumping such as competitiveness, better policies of the exporters, and difference in quality. The more inefficient the industry is, the greater is the likelihood of higher injury margins. Thus the system primarily protects inefficiency.

What is a more serious problem with this methodology from our perspective is that it is heavily biased against the developing country producers. In a recent paper, Hansen and Nielsen (2006) have developed a two-country duopoly model with international trade based on both horizontal and vertical product differentiation. Following the reciprocal dumping model framework (Brander and Krugman 1983), they assume that one producer is located in each country and because of trade costs both are price discriminating in each other country's markets (reciprocally dumping) but unlike the original model they assume that quality differences exist. The producer located in the large market specializes in producing the high-quality products (termed 'developed country producer') compared with the producer in the small market (termed 'developing country producer'). In such a case, it is the developed country producer that is creating dumping and real injury margin by underpricing his high-quality product in the developing country market vis-à-vis low-quality domestic product. Developing country producers on the other hand create only formal injury margins in the developed country market; their products are low priced due to low quality. But, it is the developed country producer who is more likely to play anti-dumping card against the small country producer on the basis of formal injury margins. This is because market integration reduces his profits unambiguously; the effect on the profits of the producer from the developing country market is ambiguous. The study concludes that the methodology is biased against developing countries.

The above ambiguities are compounded by the fact that while calculating injury margins, members practise zeroing practice. This inflates injury margins because any negative amount by which the exporting producers' price undercut those of the domestic industry are not offset with any positive amounts. In the Steel Wires case against India (12.7.1999) Indian exporters raised this issue with the EC but did not get heard. In the Polyester Staple Fibre case again Indian exporters argued that it was wrong to exclude negative price undercutting. The Commission confirmed this but since no further arguments were put forward, the claim was rejected. In the same case, certain Indian exporters argued that the injury should be calculated on the like product and not on the comparable models. The argument was based on the conclusions of the WTO AB in the bed linen case (1.3.2001). The EC, however, argued that these conclusions were drawn in the context of dumping calculations and hence were not relevant in this case.

There is no wonder then that in many cases injury margins are higher than dumping margins and that even if the lesser duty rule is applicable, dumping duties are equivalent to the full dumping margins. The effect of lesser duty rule is likely to be insignificant unless there is an unambiguous methodology of calculating injury elimination level.

We examined injury and dumping margins in almost all the cases which were investigated in the EC against Indian exporters between 1998 and 2002 and which resulted into duties. Table 3.10 summarizes the patterns. For thirty-three of the forty-eight firms[19] (69 per cent) investigated in twelve cases, injury was found to be higher than the dumping margin. In six out of the twelve cases, injury levels were higher than dumping margins for all exporters. The rule appears to have benefited exporters in only three cases (Synthetic Fibre Ropes, Hot-rolled Flat Steel, and Certain PET). Apparently the lesser duty rule is not very effective in the absence of a well-designed method of calculating injury margins.

TABLE 3.10:   Comparison of injury and dumping margins in selected EC cases investigated against India

Case	No. of exporters investigated (incl. residual category)	No. of exporters for whom injury margin > dumping margin	Col 3 as a percentage of col 2
(1)	(2)	(3)	(4)
Synthetic fibre ropes	2	0	0
Steel fasteners	4	3	75
Potassium permanganate	1	1	100
Stainless steel wires	11	8	73
Steel ropes	3	3	100
Hot-rolled flat steel	2	0	0
Certain PET	5	1	20
Cathode ray colour TV	1	1	100
PSF	3	2	67
PET film	7	7	100
Sulphanic acid	2	2	100
PTY	5	5	100
Total	48	33	

Source: *Official Journal of the European Communities*, various issues.

Duration of anti-dumping duties and undertakings   The introduction of the process of the 'sunset review' of anti-dumping orders in the Uruguay Round was perhaps one of the most important reforms in the anti-dumping process. Pre-WTO GATT rules were relatively vague about when governments were required to terminate anti-dumping duties. This meant that duties could remain in place indefinitely. Under Article 11.3 of the WTO Agreement all anti-dumping orders are to be terminated five years after their initiation unless the authorities determine in a review that the expiry would be likely to lead to a continuation of dumping and injury. Sunset review was originally deemed friendly to developing countries. However, this brought almost no gains to developing countries because Article 11.3 provides that the anti-dumping measures can be extended for successive new terms of five years if the authorities determine that the expiry of the duty would lead to recurrence of dumping and injury. This has led traditional users to renew the anti-dumping measures almost indefinitely, and they have in fact got an overwhelming proportion of anti-dumping measures in force, for which anti-dumping orders had been made several years ago. In the United States, out of 305 sunset reviews only 143 (47 per cent) have been revoked. Anti-dumping is continued in 53 per cent of the cases. There are several cases that have been continuing since the 1970s. Table 3.11 provides year-wise distribution of the US anti-dumping duties in force in the reference period. Of the 278 duties in force as of 14 August 2002, 161 (58 per cent) were ordered before 1996. In other words, these duties have been in place for more than one term. An overwhelmingly large number of such cases are against non-OECD countries. In fact, of the 161 cases, 98 (61 per cent) cases are against non-OECD countries.

TABLE 3.11:   Year-wise distribution of the US anti-dumping duties (country-specific) in force as of 14 August 2002

Order date	No. of cases currently in force	No. of cases against non-OECD countries
Before 1983	10	1
1983–6	22	20
1987–9	37	18
1990–2	35	25
1993–6	57	34
1996–2002	117	98
Total	278	

Source: USITC website: *http://usitc.gov/7ops/ad_cvd_orders.htm*

Other Issues

Special and differential treatment

As described above, a provision for special and differential treatment was incorporated in the anti-dumping agreement in the form of Article 13 during the Tokyo Round negotiations. It required developed countries to give special regard to the situation of developing countries when considering the application of anti-dumping measures but did not make any specific provision for addressing how should they do it. As stated, it was taken directly from Article 37(c) of Part IV without any revision. It is therefore not surprising that it could not be operationalized effectively. However, no refinement could be made in this provision during the Uruguay Round negotiations. Discussion on this would be taken up in detail later in this book.

Reviews

Under the provisions of the ADA, administering authorities undertake a variety of review functions. These include: Periodic Review where duty is retrospectively assessed (Article 9.3.1), Refund Review where duty is prospectively assessed (Article 9.3.2), New Shippers Review (Article 9.5), Changed Circumstances Review (Article 11.2), and the Sunset Review (Article 11.3).

The agreements do not clarify which, if any, provisions that were originally intended to apply to initial investigations also apply to the various review provisions under the agreements. In some instances the drafters of the agreements felt it necessary to explicitly state that certain provisions of the ADA with respect to initial investigations also specifically apply to reviews. For example, Article 11.4 of the ADA states that the provisions of Article 6 regarding evidence and procedure shall apply to any review carried out under this article. In others however it remains unclear (Parthasarthy 2004). These reviews are thus subject to discretion of the authorities.

Dispute settlement

The Kennedy Round Code did not provide for any separate provision for the dispute settlement. Apparently anti-dumping disputes were a part of the overall GATT dispute settlement mechanism. The Tokyo Round added Article 15 for consultation, conciliation, and dispute settlement. However it did not provide any guidelines for the panels in dispute settlement. This was done during the Uruguay Round when Article 17.6 was added to the Agreement. It provides:

(i) in its assessment of the facts of the matter, the panel shall determine whether the authorities' establishment of the facts was proper and whether their evaluation of those facts was unbiased and objective. If the establishment of the facts was proper and the evaluation was unbiased and objective, even though the panel might have reached a different conclusion, the evaluation shall not be overturned;

(ii) the panel shall interpret the relevant provisions of the Agreement in accordance with customary rules of interpretation of public international law. Where the panel finds that a relevant provision of the Agreement admits of more than one permissible interpretation, the panel shall find the authorities' measure to be in conformity with the Agreement if it rests upon one of those permissible interpretations.

Article 17.6 thus constrains the role of panels and the presence of this article distinguishes the anti-dumping regime from other WTO regimes in which common DSU rules are applicable.[20] This article ensures that panels can do nothing if establishment of facts is proper and evaluation of those facts is unbiased and objective. But even the notions of 'proper', 'unbiased and objective' establishment of the facts are not clear.

Furthermore, it allows different interpretations of the legal provisions. This is against the Vienna Convention on the Law of Treaties. While there are different possible approaches to interpretation under that Convention, its application will generally lead to one identified interpretation. Thus an application of those processes may not allow for more than one permissible interpretation.

One of the expected benefits for developing countries joining the WTO is to take advantage of multilateral mechanism to avoid any unbalanced bilateral negotiations with their powerful trading partners. However, it is faded due to powerless panels. Developed countries desperately required less interference with domestic decisions during the Uruguay Round. As a result, they strictly restricted panels' role in this Agreement compared with normal Dispute Settlement Procedure. The dispute settlement process therefore seems unlikely to provide discipline against the increasing number of antidumping restrictions against imports.

In an excellent analysis of the thirteen dispute settlement cases that reached upto the panel stage during the period from 1995 through September 2002, Durling (2004) found that only 69 out of 138 individual claims prevailed, which means that the overall success rate was only 50 per cent. This micro level analysis shows that contrary to the rhetoric that anti-dumping authorities always lose, panels have rejected almost equal number of cases against them. He concludes that both the bureaucratic and the legal momentum of dispute settlement are towards innocuous findings of procedural error that can be corrected without lifting the anti-dumping order in question (see Durling 2004 for detailed discussion).

Our calculations based on the data provided by Durling and presented in Table 3.12 yield more interesting facts. One, the success rate of those cases

TABLE 3.12: Individual claim-wise outcome of WTO challenges to anti-dumping measures

Complaining party	Target	Success rate (%)
Developing Countries	All Cases	44
Developing Countries	Developing	50
Developing Countries	Developed	36
Developed Countries	All Cases	61
Developed Countries	Developing	75
Developed Countries	Developed	54

Note: Developed countries include: United States, EC, Japan, and Canada; developing countries: India, Poland, Korea, Guatemala, Mexico, Thailand, Argentina, Egypt, and Turkey.

Source: Author's calculations based on Durling (2004).

challenging developing countries is higher than that of those cases challenging the developed countries; two, the success rate of the cases challenged by developed countries is higher than those challenged by the developing countries. This statistics simply support the argument that developing countries have been less effective in participating in the dispute settlement and are less likely to obtain significant concessions at the end (Busch and Reinhardt 2003, Besson and Mehdi 2004) and that developing countries are unlikely to obtain a favourable outcome because of asymmetric legal capacity and economic dependence via bilateral assistance.

A related issue is that of compliance. After a ruling, the prospect of Article 21.5 'compliance' panel (and possibly appeal) and Article 22 'arbitration' panel of DSU increases the incentives for foot-dragging. The Cotton Bed case may illustrate this point. Following WTO ruling in March 2001 in this case, the EC amended the original ADDs on bed linen from India in August 2001 but India was not satisfied with the EC's implementation of the anti-dumping ruling. India requested the establishment of a compliance panel challenging the implementation of the anti-dumping ruling. The WTO compliance panel, however, ruled in favour of the EC. In February 2002, upon request by the Community industry, a review was initiated. Although the review decision went in favour of India, implementation of the ruling was considerably delayed. What is more serious however is the fact that there is no way that the WTO can force a (sovereign) country to comply with the ruling. In the case of non-compliance, it can merely grant retaliation authorization to the affected country/s. If the affected country happens to be a developing country while the non-compliant country is a developed country, then retaliatory actions may be a minor irritant to the latter and it can simply choose to ignore the ruling. In the case of the 'Continued Dumping and Subsidy Offset Act', commonly known as the 'Byrd amendment', the United States refused to comply with WTO ruling even when economically powerful countries such as Canada, EU, and Japan were among the complainants. The Byrd Amendment is a US legislation whereby the federal state promises to distribute proceeds from (eventually imposed) anti-dumping and countervailing duties to all US economic operators supporting a domestic petition to impose such duties. By providing an additional financial incentive to file anti-dumping and countervailing duty cases, the law encouraged the companies to file such cases. Ten WTO members (including EU, Canada, Japan, and developing countries) successfully challenged the Byrd Amendment on the basis that it provided illegal remedies not covered in relevant WTO agreements. The WTO ruled the Byrd Amendment illegal in January 2003. The United States was given until 27 December 2003, to comply with the decision. In the wake of the failure of the US Congress to move to repeal or amend the Byrd Amendment by that deadline, complainant countries requested for retaliatory authority and were granted the authority in 2004. However, the United States endured retaliation. The United States prospectively repealed the Byrd Amendment in 2006 when the President signed the Budget Reconciliation Bill into law on 8 February 2006. The terms of the prospective repeal stipulate that Byrd Amendment distributions will continue for entries made prior to 1 October 2007. The attitude 'why should we comply?' might have become more rigid if the complainants had involved only the developing countries.

Circumvention

One of the problems with ADD on a product has been the circumvention of the duty by, inter alia, importing parts and reassembling the product in the importing country or by making minor alterations to the product subject to anti-dumping order. To prevent circumvention, EU was the first to make a legislative provision. It was then followed by the US anti-circumvention action, which in effect, amounts to imposing ADD without investigation of dumping or injury. The circumvention problem was taken up at the Uruguay Round. However, due to lack of agreement the issue was deferred. At Marrakesh the ministers adopted a decision which acknowledged lack of agreement on the problem of circumvention and referred the matter to the Committee on ADP established under Uruguay Round for resolution. However no progress has been made in this direction. Both the United States and EU in the meanwhile have provisions for 'anti-circumvention measures' under their anti-circumvention laws even though these measures are not justified under the

WTO Agreement and have the potential to impair legitimate trade and investment activities.

ANTI-DUMPING PROVISIONS AND DEVELOPING COUNTRIES: AN OVERALL ASSESSMENT

The ADA provides for the right of member countries to apply anti-dumping measures, that is, measures against imports of a product at an export price below its normal value (usually the price of the product in the domestic market of the exporting country) if such dumped imports cause injury to a domestic industry in the territory of the importing member country. The first international regulation on anti-dumping materialized in Article VI of GATT 1947. The subsequent Rounds agreement enhanced the discipline and made a number of improvements.

The Uruguay Round Agreement, which entered into force in 1994, is believed to have made a quantum leap forward. Substantively, it provides enormous guidance about the determination of dumping and injury than did the Anti-dumping Code. It sets out in substantial detail certain procedural and due process requirements that must be fulfilled in the conduct of investigations and has considerably strengthened the transparency of procedural requirements for anti-dumping cases. Nevertheless, the Agreement still represents no more than a general framework for countries to follow in conducting investigations and imposing duties. While substantive rules and basic concepts have remained unchanged the focus during negotiations had been on tightening and refining the procedural rules. Provisions of the Agreement still remain vague and can easily be manipulated. The Agreement is opaque as to permit various possible alternative approaches leaving much to the discretion of the authorities. There are ambiguities in each step of dumping margin calculations and injury determination. These ambiguities in turn have serious implications for the developing countries. Although they are not explicitly directed at developing countries, they severely damage the interests of the developing countries both directly and indirectly. Furthermore, there are many provisions that affect the developing countries asymmetrically. The definition of dumping, conditions for constructing normal vale, provisions for constructing normal value, provisions of cumulation, dispute settlement, compliance mechanism, and other practices are highly biased against the interests of the developing countries. The various Rounds made no attempt to correct asymmetries in the system. Any effort to eliminate the arbitrariness and bias against foreign exporters was opposed by the powerful developed countries Given the asymmetrical, vague, and complex provisions and ambiguities, in them developing countries could find solace in the 'special and differential treatment' but even that is not operational in this case. The Doha Round negotiations are not expected to yield any significant gains to the developing countries if these countries do not defend their interests with a more focused approach. As stated earlier, no consensus on any reform proposal has been reported until now. Given the past experience, it is feared that the two largest economies would play their cards well and block any meaningful reforms in anti-dumping rules.

Furthermore, refinements in the provisions in most cases were not taken up in earnest leaving several loopholes in the system. Anti-dumping therefore involves highly complex legal procedures, which in most cases require the assistance of legal experts familiar with the national anti-dumping system of the importing country. It is obvious that such specialized expertise is very expensive and has in some instances led small exporters from developing countries to give up particular export markets rather than pay the high legal fees required to protect their interests. Heavy financial burden, lack of expertise, poor maintenance of data are likely to keep the developing country firms away from participating in the investigations resulting in artificially high dumping against them. Creating anti-dumping capacity also requires legal expertise and massive administrative infrastructure. The absence of the required skills and resources constrain the ability of governments in these countries to use this instrument and provide protection even where it is justified. This can be illustrated effectively by an example. Though this is not directly related to anti-dumping, it offers a good illustration of how trade remedy measures affect the developing countries. The United States imposed countervailing duties/ quota on two-textile product exported from Pakistan namely, towel shops and textile and textile products. Pakistan brought the case to the Textile Monitoring Body (TMB). Since the country had no local expertise to defend the cases it hired a US firm for this purpose. The US Government refused to act on the recommendation of the TMB. Since TMB's decision was recommendatory in nature, United States was not bound to accept it. Pakistan had to approach to the Dispute Settlement Body of WTO (DSB). DSB gave the decision in favour of Pakistan. The Committee for Implementations of Textile Agreement (CITA) issued a notice to US customs and unilateral quota was removed after three years. Due to the US decision, Pakistani exports were seriously hurt but no compensation was given to Pakistani exporters. Pakistan spent US $175000 on the fee of foreign consultants.

Finally, the Agreement provides a number of specific details and procedural requirements that have themselves become subject of WTO disputes. This has resulted in an increasing number of disputes involving anti-dumping. Of 321 WTO disputes between 1995–2004, 99 (31 per cent) were accounted for by trade remedy measures (Table 3.13). Of these 54 were accounted for anti-dumping alone. This constituted 55 per cent of total trade remedy disputes. Furthermore, 78 per cent of the cases involved developing countries either as complaint or as defendant. The dispute settlement is so technical and complex that it put these countries at a disadvantage. Furthermore, in many cases anti-dumping authorities often continue their practices despite WTO rulings to the contrary (Durling 2004).

TABLE 3.13:   WTO trade disputes: 1995–10 November 2004

Trade policy	Number of disputes
Anti-dumping	54
CVD	14
Other trade remedy (e.g. safeguard)	31
Total trade remedy disputes	99
Total disputes	321

Source: WTO website.

Since safeguard measures do not require complex methods of calculating dumping margins, these countries may be forced to use safeguard measures that have much higher standards and involve compensation. This is evident in the increasing use of safeguard measures by developing countries in recent years. But the use of anti-dumping has also been increasing much more rapidly in these countries. This raises an important question as to how to explain this phenomenon. Next chapter attempts to provide a closer look at the use of anti-dumping measures by developed and developing countries to address it.

Notes

1 The first Australian Act also had a similar test.

2 Quoted in Congressional Budget Office (1994), p. 20.

3 The second era of globalization came about in the late twentieth century.

4 As a matter of fact, in the late 1950s and the early 1960s, these countries sought to bring the anti-competitive behaviour of private corporations under the discipline of the GATT trading system but failed due to the resistance from the developed countries.

5 Any developing country using these provisions, however, was expected to offer compensation or face retaliation (GATT 1954).

6 In the absence of such price it was the highest comparable price for the like product for export to any third country in the ordinary course of trade, or the cost of

production of the product in the country of origin plus a reasonable addition for selling cost and profit.

7 Part IV did not provide exemption from MFN under the GATT. The enabling provision legitimated the Generalized System of Preferences (GSP) that had come into existence in 1968 under the auspices of UNCTAD. In 1971, a GATT waiver from Article 1 (MFN) obligations was granted after the US agreed to it. The 1971 Waiver from MFN was a temporary arrangement, initially for a period of 10 years, under which developed countries could grant tariff concessions to developing countries on a non reciprocal basis. It was made permanent by the enabling clause introduced in the Tokyo Round.

8 Only 25 countries were signatories to the GATT Anti-dumping Code whereas 128 countries signed the Uruguay Round Anti-dumping Agreement (Carpenter 1999).

9 See also, papers submitted by Argentina (TN/RL/W/81), Australia (TN/RL/W/91), and Canada (TN/RL/W/47)

10 In theory, 'particular market situations' may include situations in market economies as well as in non-market economies (Bekker 2004). However, anti-dumping legislations in most countries include this provision without any explanation of the term 'particular market situations' and can use it ambiguously.

11 Baldwin and Moore (1991) had shown earlier that the use of 'facts available' nearly doubled the average US dumping margin from around 35 per cent to over 65 per cent in the pre-WTO period.

12 The case was referred to the DSB. The panel concluded that the authority must use every element of information submitted which satisfies the provision of Annex II and that members do not have unlimited right to reject all information submitted in a case where necessary information is not provided.

13 Notes and Supplementary Provisions to Article 6, Ad Article VI, Paragraph 1, note 2.

14 In this ruling the Court had referred to the following factors to rule out the existence of two separate markets: (i) the product concerned was sold on the same market and used for the same purpose; (ii) the EC producers sold the product concerned both to related and unrelated customers and charged more or less the same price; (iii) companies on the downstream market used to buy the product concerned not only from related EC suppliers but also from importers/unrelated producers.

15 These include: actual and potential decline in (i) sales, (ii) profits, (iii) output, (iv) market share, (v) productivity, (vi) return on investment, (vii) utilization of capacity, (viii) factors affecting domestic prices, (ix) the magnitude of margin of dumping, (x) actual and potential negative effects on cash flow, (xi) inventories, (xii) employment, (xiii) wages, (xiv) growth, (xv) ability to raise capital or investment.

16 This point was brought out in a conversation with a practitioner.

17 Article 7.3 stipulates that provisional measures shall not be applied sooner than 60 days from the date of initiation of the investigation.

18 For instance, while the EC statute has made this rule mandatory, in the US and Canada once injury is proved and its causal effect is established anti-dumping duty equivalent to the dumping margin is imposed.

19 This includes the category of residual exporter firms.

20 Article 1 of the DSU indicates that it applies to the disputes under the covered agreements subject to such special or additional rules as are identified in Appendix 2. Articles 17.4 to 17.7 of Anti-dumping Agreement are identified as special or additional rules and procedures in Appendix 2 of the DSU.

4 Patterns of Anti-dumping Use
Developed vs Developing Countries

This chapter provides a comprehensive assessment of the anti-dumping use. It investigates the trends and time patterns of anti-dumping use in developed and developing economies for a period of over twenty-four years from 1980 to June 2004. The spread and proliferation of anti-dumping use around the world has been well-documented in literature (Miranda et al. 1998, Prusa 2001, Finger et al. 2001, Zanardi 2004). However, most existing studies focus on the initiations/measures imposed per year. They do not really reflect the rigour with which the tool is used, which is in fact captured by various aspects such as the number of measures in force (actual measures), duration of the duties, duty rates, and trade weighted initiations. But these aspects are generally ignored as data are not readily available and hence present a misleading picture. To correct this bias, we collected information on some of these aspects of anti-dumping use and presented it in this chapter.

From the beginning of 1980 the Anti-dumping Code of the GATT required its signatories to submit reports of their anti-dumping activity to the GATT Committee on ADP every six months. As a result, the Rules Division of the WTO has created a detailed database on anti-dumping cases. This database is multidimensional. It provides information on anti-dumping activity of WTO members by initiating country, targeted country, targeted vs initiating country, sector, and year. This study uses the data set provided by the rules division of WTO.[1] However, the data is subject to various errors, omissions, and inconsistencies (CBO 2001) and before turning to analysing this data, it is important to highlight these limitations. First, even though the Uruguay Round ADA made it compulsory for all member countries to report this information, this requirement is not binding. As a result, many countries fail to notify their anti-dumping status and activities to the WTO. Second, the database does not cover the countries that are not WTO members thereby presenting an incomplete picture. The exclusion of Taiwan and China until recently for instance provided a highly misleading picture. Taiwan implemented an anti-dumping law in 1984 and between 1984–2001 it initiated seventy-three cases. Similarly, China implemented a law in 1997 and within four years (before it came a WTO member) initiated twenty-two cases. Zanardi (2004) suggests that the number of anti-dumping initiations and measures provided by the data should be considered as a lower bound. Finally, while the WTO collects information in addition to the number, on various other aspects of anti-dumping investigation initiations and measures imposed, it is not readily available.

Despite all these limitations, the WTO database remains the most comprehensive source of international data available on anti-dumping activity. The present study makes use of this database for analysing broad trends in anti-dumping actions and supplements it with other sources. Using the World Bank classification, it classifies initiating and targeted developing countries by level of development, that is whether such countries are low-income countries, lower middle-income countries, upper middle-income countries. Developed countries are categorized as OECD or non-OECD high-income countries. In all, the paper identifies five categories of countries: low-income, lower middle-income, upper middle-income, OECD, and non-OECD developed countries (Appendix Table 4A). The study analyses the patterns of anti-dumping use across these different categories of countries. The sector disaggregation in the database follows the HS Classification[2] of trade and is provided at the two-digit level. We thus had data of anti-dumping activities for twenty-one sectors. We rearranged this data into four broad categories—resource-intensive sectors, labour-intensive sectors, science-based, and miscellaneous sectors. Science-based sector was further reclassified into differentiated and scale-intensive sectors. While doing so we broadly followed the World Bank sectoral classification (Appendix Table 4B). The analysis provided in the chapter covers the period from 1980 to June 2004. This was the period for which data was available at the time of writing this chapter. Though the data for the years 2004 and 2005 are also available now, broad patterns discussed here are not expected to have undergone major changes. As described in Chapter 2, anti-dumping still remains the most contentious issue. While the total number of anti-dumping cases has declined, it still remains phenomenally high. In fact, the decline in the number of CVD and safeguard is much sharper.

Our analysis in this chapter suggests that developing countries might have increased the use of anti-dumping in terms of the number of initiations and measures per year but they are yet not in a position to exploit the gaping loopholes of the anti-dumping agreement as much skilfully as their developed country counterparts can, due to lack of legal expertise and financial resources. The study also presents preliminary evidence that suggests that the effect of anti-dumping actions by developed countries is likely to be much more dramatic than those of developing countries. Thus one anti-dumping investigation initiated by a large country like the United States does not correspond with one anti-dumping investigation initiated by a small developing economy in terms of its effect on the world trade.

The first section of this chapter documents the trends and patterns of anti-dumping initiations broken down by reporting country/country group and by time period. The next section analyses the trends and patterns of anti-dumping use broken down by target country/country group and by time period. The third section reveals who targets whom. The penultimate section provides an analysis of anti-dumping activity by sector both globally and within each initiating and targeted country group. Finally the last section concludes the analysis.

USE OF ANTI-DUMPING: BY REPORTING COUNTRY

Initiations: By Country Group

The extent of anti-dumping activity is generally gauged from the number of worldwide anti-dumping initiations. To begin with we also follow this tradition. Figure 4.1 shows the trends of worldwide anti-dumping actions over the past two decades. Since the number of anti-dumping initiations is characterized by wide yearly fluctuations, we have plotted 3-yearly moving averages. Two observations may be made. First, there has been a phenomenal growth in the use of anti-dumping activity since the early 1990s. A total number of 668 cases were reported over the period 1986–1990. In the early

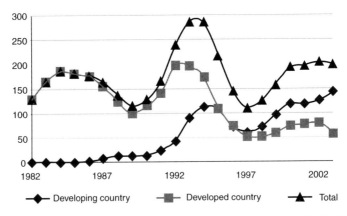

FIGURE 4.1:   Initiations by country group: 3-yearly moving average (1980–June 2004)

Source: WTO Secretariat Rules division database.

1990s however, the number of anti-dumping initiations shot up to 1240. Following years witnessed further growth in anti-dumping investigations. During 1996–2000, the total number of anti-dumping cases reported was 1372 while in the first three and a half years of the early 2000s, 1008 cases were reported. Even though the number of anti-dumping cases initiated declined in 2002 and 2003, the average number of cases per year during the early 2000s remained 288 as compared with 274 during the late 1990s. Second, before the Uruguay Round went into effect developed countries were more significant users of this law; since this agreement went into effect in 1995, developing countries have been using the law more aggressively than their developed country counterparts. Thus, the use of anti-dumping activity that was confined only to developed countries spread across different country groups during the late 1990s.

Table 4.1 provides summary information on anti-dumping initiations between 1980 and 30 June 2004 broken down by country group and time period. The data have been rearranged for summary information in five time periods of five-years each (the last period is the three and a half year period) to avoid the problem of year-to-year fluctuations that characterize anti-dumping investigations. The table shows that until 1984, all the cases were initiated by OECD countries; developing countries did not participate in this activity. During the late 1980s, upper-income developing countries also started initiating/filing anti-dumping cases but their share remained mere 9 per cent. In the early 1990s, there was a sharp increase in cases opened by these countries and their share in total cases initiated increased to around 30 per cent. A cyclical downturn was observed around that time in the world prices of many commodities. It appears that it induced new users, upper middle-income countries in particular, to use the instrument of anti-dumping to protect their industries (see Miranda et al. 1998). The late 1990s witnessed a sharp increase in anti-dumping initiations by low- and lower middle-income developing countries also. The number of anti-dumping initiations for low-income countries over 1996–2000 was ten times that of what it was in the early 1990s. The cases reported by OECD and upper middle-income countries declined marginally during this period; but increase in the cases in low- and lower middle-income countries more than compensated the decline. Thus, developing countries of all stages of development and industrialization joined the ranks of active anti-dumping users by the late 1990s and fuelled the surge in anti-dumping cases. They together accounted for 61.5 per cent of the total cases during the early 2000s. In the pre-WTO regime, GATT specifications of trade restrictions were of limited relevance to developing countries. Many developing countries had bound only a few of their tariffs; hence they could increase these tariffs without violating the GATT obligations. However, under WTO, all parts of agreements are applied to all member countries. Developing countries all submitted the schedules of bound tariff rates. It could be that these countries started using anti-dumping in order to avoid some of the adverse effects of liberalization and in order to reassure domestic political interests that some form of 'safety net' remains in place. This proposition will be empirically investigated in the next chapter. The above analysis indicates that anti-dumping is no longer a law that is used by the developed country group alone.

TABLE 4.1:   Anti-dumping initiations by country group—Number of cases: 1980–June 2004

Year	No. of cases				
	1980–5	1986–90	1991–5	1996–2000	2001–June2004
Developing countries					
Low	0	0	21	169	212
	(4)	(34)	(61)		
	[1.7]	[12.3]	[21.0]		
Middle	0	0	66	278	293
	(13)	(56)	(84)		
	[5.3]	[20.2]	[29.1]		
Upper	0	63	369	351	115
	(13)	(74)	(70)	(33)	
	[9.4]	29.8]	[25.6]	[11.4]	
Developed countries					
OECD	930	605	774	553	379
	(186)	(121)	(155)	(111)	(108)
	[100]	[90.6]	[62.4]	[40.3]	[37.6]
Non-OECD	0	0	10	21	9
	(2)	(4)	(3)		
	[0.8]	[1.5]	[0.9]		
Total	930	668	1240	1372	1008
	(186)	(133)	(248	(274)	(288)
	[100]	[100]	[100])	[100]	[100]

Note: Parentheses () show cases per year; parentheses [ ] show the per cent of total cases.

Source: Author's computations based on WTO Secretariat Rules division database.

Patterns of anti-dumping use changed significantly even within the group of developing countries. Figure 4.2 shows that prior to the Uruguay Round, among developing countries, upper middle-income countries were the heaviest users of this law. In the post-Uruguay Round period however, the number dropped for them. In contrast, the number of cases opened by low- and lower middle-income countries continued to rise reducing the gap in anti-dumping filings across different developing country groups.

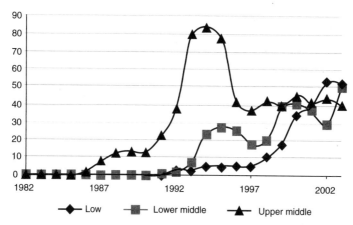

FIGURE 4.2:   Anti-dumping initiations by developing country groups: 3 years' moving average (1980–June 2004)

Anti-dumping Measures Imposed Per Year: By Country Group

The fact that an anti-dumping investigation has been initiated does not mean that an ADD will be imposed on the product. The investigation may be terminated without any duty for a variety of reasons (Chapter 3). It is therefore important to analyse the trends and patterns of anti-dumping measures also. Table 4.2 summarizes this information. It reveals that the share of developing countries also increased in anti-dumping measures adopted. Their share in total anti-dumping measures was 61 per cent during 1996–2000. It increased to around 70 per cent by the early 2000s. In fact, the share of developing countries was higher in the measures imposed than in initiations reflecting the fact that the success rate of anti-dumping initiations had been higher in developing countries. One may be alarmed by this and argue that lower investigation standards could be responsible for such trends. But it is also possible that it is due to the problem of non-response by subject country exporters, which confront the developing countries. The share of these

TABLE 4.2:   Anti-dumping measures by reporting country groups: 1996–2004

Year	No. of cases	
	1996–2000	*2001–4*
Developing countries		
Low	112	163
	(22.4)	(46.6)
	[14.1]	[24.9]
Middle	160	168
	(32)	(48)
	[20.2]	[25.6]
Upper	210	127
	(42)	(36.3)
	[26.5]	[19.4]
Developed countries		
OECD	301	191
	(60.2)	(54.6)
	[29.2]	[29.2]
Non-OECD	10	6
	(2)	(1.7)
	[1.3]	[0.9]
Total	793	655
	(158.6)	(187.1)
	[100]	[100]

Note: Parentheses () show cases per year; parentheses [ ] show the per cent of total cases.
Source: Author's computations based on WTO Secretariat Rules division database.

countries in subject countries' trade is generally so small that the cost of defending the case is higher than the benefits gained from defending and winning the case. Exporters therefore choose not to respond to the questionnaires sent by investigation authorities of the developing countries. As a result, the authorities are forced to depend on the 'best facts available' that frequently result in positive dumping finding. India for instance reported 379 initiations until March 2003. In 225 (or 59.5 per cent) of these investigations, there was either no response from the exporting country firms or the investigations were incomplete. Of the remaining 145 cases, only 107 (28 per cent) cases were based on the information provided by the exporters. For the rest there was no discernible information. Furthermore, lower success rates in anti-dumping cases initiated by developed countries do not indicate that they have adopted higher standards of investigation. Lower success rates also suggest that these countries might be using the tool to exploit for its harassment effect. Evidence suggests that anti-dumping petitions have a profound impact on imports even if they do not result in duties (Staiger and Wolak 1994, Prusa 2001). Imports fall dramatically during the investigation period regardless of the case's ultimate outcome.[3] Legal scholars often refer to this as the 'harassment' effect of an anti-dumping investigation. Though it cannot be established what exactly the reason for relatively lower success rates in developed countries has been, one cannot rule out the possibility that they may be initiating the cases for harassment. These possibilities notwithstanding, a little noticed trend in US anti-dumping protection is the rapid increase in the percentage of cases ruled affirmative by the USITC over time. The success rate has risen from about a 45 per cent in the early 1980s to a 60 per cent rate by 2000.[4] Empirical analysis reveals that this could be attributed to the increasing use of discretionary policies (Blonigen 2002). Thus, the success rate of the cases initiated by major developed countries has been relatively much higher in the post-Uruguay period in comparison with the 1980s.

Howsoever one explains these patterns, the fact remains that the developing countries are more frequent users of this tool than the developed countries at least in terms of the number of initiations/measures. Since the share of these countries in world trade has been much lower than that of the developed countries,[5] this unmistakably means that the intensity of anti-dumping use has also been higher in these countries (see also Finger et al. 2001). Developing countries thus appear to have become more active and more intense users of the tool than their developed counterparts. More frequent use of anti-dumping measures by developing countries is indeed contrary to the expectations. As has been argued in previous chapters, rather complicated legal and administrative rules and procedures put developing countries at a disadvantage. A sophisticated legal regime requires that a country has access to substantial financial and legal resources to use the measure and protect itself from the use of the tool against it. Developing countries have both limited legal capacity and financial resources putting them at a disadvantage. Where price comparison is concerned, complex exercise is needed to determine how costing and accounting calculations are to be made, what adjustments are needed to allow for appropriate comparisons, how to deal with related party transactions, how to deal with and value imports from NME, and how to deal with cases where there is insignificant or unreliable data. Where injury is concerned, equally complex rules or methods are needed to identify various injury factors and to outline the level of causative effect and the methodology by which causation is to be identified. This raises the fundamental question of whether the use of anti-dumping is actually widespread among the developing countries. The following subsections address this question by digging deeper into the data.

Analysis of Initiation: By Country

Analysis of countrywise initiations suggests that anti-dumping cases till 1985 were initiated by the four contracting parties of the GATT—Australia, Canada, EU, and the United States—all OECD countries. In the late 1980s, Mexico, an upper-income country, joined the anti-dumping club as a major user of such actions. Other Latin American countries—Argentina, Brazil, Columbia—followed Mexico in the early 1990s. By the late 1990s, lower middle-income countries such as South Africa, Egypt, Peru, and Philippines and low-income countries such as India also started using anti-dumping in a major way. While in 1980 only four countries reported anti-dumping initiations, in 1990 the number increased to ten. From 1995 through 2004, forty-one countries reported initiating new anti-dumping investigations. Of these, six were OECD and five non-OECD developed countries; the rest were developing countries. Only thirty developing countries have reported one or more cases over the post-Uruguay Round period. Furthermore, the distribution of anti-dumping user countries has been highly skewed. In all, only twelve countries have been using these actions actively (Table 4.3). These countries accounted for over 80 per cent of the total cases initiated during 1996–2004. The four traditional users of anti-dumping namely the United States, EU, Australia, and Canada still account for over one-third of the total cases initiated in the world. These users accounted for over 95 per cent of the total cases initiated by OECD countries during 1995 to 2004. Among the upper-income countries, three Latin American countries along with Korea accounted for around three-fourth of the cases initiated in that country group. Three lower middle-income countries: South Africa, China and Turkey initiated 80 per cent of the cases in that category. Finally, only one developing country namely India has been responsible for initiating most cases in the low-income country group.

The above analysis indicates that the surge in anti-dumping cases was indeed fuelled by the developing countries in the late 1990s, but the use of anti-dumping mechanism was still not widespread among these countries. There is not, as yet, an explosion in the number of developing countries using the anti-dumping law. According to an estimate (Zanardi 2004), around forty developing countries have not initiated an investigation even if they have an anti-dumping law. This number is as large as the number of total users of anti-dumping. Very few low- and lower-income countries use this tool. India

TABLE 4.3:   Top 12 anti-dumping users: 1996–June 2004

Country	% in total cases	Ranking in anti-dumping use	Share within the country group (%)
OECD			
United States	14.1	2	37.37
EU	10.3	3	27.25
Australia	6.7	5	17.80
Canada	4.8	7	12.79
Upper middle			
Brazil	4.6	8	20.41
Argentina	6.7	4	29.96
Mexico	3.0	11	13.48
Korea	2.8	12	
Lower middle			
South Africa	6.6	6	36.53
China, P.R.	3.5	9	19.44
Turkey	3.2	10	18.03
Low income			
India	14.2	1	88.45

Source: Author's computations based on WTO Secretariat Rules division database.

and to some extent Nicaragua and Pakistan are the only low income countries. Many such countries including Bangladesh, Nepal, Zimbabwe, Malawi, Mozambique, and Vietnam who have been targeted in these cases could not yet initiate the use of this tool. Bureaucratic hassles, financial implication, and the lack of expertise could be some of the reasons why these countries could not use the tool. Vermulst (2005) notes that complex methodology related to the calculation of dumping and injury margins, as well as the very detailed procedural requirements that authorities need to comply with before taking anti-dumping action make the ADA difficult to apply and understand in practice.

Measures in Force: Developed vs Developing Countries

Table 4.4 presents the number of active measures as on 30 June of each year since the inception of the WTO. This information is not readily available. It is based on two sources: Zanardi (2004) and various semi-annual reports submitted to the Anti-dumping Committee. Since there were gaps in the WTO

TABLE 4.4: Measures in force (definitive duties and price undertakings) as on 30 June

	1995	1996	1997	1998	1999	2000	2001	2002	2003	2004
Low	5	13	19	32	62	92	121	150	210	216
	(0.61)	(1.43)	(1.9)	(3.11)	(5.29)	(7.62)	(9.82)	(12.6)	(15.87)	(15.98)
Middle	66	69	113	137	175	199	209	223	295	331
	(8.03)	(7.61)	(11.3)	(13.3)	(14.9)	(16.5)	(17)	(18.8)	(22.29)	(24.54)
Upper	81	123	186	187	214	232	232	152	168	166
	(9.85)	(13.6)	(18.6)	(18.2)	(18.2)	(19.2)	(18.8)	(12.8)	(12.69)	(12.28)
OECD	661	690	663	659	694	667	645	655	641	629
	(80.4)	(76.1)	(66.2)	(64)	(59.2)	(55.2)	(52.4)	(55.1)	(48.45)	(46.55)
Non-OECD	9	12	20	15	28	18	25	9	9	9
	(1.09)	(1.32)	(2)	(1.46)	(2.39)	(1.49)	(2.03)	(0.76)	(0.680)	(0.666)
Total	822	907	1001	1030	1173	1208	1232	1189	1323	1351

Source: Zanardi (2004), semi-annual report submitted to the Anti-dumping Committee.

data in the initial years, we used Zanardi (2004) for the period 1995–2001. The data for 2002, 2004, and 2005 is based only on WTO database. The table shows that even though the share of developing countries in initiations and measures taken annually is above 60 per cent, in measures-in-force it is much less. During 2001–2004, the share of developing countries in total initiations was over 62 per cent; in active measures it was less than 50 per cent. Thus a handful of OECD countries were responsible for over half of the active anti-dumping measures during the early 2000s. At least one of the reasons for this could be that the duration of active anti-dumping measures is longer in developed countries as compared with developing countries. The United States for instance had no provision for regular sunset reviews before the Uruguay Round Agreement. The Agreement required the United States to implement them but not until 1 January 2000 and the United States waited until that deadline to carry out its first terminations.[6] It is therefore important to examine the duration of anti-dumping measures in developed and developing countries.

Duration of Anti-dumping Measures: Developed vs Developing Countries

Information on anti-dumping durations is collected from CBO (2001). It suggests that durations-to-date of anti-dumping measures have been longer in developed countries as compared with developing countries (Table 4.5). The mean duration-to-date of active anti-dumping measures in developed countries as on 1 January 2000 was 6.24 years, the median was 5.6 years. On the other hand, the mean duration of active measures on 1 January 2000 for developing countries was only 2.62 years, the median was 2.67 years. Country-wise analysis suggests that the measures imposed by the United States lasted much longer than those by any other country. The United States was followed by New Zealand, Australia, Canada, Japan, and the EU. Developing countries barring few exceptions have short-lived measures. Durations-to-date of active anti-dumping measures in two developing countries namely, Mexico and Turkey compare favourably with those in the developed countries. All other developing countries have comparatively short duration of anti-dumping measures. A given country with short mean and median durations might have enacted a large number of measures recently perhaps because it has lately begun enforcing anti-dumping laws. However, in the sample of developing countries, there are several countries which started using the anti-dumping tool in the late 1980s itself. One may therefore conclude that on an average durations-to-date are longer for developed countries.

TABLE 4.5:   Duration to date of active anti-dumping measures on 1 January 2000

Measures imposed by	Number of measures		Duration to date (years)		
	Total	Of known duration	Mean	Median	Longest
Industrialized countries					
North America					
Canada	79	79	6.31	5.45	24.93
United States*	325	325	9.72	8.86	33.3
(United States)	(267)	(267)	(8.23)	(7.16)	(26.21)
Asia and South Pacific					
Australia	38	38	4.59	5.87	7.94
Japan	1	1	4.41	4.41	4.41
New Zealand	21	21	6.24	7.3	11.58
EU	148	147	4.44	3.72	14.21
Developing countries					
North America					
Guatemala	1	1	2.89	2.89	2.89
Mexico	71	71	4.53	4.39	9.26
South America					
Argentina	43	43	2.19	1.93	4.96
Brazil	39	39	3.63	3.67	7.48
Chile	2	2	2.69	2.69	2.69
Colombia	14	14	3.26	2.65	7.63
Peru	8	8	2.25	2.74	4.41
Trinidad and Tobago	4	4	0.8	0.66	1.79
Venezuela	12	12	1.48	0.57	4.81
Asia and South Pacific					
India	60	60	1.83	1.55	5.81
Israel	9	9	0.8	1.04	1.77
Malaysia	9	9	2.27	1.74	3.79
Singapore	2	2	4.25	4.25	4.42
South Korea	26	26	2.91	2.62	6
Thailand	4	4	2.78	2.14	5.14
Europe					
Poland	1	1	1.15	1.15	1.15
Turkey	35	35	6.71	6.98	9.09
Africa					
Egypt	18	18	0.59	0.24	1.51
South Africa	94	94	2.67	1.95	10.71

Note: * As on 1 January 2000 (when the sunset clause became applicable in the US).
Source: CBO (2001).

The Magnitude of Anti-dumping Duties:
Developed vs Developing Countries

The mean and median duty rates for developed and developing countries are provided in Table 4.6. These rates are unweighted averages and not trade weighted averages. These are indicators of the tendencies and propensities of the anti-dumping laws and procedures. In the five years since the Uruguay Round went into effect, initial duty rates in OECD countries were somewhat higher than they were in developing countries. While the mean initial duty rate for developed countries was 46.2 per cent for developing countries it was 40.2 per cent. Among the developing countries Latin American countries had the highest mean duty rates. If these countries are excluded from the analysis then the mean duty rate for the developing countries drops to 25 per cent. Looking at medians rather than means does not change significantly the picture.

In a recent study, Blonigen (2002) has shown that there has been a rapid increase in average dumping margins calculated by the USDOC. Average US ADDs have risen from around 15 per cent in the early 1980s to over 63 per cent by 2000. Statistical analysis carried out by him finds that discretionary practices by the US agencies have evolved over time and this has played a major role in rising anti-dumping margins.

Trade Weighted Initiations/Measures:
Developed vs Developing Countries

Trade weighted initiations/measures is another indicator of the severity of anti-dumping. This is because the number of petitions must be related to the total volume of imports for each country. In other words, 5 petitions in five years by Trinidad and Tobago may be relatively more important than 100 investigations by the United States in the same period, given the total value of imports for these countries. Finger et al. (2001) addresses this issue by constructing an index of initiations (impositions) relative to imports (exports) over the period 1995–9. Using this index, they show that in relative terms, developing countries are the most intense users of anti-dumping, while the United States and the EU (and industrial economies in general) are among the least intense users.

Since anti-dumping measures are often criticized on the ground that they restrict market access of targeted countries and in turn reduce world trade, it is important to examine the proportion of trade affected by anti-dumping actions initiated by each country. Since developed countries account for a large share of trade, any trade restrictive measure imposed by them is likely to

TABLE 4.6:   Duty rates: By level of development

Country	Duty rate (per cent)		Number of cases	
	Mean	*Median*	*Duties imposed*	*Duty rates reported*
Duties imposed, 1995–9				
Developed countries (OECD)				
Australia	59.3	59.3	14	2
New Zealand	51.9	23	9	9
United States	47.6	30.9	72	70
Canada	44.7	49.2	33	24
South Korea	28.9	32.4	18	3
EU	27.7	24.8	106	63
Developed countries (non-OECD)				
Israel	16.2	16.4	8	4
Developing countries (upper middle)				
Trinidad and Tobago	260	260	3	1
Argentina	84.8	86.3	50	12
Mexico	59.1	48	39	35
Venezuela	57.2	56.3	12	12
Malaysia	28.8	18.5	9	9
Chile	8.8	9	4	4
Developing countries (lower middle)				
Guatemala	89.5	89.5	1	1
Colombia	62.1	59.4	9	9
Brazil	53.2	45.5	27	24
South Africa	45.2	31.5	75	44
Peru	40.2	39.1	9	8
Thailand	27.4	27.8	3	3
Egypt	24	17.6	18	18
Turkey	10.6	10.6	13	1
Developing countries (low)				
India*	27.6	23.2	5	5

Note: * These rates are averages over 1992–4.

Source: CBO (2001).

significantly reduce the trade flows of the products concerned. The correct method would therefore be to give greater weight to initiations that affect larger quantities of targeted countries' trade. In other words, it is not the number of initiations but the proportion of targeted countries' trade affected by anti-dumping measures that matters. This requires highly disaggregated country-level information. We attempted to get some estimates in this regard for cases initiated by/against India.

Tables 4.7 and 4.8 show the proportion of trade affected by the anti-dumping cases initiated by and against India by EU and United States, respectively.

These tables reveal that cases initiated by India have affected on an average around 1 per cent of the United States and the EU trade. As one can see, in most individual cases it is much less than 1 per cent. On the other hand, when the EU and the United States initiate cases against India, a large proportion of India's trade is affected. Sometimes it is as high as 98 per cent (as in Ring binder mechanism initiated by the EU) or 95 per cent (as in the synthetic fibre of polyester case again initiated by the EU). Apparently, the cases initiated by developed countries against the developing countries are capable of destabilizing their trade in a major way. While commenting on the patterns of anti-dumping use, Zanardi (2006, p. 17) observes

...the usual confrontation between developed and developing countries is partly misleading since much of the action from developing countries is directed towards other developing countries.

Our argument however is that when viewed from the perspective of the trade effects of anti-dumping measures, the cases initiated by developed countries are likely to have much more pronounced effects on trade flows and have much greater weightage and hence, mere comparison of numbers does not present the correct picture.

Trade Deflection and Developing Countries

One may argue that there is a possibility of trade deflection also, which means that it is possible that in case of the anti-dumping duty, the subject country will shift its exports to other markets to make up for the lost market in the original importing country. For instance, if country A imposes an ADD on country B, then country B can deflect the trade to a third country say country C. Economic theory (Bown and Crowley 2003) suggests that exporting countries will seek out new markets if their existing markets are shut off. In a study on hot-rolled steel, Durling and Prusa (2004) found that an anti-dumping action in one market causes the subject suppliers to increase their

TABLE 4.7: Trade affected by anti-dumping use—India vs the EU

Cases initiated by India against the EU	EU trade affected (% of total in each category)	Cases initiated by the EU against India	India's trade affected (% of total in each category)
Caustic Soda IV	0.07	Hot-rolled Flat Products of Non Alloy Steel	27.047
HAS	2.875	Quarto Plates)	77.03217
Sodium Nitrite II	0.009	Stainless Steel Bright Bars	64.73163
Potassium carbonate	0.014	Potassium Permanganate	28.835
Sodium Ferrocynide II	0.005	Graphite Electrode System	47.51519
Methylene Chloride I	5.302	Sulphanilic Acid	57.77028
Iso Propyl Alcohol	0.016	Pet Films	42.96948
Oxo Alcohols I	1.428	Pet Films	41.56364
Phenol	0.563	Unbleached Cotton Fabric	48.6
Bisphenol IV	0.222	Unbleached Cotton Fabric-II	47.77633
Aniline II	2.834	Polyester Textured Fillament Yarn	95.16667
Choline and its salts	0.197	Synthetic Fibres of Polyester	53.65989
Vitamin A	2.54	Polyester Staple Fibre	98.1445
Vitamin C II	1.527	Ring Binder Mechanism	15.45082
Theophylline and Caffeine II	0.254	Synthetic Fibre Ropes	10.98075
Para Hydroxy Phenyl Glyvine Base II	1.19	Synthetic Fibre Ropes-II	27.74694
Polyisobutylene	0.014	Stainless Steel Fasteners and Parts	13.66555
Flexible Isobutylene	0.435	Compact Disk (Recordable)	

Contd

Table 4.7 Contd

Cases initiated by India against the EU	EU trade affected (% of total in each category)	Cases initiated by the EU against India	India's trade affected (% of total in each category)
HSR	1.001	Cotton Type Bed Linen	38.98126
TSP-1	0.28	Flat Rolled Products of Iron and Non Alloy Steel	27.43526
Acrylic Fibre IV	0.115	Stainless Steel Stranded Ropes and Cables	22.56938
X-Ray baggage System	2.452	Cathode Ray Colour Television Picture Tube(CPTs)	19.80905

Source: DGCIS (India) and WITS (UNCTAD), 2004–5.

TABLE 4.8: Trade affected by anti-dumping use—India vs the US

Cases initiated by India against the US	US trade affected (% of total in each category)	Cases initiated by the US against India	India's trade affected (% of total in each category)
Caustic Soda I	1.089	Allura Red	8.460438
HAS	4.801	Silico Manganese	38.70916
Sodium Cyanide I	0.196	Welded Carbon Steel Pipe and Tubes	28.68217
Iso Propyl Alcohol	6.618	Steel Wire Rope	26.98044
Oxo Alcohols I	1.636	Sulphanilic Acid	22.2369
Bisphenol A-III	0.956	Elastic Rubber Tape	46.3678
Aniline I	0.264	Pet Films	31.62657
Vitamin C III	0.649	S.S. Flanges	72.6252
Graphite Electrode	0.155	Hot Rolled Coils/Plates	26.28876
Flexible Slabstock I	0.22	Cold Rolled Carbon Steel Flat Products	26.74024
SBR	0.051	Carbon Steel Plates	19.06413
		S.S. Bar	21.34857
		Stainless Steel Round Wires	29.11051

Source: DGICS (India) and WITS (Unctad), 2004–5.

shipments to other markets by about 25–30 per cent in the years following the investigation. It is however interesting to note that they did not find evidence of trade deflection resulting from the US anti-dumping activity. A Bown and Crowley study (2003) assembled a ten-year panel of Japanese exports to various destination markets (by tariff code); it then estimated the bilateral trade effects as Japanese exporters experience anti-dumping protection in one (or more) foreign markets. It documents a significant deflection: the imposition of a US ADD on Japan for instance results in Japanese exporters increasing their shipments to non-US markets by 11–22 per cent. Two observations can be made. One, there is, in general, little possibility of trade deflection by exporters from the targeted countries, if large importers like the United States impose anti-dumping measures. Two, developed countries' exporters are in a better position than their developing countries' counterparts to exploit whatever little possibility of deflection arises, to partly offset the effects of anti-dumping measures against them. Although there is no study on trade deflection for the developing countries, we believe that such trade deflection effect are not prominent in developing countries. Exploring new markets entails costs and risks, which may be significant and exporting firms in developing country members are generally too small to bear these costs. Thus any anti-dumping move is likely to affect their exports significantly. An analysis of Chinese exports to EU of the commodities subject to anti-dumping actions reveals that anti-dumping measures are generally very trade restrictive. According to a study by Mai (2001), from 1995 to 1998 total Chinese exports to EU increased by about US $9,051. However, coincident to the imposition of provisional and definitive anti-dumping measures by EU between 1995 and 1998, Chinese exports to EU of the targeted products reduced by about US $342 million, about 4 per cent of the total increase in Chinese exports to EU between 1995 and 1998. Furthermore, Aggarwal (2006) in an empirical study of the trade effects of anti-dumping investigations initiated by India reveals that trade-reducing effects of anti-dumping measures for developing countries are more significant than for the developed countries.

Thus, the effect of any anti-dumping initiation initiated against a developing country is likely to be much larger on its economy than that of an investigation initiated against a developed country.

ANTI-DUMPING USE: BY TARGET COUNTRY

Targets: By Country Group

Figure 4.3 shows 3-yearly moving averages of anti-dumping cases broken down by targeted country group. Whilst the numbers of anti-dumping cases targeted against developed countries showed a downward movement, those targeted against developing countries followed a consistent upward trend. Until 1992, more cases were targeted against developed countries than against developing countries. Thereafter the situation reversed. During 1996–2004 developed countries were targeted in 36 per cent of the cases while 64 per cent cases were opened against developing countries. The proportion changed further in favour of the developed countries during the period 2000 to June 2004 when the developed countries were targeted in 35 per cent of cases against 65 per cent opened against the developing countries.

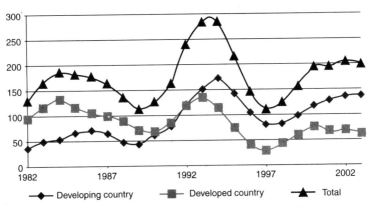

FIGURE 4.3:   Anti-dumping cases by targeted country group: 3 years' moving average (1980–June 2004)

Source: WTO Secretariat Rules division database.

Among developing countries (Figure 4.4), the number of cases targeted against the middle income country groups followed a strong upward movement. However, the increase in the number of cases against the upper income country group was not so dramatic and was marked by wide fluctuations.

Table 4.9 provides summary information on anti-dumping actions broken down by targeted country group. It shows that in the early 1980s, around 60 per cent of the anti-dumping cases were against OECD countries. Nearly 22 per cent cases were reported against the upper middle income group of developing countries. Low- and lower middle-income country-groups together constituted around 12 per cent of the cases. In the late 1980s, these patterns remained the same. In the early 1990s, however, there was a quantum jump in the number of cases targeted against low- and lower middle-income countries. While in the late 1980s, only 17.5 per cent of the cases were directed

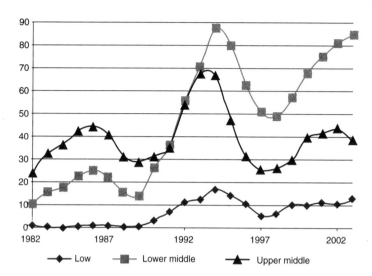

FIGURE 4.4:   Anti-dumping targets within developing country groups (1980–
June 2004)

against them, in the early 1990s, their share doubled to 34 per cent. In contrast, the proportion of cases opened against upper middle-income and OECD countries during this period declined. Post-Uruguay Round period did not see reversal in this pattern. As a results, the proportion of anti-dumping cases targeted against low- and lower middle-income countries increased further. During 2001–June 2004, 46 per cent of the cases were against low- and middle-income countries alone. Upper-middle and OECD countries were targeted in 18 per cent and 25 per cent of the cases, respectively. Apparently, developing countries in general, low- and middle-income countries, in particular remain more frequent targets of anti-dumping cases.

Targets: By Country

Our country-level analysis of anti-dumping targets suggests that victims were more diverse than those victimizing. In 1980, anti-dumping cases were targeted against twenty countries. The number of targeted countries increased to seventy-six by the late 1990s. This could partly be due to the break-up of Czechoslovakia, the USSR, and Yugoslavia; however, mainly it shows that an increasing number of countries were becoming victims of anti-dumping measures (Miranda et al. 1998). In the low-income group ten countries were targeted in the late 1990s. The corresponding figures for the lower

TABLE 4.9:   Anti-dumping initiations by targeted country group: 1979–80
              to 2004

Year	1980–5	1986–90	1991–5	1996–2000	2001–4
Developing countries					
Low	37	42	240	77	75
	(7.4)	(8.4)	(48)	(15.4)	(21.4)
	[4]	[6.3]	[19.4]	[5.6]	[7.4]
Middle	70	75	183	482	396
	(14)	(15)	(36.6)	(96.4)	(113.1)
	[7.5]	[11.2]	[14.8]	[35.1]	[39.3]
Upper	210	171	288	306	184
	(42)	(34.2)	(57.6)	(61.2)	(52.6)
	[22.6]	[25.6]	[22.3]	[22.3]	[18.3]
OECD	562	302	441	403	252
	(112.4)	(60.4)	(88.2)	(80.6)	(72)
	[60.4]	[45.2]	[35.6]	[29.4]	[25]
Non-OECD	60	78	88	104	101
	(12)	(15.6)	(17.6)	(20.8)	(30)
	[6.5]	[11.7]	[7.1]	[7.6]	[10]
Total	930	668	1240	1372	1008
	(186)	(133.6)	(248)	(274.4)	(288)
	[100]	[100]	[100]	[100]	[100]

Note: Parentheses ( ) show number per year, Parentheses [ ] show the percentage of total cases.
Source: Author's computations based on WTO Secretariat Rules division database.

middle-income group, upper middle-income group, OECD, and non-OECD groups were twenty-one, eighteen, nine, and seven, respectively.

Table 4.10 suggests that the EU as a whole emerged as the most targeted region during the late 1990s followed by China. Individually however, China is the most adversely affected country. Only three OECD countries figure in the list of top targets and their share is mere 17 per cent. Among the developing countries, Korea, Indonesia, India, Russia, and Thailand have been prominent targets of the anti-dumping tool. Of the fourteen major targets, three were transition economies while six were market based East Asian countries. This raises a question whether East Asia and economies-in-transition are major victims of anti-dumping measures. To address this question we reclassified

TABLE 4.10:   Top targets in anti-dumping actions: 1996–2004

Country	% in total cases	Target rank
OECD		
United States	5.75	3
Japan	4.45	5
EU	6.60	11
Upper middle		
Korea, Rep. Of	7.65	2
Brazil	2.92	10
Malaysia	1.97	15
Lower middle		
China, P.R.	15.21	1
Indonesia	4.06	7
Thailand	3.78	8
Russia	3.63	9
Ukraine	2.01	13
South Africa	1.97	14
Low income		
India	4.14	6
Non-OECD		
Taiwan	5.44	4

Source: Author's computations based on WTO Secretariat Rules division database.

the countries as transition economies, market-based East Asian countries, and the rest. During 1996–2000, nearly 57 per cent of the total cases were initiated against these countries (Table 4.11). Their share in total cases initiated increased further to over 60 per cent in the early 2000s. While transition economies faced 29 per cent of the total cases initiated, market economy based East Asian countries were targeted in 31 per cent of these cases.

Economies in transition constitute Central and Eastern Europe, erstwhile Soviet Union States, China, and Vietnam. Their non-market economy status in many countries of the world is the decisive reason for a disproportionately high anti-dumping cases against these countries. As discussed in the previous chapter, legal provision makes the NME particularly vulnerable to dumping findings. The ADA allows the investigating authorities to ignore the nominal prices or costs in the NME and base the normal value estimated on the price or cost of a producer of the like product in an 'surrogate market economy'

TABLE 4.11:   Anti-dumping initiations targeted against economies in transition and East Asia: 1980–June 2004

Country code	1991–5	1996–2000	2001–4
Transition economies	303	388	296
	(24)	(28.3)	(29.4)
East Asian	240	392	316
	(19)	(28.6)	(31.3)
Rest of the world	697	592	396
	(56)	(43.3)	(39.3)
Grand total	1240	1372	1008
	(100)	(100)	(100)

Note: Parentheses show the per cent of total cases.

Source: Author's computations based on WTO Secretariat Rules division database.

which may be regarded as a substitute for the purposes of the investigation. If the surrogate market economy is highly protected/ the industry is highly concentrated/ it is at a high level of development than the defendant country then the constructed value is apt to be high and an affirmative finding is likely. In cases where the investigating country itself is the surrogate economy, finding dumping is almost a foregone conclusion. Not only that, this NME system has the effect of yielding high ADD also. The National Board of Trade, Sweden has recently, completed a study of how NME are treated in EU anti-dumping investigations. By examining 200 recent applications by individual firms for market economy status, the study found that being granted market economy treatment yields, on average, a 28 percentage point lower duty compared to the firms not granted market economy status. Interestingly, the United States is the most frequently used analogue country in EU anti-dumping proceedings. Oleksiy and Shcherbakov (2001) in an empirical study provide support to the hypothesis about discrimination against transition economies at the international trade markets.

The growth of anti-dumping investigations against East Asian countries was attributed to the Asian financial crisis that started in April 1997. As domestic demand in South East Asia declined sharply, they directed their production into export markets. However, the share of these countries in anti-dumping impositions increased further in the early 2000s. These countries appear to be penalized for rapid growth in their exports.

Anti-dumping Measures Per Year: Targeted by Country Group

Looking at measures imposed per year rather than initiations does not change the overall scenario significantly. One must however observe that the share of developing countries in new measures imposed per year has been higher than that in total initiations. While over 62 per cent of the cases initiated during 1996–2000 were directed against the developing countries, 65 per cent of total measures were imposed against them. These trends were reinforced in the early 2000s. During this period, the share of developing countries in total measures imposed increased to 70 per cent even though in cases initiated their share was 65 per cent. Apparently, success rates in the cases initiated against

TABLE 4.12: Anti-dumping measures by targeted country group: 1980–June 2004

	No. of cases	
Year	1996–2000	2001–4
Developing countries		
Low	40	43
	(8)	(12.3)
	[5]	[6.6]
Middle	301	284
	(60.2)	(81.1)
	[38]	[43.4]
Upper	170	129
	(34)	(36.9)
	[21.4]	[19.7]
Developed countries		
OECD	222	136
	(44.4)	(38.9)
	[28}	[20.8]
Non-OECD	60	63
	(12)	(18)
	[7.6]	[9.6]
Total	793	655
	(158.6)	(187.1)
	[100]	[100]

Note: Parentheses ( ) show number per year, Parentheses [ ] show the per cent of total cases.
Source: Author's computations based on WTO Secretariat Rules division database.

them is higher than those in the cases initiated against developed countries. The following subsection examines success rates in anti-dumping investigations broken down by country group.

Success Rates: By Targeted Country Group

The ratio of anti-dumping measures to cases opened with one-year lag, broken down by targeted country group and time period rate is presented in Table 4.13. It can be seen that the proportion of anti-dumping cases contested successfully against developing countries has consistently been higher than that against the developed countries. The success rate against OECD countries has always been lower than the overall average success rate. Clearly, developing countries stand to lose in this game.

TABLE 4.13:   Success rates by targeted country: 1980–2003

Year	1980–5	1986–90	1991–5	1996–2000	2001–3
Developing countries					
Low	75.7	64.3	56.7	58.4	63.1
Middle	50.0	45.3	48.6	73.1	66.2
Upper	57.1	49.1	47.6	64.1	59.7
Developed countries					
OECD	50.6	49.0	40.6	55.0	55.8
Non-OECD	61.7	38.5	36.4	63.8	65.9
Total	53.8	48.4	47.6	63.3	61.9

Source: Author's computations based on WTO database.

Considerable time and expense are required by a company to defend itself against dumping charges (see Yano 1999). Firms from low- and lower middle-income countries are less equipped to cope up with these difficulties. Lack of expertise, lack of financial resources, and lack of manpower are some of the handicaps they face. As a result, many firms may choose not to defend. It is therefore expected that most cases contested against these countries are likely to result in definitive measures. There is another reason why low and lower middle income countries risk anti-dumping finding against them. As discussed earlier, home market prices for domestically produced goods might be higher in these countries than those in the export markets. This could be due to inefficient cost structure or because of tariffs and fiscal taxes. Furthermore, most transition economies are in the low- and lower middle-income country groups. As discussed above, exporters from these economies are more vulnerable to affirmative findings. Therefore, the presence of these countries in the low and lower middle income groups could also have affected the success rates in these country groups.

Measures in Force in the EU and the US: By Targets

Table 4.14 shows that developing countries have been the major victims of anti-dumping actions by two major trading countries of the world namely the EU and the United States. While 62 per cent of the active US measures (as of 15 April 2005) were directed against the developing countries, EU targeted them in 86 per cent of the cases (as of 31 March 2005). It is already discussed above how significantly such actions by developed countries reduce the trade flows of these countries.

TABLE 4.14:   Active measures in the EU and the US—By targets

Country group	AD measures imposed by US in force as on 15 April 2005	AD measures imposed by EU in force as on 31 March 2005
Developing countries		
Low	27	15
	(7.8)	(11.0)
Middle	111	82
	(32.1)	(60.3)
Upper	76	20
	(21.9)	(14.7)
Developed countries		
OECD	113	9
	(32.6)	(6.6)
Non-OECD	19	10
	(5.5)	(7.6)

Source: Author's computations based on Interim Annual Report submitted to the European Parliament (EU) and ITC data (US).

A large proportion of cases against developing countries in active measures of the United States and the EU also indicates that the cases against developing countries in these two countries have longer duration. Bown et al. (2003) in an empirical study of the patterns of the US anti-dumping activity has confirmed that the anti-dumping duties against developing countries are indeed are of longer duration.

Confrontation Ratio: By Country Group

We divided the number of cases initiated by each country group by the number of cases targeted against it. This ratio termed 'confrontation ratio' is presented in Table 4.15 broken down by time period. As can be seen, this ratio has always been greater than 1 for OECD countries. Clearly the number of cases initiated by them have been greater than the number of cases targeted against them in all time periods. This is thus the least vulnerable group of all. In contrast, non-OECD group appeared to be the most vulnerable group. It could perhaps be due to the presence of some East Asian economies in this group. These countries are followed by the developing countries. For the upper middle income group, the ratio exceeded 1 during the 1990s but then declined. The lower middle income group remains the most vulnerable group among developing countries perhaps due to the presence of several transition economies. A high confrontation ratio for the low income developing countries may be due to the presence of India in this group and therefore does not present the right picture. If this group is excluded, one may conclude that the developing countries might have been increasing confrontation over time, they are still behind the OECD countries who are known for their competitiveness and trade openness in the industrial sector.

TABLE 4.15:   Confrontation ratio—By country group: 1980–2004

Year	No. of cases				
	1980–5	1986–90	1991–5	1996–2000	2001–4
Developing countries					
Low	0	0	0.09	2.19	2.83
Middle	0	0	0.36	0.58	0.74
Upper	0	0.37	1.28	1.15	0.63
Developed countries					
OECD	1.65	2.00	1.76	1.37	1.50
Non-OECD	0	0	0.11	0.20	0.09

Source: Author's computations based on WTO Secretariat Rules division database.

WHO TARGETS WHOM: ANALYSIS BY COUNTRY GROUP

Anti-dumping Initiators: By Target Country Group

Table 4.16 relates initiating and targeted countries. The top row indicates countries initiating anti-dumping cases while the first column shows countries targeted by their investigations. During 1995–June 2004, developing countries together launched 1518 cases, out of which around 61 per cent were against other developing countries. But at the same time, OECD countries also targeted 68.7 per cent of the cases against developing countries. Apparently, even though there is substantial intra-developing country group anti-dumping activity, OECD countries targeted developing countries more frequently. In contrast, OECD countries were least frequently targeted by other OECD countries. Of the total 984 cases initiated by the OECD countries, only 232 cases were targeted against the OECD countries; this formed 23.6 per cent of the total cases. Low, lower middle- and upper middle-income countries targeted OECD countries in 29.5 per cent, 26.7 per cent, and 33 per cent of the cases initiated by them, respectively. Thus, developing countries targeted a majority of cases against other developing countries but the developed countries directed even a larger proportion of investigations against these countries. Though it is a matter of concern that there have been substantial intra low- and lower middle-income country group filings, its roots lie in the fact that developing countries are soft targets. Some argue that as long as the traditional users continue to use this tool against the developing countries, anti-dumping capabilities will need to be developed by these countries to have the ability to hit back (see for instance Vermulst 1997) and perhaps they do so by first targeting other developing countries.

TABLE 4.16: Anti-dumping targets—By initiating country group: 1995–June 2004

Initiating country → Targets ↓	Low	Low middle	Upper middle	OECD	Non-OECD
Low	7 (1.8)	56 (10.0)	23 (4.0)	75 (7.6)	0 0.0
Low middle	152 (39.3)	180 (32.2)	204 (35.7)	385 (39.1)	8 (22.9)
Upper middle	57 (14.7)	122 (21.8)	126 (22.0)	216 (22.0)	6 (17.1)
OECD	114 (29.5)	149 (26.7)	190 (33.2)	232 (23.6)	21 (60.0)
Non-OECD	57 (14.7)	52 (9.3)	29 (5.1)	76 (7.7)	0 0.0
Total	387 (100.0)	559 (100.0)	572 (100.0)	984 (100.0)	35 (100.0)

Note: Parentheses show the percentage of total cases.

Source: Author's computations based on WTO Secretariat Rules division database.

Anti-dumping Targets: By Initiating Country Group

Table 4.17 investigates the patterns of anti-dumping targets by initiating country group. It shows that a total of 1617 cases were targeted against developing countries over the period. Of them 690 (43 per cent) of the cases directed against developing countries were initiated by OECD countries while only 33 per cent of the cases targeted against OECD countries were filed by these (OECD) countries. While developing countries were targeted principally by other developing countries, the share of OECD countries in anti-dumping activity against them remains higher than that in cases against other OECD countries. This while combined with the results of Table 4.16 suggests that intra-OECD country group anti-dumping activities are much lower than intra-developing country group or even inter developing and developed (OECD) country groups anti-dumping filings. Though much has been said on intra-developing country anti-dumping activities, OECD countries are also directing these cases mainly against developing countries. This is despite that fact that they are passionately teaching lessons of liberalization to developing countries.

TABLE 4.17:   Anti-dumping targets—By initiating country group: 1995–June 2004

Initiating country targets	Low	Low middle	Upper middle	OECD	Non-OECD
Low	7	152	57	114	57
	(4.3)	(16.4)	(10.8)	(16.1)	(26.6)
Low middle	56	180	122	149	52
	(34.8)	(19.4)	(23.1)	(21.1)	(24.3)
Upper middle	23	204	126	190	29
	(14.3)	(22.0)	(23.9)	(26.9)	(13.6)
OECD	75	385	216	232	76
	(46.6)	(41.4)	(41.0)	(32.9)	(35.5)
Non-OECD	0	8	6	21	0
	0.0	(0.9)	(1.1)	(3.0)	0.0
Total	161	929	527	706	214
	(100.0)	(100.0)	(100.0)	(100.0)	(100.0)

Note: Parentheses show the percentage of total cases.

Source: Author's computations based on WTO Secretariat Rules division database.

ANTI-DUMPING CASES: BY SECTOR

Anti-dumping Initiations: By Sector

A sectoral breakdown of global anti-dumping initiations is shown in Table 4.18. It is evident that a majority of cases were initiated in the resource intensive and science-based sectors. Within the resource intensive sector, base metals was the leading sector targeted. This could be due to a very high incidence of anti-dumping filings in the steel industry. In the science-based sector, scale intensive—chemicals, plastic, and rubber—dominated anti-dumping filings over the period 1980–2004. Why dumping cases tend to be concentrated in these sectors? Miranda et al. (1998) argued that 'the world markets for steel, base chemicals and plastics are highly cyclical. Thus, at the bottom of a cycle, firms operating in these markets may turn to pricing sales below cost' (Miranda et al. 1998, p. 16). It is also possible however that at the

TABLE 4.18:   Anti-dumping cases by sector: 1980–June 2004

	1980–4	1985–9	1990–4	1996–2000	2001–4
Resource intensive	293	283	587	664	471
	(40.5)	(39.9)	(47.0)	(48.4)	(46.7)
Base metals and	213	168	374	424	303
products	(29.4)	(23.7)	(29.9)	(30.9)	(30.1)
Labour intensive	64	51	149	153	89
	(8.8)	(7.2)	(11.9)	(11.2)	(8.8)
Textiles	45	30	100	110	64
	(6.2)	(4.2)	(8.0)	(8.0)	(6.3)
Science based	333	360	503	544	447
	(46.0)	(50.8)	(40.3)	(39.7)	(44.3)
Scale intensive	216	171	347	394	393
	(29.8)	(24.1)	(27.8)	(28.7)	(39.0)
Differentiated	105	170	140	150	54
	(14.5)	(24.0)	(11.2)	(10.9)	(5.4)
Miscellaneous	34	15	10	11	1
	(4.7)	(2.1)	(0.8)	(0.8)	(0.1)
Total	724	709	1249	1372	1008
	(100.0)	(100.0)	(100.0)	(100.0)	(100.0)

Note: Parentheses show the per cent of total cases.

Source: Author's computations based on WTO Secretariat Rules division database.

downturn, domestic firms in importing countries use anti-dumping law to protect themselves and since there is a very high probability of affirmative injury findings during this period, they rush to file anti-dumping cases.

It may also be observed that there has been an obvious shift away from science based sectors to resource and labour intensive sectors during the early 1990s. Resource and labour sectors accounted for less than 50 per cent of the cases in the 1980s, their share increased to roughly 60 per cent in the late 1990s. During the early 2000s, it was 55 per cent. In contrast, the share of science based sectors declined sharply from 51 per cent in the late 1980s to 40 per cent during 1996–2000 but then increased slightly to 44 per cent. Even within the science-based sector, there was a sharp decline in the proportion of cases initiated in the differentiated sector. The share of the scale intensive sector increased sharply. These broad patterns suggest that ADDs are concentrated in the sectors which are of direct interest to the developing countries.

Anti-dumping Cases by Sector and Initiating Country Group

Table 4.19 shows the sectoral distribution of anti-dumping initiations within each country group over the period 1995–June 2004. Two observations may be made. First, resource intensive and science-based sectors dominated anti-dumping filings in all country groups. Second, low income countries initiated a higher proportion of cases in science based sectors (65.4 per cent of the total) than in resource intensive sectors (22 per cent). Lower middle income countries reported almost the same proportion of cases in both these sectors while upper middle, OECD, and non-OECD developed countries reported a larger proportion of cases in resource intensive sectors than in science-based sectors. These trends can be explained within the framework of the theory of comparative advantages. Apparently, countries used the anti-dumping mechanism to protect the industries where they did not have comparative advantages.

TABLE 4.19:   Sectoral distribution of anti-dumping cases—By country group: 1995–June 2004

	Low	Lower middle	Upper middle	OECD	Non-OECD
Resource intensive	85 (22.0)	287 (42.6)	210 (53.3)	594 (56.7)	24 (68.6)
Labour intensive	45 (11.6)	79 (11.7)	37 (9.4)	90 (8.6)	4 (11.4)

Contd

Table 4.19 Contd

	Low	Lower middle	Upper middle	OECD	Non-OECD
Science based	253	307	142	362	6
	(65.4)	(45.6)	(36.0)	(34.5)	(17.1)
Scale intensive	222	275	87	251	4
	(57.4)	(40.9)	(22.1)	(24.0)	(11.4)
Differentiated	31	32	55	111	2
	(8.01)	(4.7)	(13.95939)	(10.5916)	(5.714286)
Miscellaneous	4.0	0.0	5.0	2.0	1.0
	(1.03)	0	(1.27)	(0.19)	(2.86)
Total	387	673	394	1048	35
	(100.0)	(100.0)	(100.0)	(100.0)	(100.0)

Note: Parentheses show the per cent of total cases.

Source: Author's computations based on WTO Secretariat Rules division database Anti-dumping Cases by Sector and by Targeted Country Group.

Table 4.20 shows the sectoral distribution of anti-dumping initiations within each targeted country group. In low- and lower middle-income countries resource- and labour-intensive sectors were targeted most frequently. Of the total 1423 cases targeted against the developing countries, 858 were filed in these sectors. This accounted for over 65 per cent of the total cases. In contrast, developed countries (both OECD and non-OECD) were more frequently targeted in science based sectors. More than 50 per cent of the cases targeted against these countries were filed in this sector alone. The frequency with which both 'differentiated sectors' and scale-intensive sectors were targeted was relatively high for developed countries. Evidently, countries were more frequently targeted in the sectors where they had comparative advantage.

Such patterns have serious implications in particular for the developing countries. They clearly show that the crucial efficiency gains from trade liberalization have been severely limited by lingering protection in the very sectors where developing countries often have comparative advantages. While developed country firms are equipped to counter such measures through trade deflection and other measures, developing country firms are highly vulnerable to such actions.

Table 4.20:   Distribution of anti-dumping cases by sector and targeted country
group: 1995–June 2004

	Low	Lower middle	Upper middle	OECD	Non-OECD
Resource intensive	74	541	149	363	73
	(46.0)	(53.0)	(61.8)	(40.3)	(34.1)
Labour intensive	27	116	21	60	31
	(16.8)	(11.4)	(8.7)	(6.7)	(14.5)
Science based	60	358	71	473	108
	(37.3)	(35.1)	(29.5)	(52.6)	(50.5)
Scale intensive	50	276	59	375	79
	(31.1)	(27.0)	(24.5)	(41.7)	(36.9)
Differentiated	10	82	12	98	29
	(6.2)	(8.0)	(5.0)	(10.9)	(13.6)
Miscellaneous	0	6	0	4	2
	(0.0)	(0.6)	(0.0)	(0.4)	(0.9)
Total	161	1021	241	900	214
	(100.0)	(100.0)	(100.0)	(100.0)	(100.0)

Note: Science-based comprises scale intensive and differentiated sectors; parentheses show the per cent of total cases.

Source: Author's computations based on WTO Secretariat Rules division database.

CONCLUSION

Anti-dumping emerged as a global phenomenon in the past decade and is now used extensively by developed and developing countries alike. This study shows that the total number of cases being opened throughout the world is increasing rapidly. Moreover, there has been a significant change in the patterns of anti-dumping activity over the period of past twenty-five years. Important observations gleaned from this chapter are as follows.

One, in the 1990s the surge in anti-dumping cases was largely fuelled by the developing countries. However the use of anti-dumping is not still widespread among these countries. Very few developing countries are using it frequently. Several developing countries that have acquired the anti-dumping legislation have not yet initiated a single case.

Two, when a developed country initiates a case its impact may be much more dramatic especially on developing countries than when a developing country initiates a case. Since developed countries account for a large share of trade, any trade restrictive measure imposed by them is likely to significantly reduce the trade flows of the products concerned. Giving equal weight to anti-dumping activity by developed and developing countries therefore is not appropriate. The correct method would be to give greater weight to initiations that affect larger quantities of subject countries' trade. In other words, it is not the number of initiations but the proportion of subject countries' trade affected by anti-dumping measures that matters.

Three, developed countries impose measures for longer durations and with higher duty rates against the developing countries. In terms of the number of measures-in force they far outdistance even the most active developing countries. Besides, the fact that a high percentage of anti-dumping investigations and complaints that do not lead to duties in developed countries suggests that perhaps the practice is being used for purposes of harassment.

Four, the number of cases targeted against developing countries also increased sharply in the 1990s. In fact the number of cases initiated against low- and lower middle-income countries increased faster than the number of cases initiated by them. WTO records show that around 65 per cent of the cases initiated during 2000–4 were directed against the developing countries. Transition economies and East Asian countries were found to be the worst hit by anti-dumping use. An analysis of the number of ADDs, currently in force in the United States and the EU against developed and developing countries, yields startling revelations. In the United States, two-thirds of the ADDs are imposed against the developing countries while in the EU around 86 per cent of all impositions are against these countries. It was also observed that there was a distinct rise in the success rates of anti-dumping initiations during the late 1990s against these countries.

Five, evidence suggests that low- and middle-income developing countries were targeted mainly by OECD countries while they themselves were targeting other developing countries. Intra-OECD country group anti-dumping activities are relatively much smaller than intra-developing country group or inter-OECD and developing country group anti-dumping activities. Apparently, developing countries emerge as the major victim of the tool. Perhaps the use of the tool against these countries by developed countries itself is responsible for a high proportion of intra-developing country use of the tool.

Finally, analysis of the sectoral patterns of anti-dumping initiations suggests that a majority of cases were initiated in resource-intensive and science-based sectors. Base metals was the leading resource-intensive sector targeted. This could be due to a very high incidence of anti-dumping filings in the steel industry. In the science-based sector, scale-intensive—chemicals, plastic, and rubber—dominated anti-dumping filings over the period 1995–2004. The study also observes that countries were targeted primarily in the sectors where they had comparative advantage and they tended to use this mechanism primarily in the sectors where they did not have comparative advantage. Such trends have serious implications for the developing countries. These countries have recently started opening up their economies. But gains from trade liberalization may be reversed for them if they are targeted in the sectors where they have comparative advantage. Developed countries which are preaching trade liberalization to these countries are themselves turning to anti-dumping to protect their markets against the exports of developing countries. This may lead to marginalization of these countries in the process of globalization and defeat the purpose of the multilateral agreement.

APPENDIX

TABLE A4.1:   Classification of countries

Low income countries
Bangladesh, India, Kazakstan, Korea PDR, Malawi, Moldova, Mozambique, Nepal, Nicaragua, Nigeria, Pakistan, Uzbekistan, Vietnam, Zimbabwe

Lower middle income countries
Algeria, Belarus, Bosnia Herzegovina, Bulgaria, China, P.R.*, Colombia, Cuba, Dominican Republic, Ecuador, Egypt, Georgia, Guatemala, Honduras, Indonesia*, Iran, Jordan, Macedonia, Paraguay, Peru, Philippines, Romania, Russia, Serbia and Montenegro, South Africa, Sri Lanka, Thailand, Turkey**, Ukraine, Yugoslavia

Upper middle income countries
Argentina, Brazil, Chile, Costa Rica, Croatia, Czech Republic, Estonia, Hungary, South Korea, Rep. of, Latvia, Libya, Lithuania, Malaysia, Mexico, Oman, Poland, Saudi Arabia, Slovak Republic, Trinidad and Tobago, Uruguay, Venezuela

OECD
Australia, Austria, Belgium, Canada, Denmark, European Community, Finland, France, Germany, Greece, Ireland, Italy, Japan, Luxembourg, Netherlands, New Zealand, Norway, Portugal, Spain, Sweden, Switzerland, United Kingdom, United States

Non-OECD developed
Bahrain, Chinese Taipei, Faroe Islands, Hong Kong, Israel, Liechtenstein, Macau, Qatar, Singapore, Slovenia, United Arab Emirates

Note: * China and Indonesia were included in the low-income group prior to 1995.
** Turkey was in the upper middle-income group prior to 1995.

TABLE A4.2:   List of sectors

Sectors	
Resource intensive	Live animals, animal products, vegetable products, animal or vegetable fats and oils, tobacco and manufactured tobacco products, mineral products, raw hides and skins, wood and articles of wood, articles of stone, plaster, cement or similar, base metals and articles of base materials
Labour intensive	Textile articles footwear, headgear and the like, miscella-neous manufactured articles
Science based	
Differentiated	Machinery and mechanical appliances, vehicles, aircraft and associated transport

Contd

Table A4.2 Contd

Scale intensive	Products of chemical or allied industries plastics and articles, rubber and articles optical, photographic and accessories thereof
Miscellaneous	Arms and ammunition, works of art, collectors' pieces and antiques

Notes

1 We thank Raul Torres of the World Trade Organisation (Switzerland) for providing us the desired information from this database.

2 The Harmonized System (HS), developed under the auspices of the Customs Cooperation Council, standardizes the description and classification of goods for import and export. Both export and import statistics are classified and published according to the Harmonized Commodity description and Coding System. The HS nomenclature is logically structured by economic activity or component material. The nomenclature is divided into 21 sections, which in general groups goods produced in the same sector of the economy. Each section comprises of one or more chapters, with the entire nomenclature being composed of 99 chapters.

3 Using extremely disaggregated trade data, Prusa (2001) found that even when an anti-dumping dispute was ultimately rejected, imports fell by 15–20 per cent.

4 Based on the database provided by Blonigen (2003a) we find that the proportion of AD cases with affirmative findings has increased in Canada and Australia as well. In Canada it increased from 54.7 per cent in the pre 1995 period to 58.5 per cent in post 1995 period while in Australia it climbed up from 31 per cent to 35 per cent over the same period. In the US, the success rate during 1995-2004 had been as high as 72 per cent.

5 The share of the developing countries in world merchandise exports was 31 per cent in 2004 (WTO 2005).

6 On that day the number of US active measures dropped from 326 to 267.

5 Economics or Politics?
An Empirical Analysis of Anti-dumping Use

What is the rationale behind anti-dumping policy? The rhetoric of anti-dumping is that it disciplines 'unfair trade practices'. This raises another question: what is an 'unfair trade practice'? The Agreement specifies that price discrimination is an unfair trade practice if it causes injury to the domestic industry. This leads to yet another question: Should price discrimination practiced by foreign exporters be labeled as an unfair trade practice and be punished by slapping ADD if the domestic industry is not doing well? There is no simple answer to this question. Several alternative explanations have been given to justify the use of anti-dumping against price discrimination. The politicians, economists, and lawyers have all participated in this debate. Most politicians and lawyers strongly defend anti-dumping as a trade remedy that is necessary for ensuring fair trade. They believe that international price discrimination per se is objectionable. If left unchallenged it confers an unfair competitive advantage on exporters, which they exploit with considerable negative consequences on domestic industry. In contrast, economists argue that without a showing of predatory intent, price discrimination cannot be held to be an unfair trade practice. Since there is no such pre-requisite of anti-dumping use, it itself is an unfair policy that blocks fair competition.[1] Some observers however take the middle course and justify the use of anti-dumping on the 'second best' grounds. According to them anti-dumping is an instrument that is necessary for the maintenance of the multilateral trading system. They argue that by ensuring protection in case of trade destabilization, it acts as a safety valve that ensures domestic political support to trade liberalizing initiative. Anti-dumping, in their view, is the price to be paid for the maintenance of an open trading system among nations (see for instance, Bhagwati 1988; Boltuck and Litan 1991; p. 13, Dam 2001, p. 156). They thus emphasize the interactions between political compulsions and economic choices and provide political economy perspective to the use of anti-dumping.

These explanations can be summed up in three broad perspectives.

- Political perspective: Anti-dumping is a trade remedy for domestic producers injured by cheap imports.

- Economic perspective: It is a tool that discourages predatory dumping.
- Political economy perspective: Anti-dumping is a GATT/WTO legal tool that is used to grant protection to the import competing domestic industry, which is affected adversely by free trade.

This chapter examines theoretical explanations of the three perspectives and reviews the existing empirical literature in regard to each of them. Drawing on the review, it empirically investigates the relevance of the political economy approach of the anti-dumping policy for the developed and developing countries. It identifies a number of possible macroeconomic factors that may instigate the use of trade remedy and empirically examines, using a panel data set of ninety-nine countries[2] over the period 1980–2000, which of the factors explain the use of anti-dumping tool in developed and developing countries.

The first three sections of this chapter provide the theoretical discussion and present empirical evidence on various justifications of anti-dumping use from three perspectives: the political, the economic, and the political economy. The next section empirically analyses the macroeconomic factors that motivate the use of anti-dumping and the last section concludes the analysis.

THE POLITICAL PERSPECTIVE

The political perspective of anti-dumping is that it is a response to unfair trade practices of exporters that results from their home country government trade distorting policies and consequent market imperfections (US 2002).[3] According to this approach, government-imposed trade barriers and government-tolerated anti-competitive activities permit domestic producers to create monopolies in their home markets. This enables them to charge low prices in export markets and compensate the loss by charging higher prices in the domestic markets without attracting foreign entry. Dumping of goods creates an artificial comparative advantage for the exporters over their competing rivals in the importing country. It is artificial because the lower export price does not result from cost-efficiency, which is based on natural resources, labour skills, availability of capital, and technological innovations. Rather, it results from the government policies. The consequence is the distortion of the market signals to producers in the importing country because the prices suggest that adequate returns will not be achieved for the dumped product. Countries with a real comparative advantage lose the capacity and capability to produce such products. Producers in importing countries fail to expand capacity, to improve productivity, and to use all other resources efficiently. The distorted price signals in the market thus stimulate overproduction of the exportable goods and underproduction of importable goods. This in turn leads to chronic oversupply by inefficient producers on the one hand and the closure of otherwise efficient and competitive facilities on the other reducing worldwide efficiency. ADDs restore relative pricing to prevailing world market conditions and hence efficient resource allocation.

The 1998 US submission to the WTO (WTO 1998) identifies several industrial policies as possibly giving rise to dumping. These include: high tariff or non-tariff barriers that exclude foreign competition, regulations that restrict domestic competition, the absence of adequate competition laws to counteract private anti-competitive conduct, price controls that set artificially high prices for the exported product or artificially low prices for inputs for the exported product, and government subsidies that give foreign producers an artificial cost advantage or that result in excess capacity. The 1998 paper goes on to address how differences in national economic systems can result in dumping. For example, in countries in which social pressures or policies inhibit layoffs during downturns, labour costs are more fixed than variable. In such settings, producers may choose to sell below full costs instead of laying off unneeded workers. In other words, they will 'export [their] unemployment to the other country's industry.' In another scenario, producers rely more heavily on debt in countries with poorly developed equity markets. They may find it necessary to sell below cost to service their debt obligations, whereas producers with lower debt-equity ratios might cut back production during slumps. The paper also identifies other situations—the presence of large, conglomerate business groupings with non-commercial access to financing; cut-throat pricing encouraged by a policy of adopting 'market stabilization' cartels on the basis of pre-cartel production levels and state planning regimes with quantitative export targets—in which differences in national economic structures can lead to dumping. Mastel (1998) empasized that closed (or sanctuary) markets encourage the practice of dumping to open economies where the firms do not enjoy the 'luxury' of protection.

The use of anti-dumping measures enables the domestic producers to offset, quantitatively, the artificial advantages realized by the exporting country's producers so that they may compete on an equal footing with the exporting country's producers. Anti-dumping law, therefore, is largely a mechanism to provide a level playing field. This law provides a form of protection that is compatible with the major objectives of the GATT/WTO of ensuring fair and undistorted competition in the sense of equal competitive opportunities to all producers. This is needed so long as market conditions are not symmetrical across borders and foreign firms have scope for practices, which domestic firms do not and which may give them an asymmetrical advantage.

Empirical evidence

There has been intensive empirical research on the motives of using anti-dumping measures. This research focuses mainly on the economic and political economy justification of anti-dumping use. Few empirical studies examined the use of anti-dumping from the political perspective. However, the political perspective of anti-dumping cannot be ignored as the defenders of the tool use this viewpoint to support the Agreement in its current form. It is important to address the question whether the use of this so called trade remedy be justified using the political perspective. According to this viewpoint anti-dumping measures are needed to offset artificial competitive advantages created by market-distorting government policies and the market imperfections that result from such policies and restore the so-called level playing field. From the empirical perspective the question is whether anti-dumping measures are really targeting artificial competitive advantages that result from the above government policies. Though there is no empirical analysis, one can argue that 'there is a serious mismatch between what the AD measures actually do and what they are supposed to do within this framework' (Lindsey and Ikenson 2002b). They are supposed to identify the instances of price discrimination that are consequences of underlying market distorting policies. But in practice they target any price discrimination that results in surge of imports. There is no mechanism in the tool that distinguishes normal price discrimination from dumping caused by market disporting government policies. Furthermore, the ASCM itself addresses the issue of trade distorting subsidies. There is no justification of another tool with the same purpose within the same Multilateral Framework. Clearly, the use of anti-dumping measures cannot be explained within the framework of the political perspective.

THE ECONOMIC PERSPECTIVE

The early view of anti-dumping in economics was to justify anti-dumping measures on the grounds of economic effects of dumping. Viner published his seminal study on the subject in 1923. In this study (Viner 1923) he viewed anti-dumping as a tool against dumping, which he believed was harmful to the importing country. He introduced a distinction between the following three forms of dumping.

- sporadic dumping,
- temporary dumping, and
- permanent dumping.

    The classification was based on the degree of continuity of dumping and its effects. Sporadic dumping is for a very short time period. It occurs when a producer intends to dispose of the casual overstock. Sales in the specified period may not be as good as expected and the producer finds himself with surplus stock. He finds it difficult either to dispose it off in the domestic market or to hold it for the next season for various reasons. He therefore tries to sell it in the foreign markets at lower prices to recover some cost, which results in dumping. Sporadic dumping may also be unintentional. It could be due to currency fluctuations or due to inexperience of the exporters. This is rectified as early as it becomes known.

Short-term dumping or temporary dumping is for longer duration than sporadic dumping. It occurs when a producer attempts to maintain connection in a market where prices are considerably lower or he sells the product at a lower price in export markets to build trade connections in a new market. He may also dump the product in an import market with predatory intents, that is he cuts prices to drive his rivals out. Once he obtains monopoly powers, he raises prices to recoup his early losses. Thus, predatory dumping is also one of the forms of transitory dumping.

Permanent dumping is continuous for many years. It occurs when a producer intends to obtain full production from the existing capacity without cutting the domestic prices or he intends to obtain economies of larger scale of production without cutting the domestic prices. In sectors where scale economies are important, firms can limit the domestic supply to charge higher prices to maximize profits. For operating at the full capacity or avail economies of scale advantages, however, they look for export markets. Since their market power is less in export markets they charge lower prices in these markets. Thus, the firms produce a surplus output with an intent to dump on to export markets. Though this type of dumping is generally permanent, it could also be temporary. Dumping motivated by mercantilistic approach of the government however is always long term and continuous. This occurs when the government provides direct or indirect assistance to exporters by way of subsidies, cheap loans, and undervalued currency to confer on them artificial advantages in order to stimulate exports.

Sporadic dumping according to Viner is very short lived and benign. It is for such a short period that it cannot have injurious effects on domestic producers and cannot even allow anti-dumping investigations to complete. Permanent dumping, he argued, generates greater advantages to the consumer than the injury to the domestic producer in the importing country. But when dumping is temporary, he believed it is harmful to the importing country. Transitory dumping he pointed out results in greater injury to domestic industry than benefit to consumers. He reasoned that transitory dumping imposes adjustment costs on the importing nation because it leads resources to become idle while waiting for it to stop and that such costs exceed the benefits of temporarily cheaper imports (Viner 1923). This according to him is the prime justification for acting against dumping. Viner also believed that 'it is not a matter of importance whether dumping in general or any particular species of dumping should be classified with unfair competition or not. What is important with respect to dumping is its economic effect, which is not greatly dependent upon what happens to be its motive'.

Haberler (1936) supported Viner's arguments and argued that dumping occurs in spasm and spasm lasts long enough to bring about a shifting of production in the importing country, which must be reversed when the cheap imports cease. Haberler thus shifted the emphasis from the cost of idle resources to the cost of moving the resources back and forth between industries due to dumping. But the basic argument remained much the same.

This argument was found to be flawed by economists who eventually began to question the basic assumption that dumping is transitory. They argued that dumping need not be transitory (as when different markets have different demand elasticities), and even when it is, nothing in Viner's work (or since) demonstrates that temporarily cheap imports necessarily impose adjustment costs that exceed the welfare gains to the importing country from temporarily cheaper imports (Sykes 1999).

Gradually, the debate, which was previously dominated by the traditional approach of Viner, tended to shift from economic effects to motives of price discrimination and from producers' to consumers' welfare. Dumping was classified into several categories depending on the motivation of the exporters and the characteristics of the markets that underlie them. These are as follows.

- market-expansion-related dumping,
- promotional dumping,
- cyclical dumping,
- predatory dumping,
- strategic dumping.

Market expansion dumping occurs when a company expands its export sales by charging lower price in the export markets than in the domestic markets. The motivation behind this behaviour is that the additional profits may be earned by charging higher prices in markets with lower price elasticities of demand, but lower prices in markets with higher price elasticities of demand. If the lower price elasticities of demand occur in the company's home market relative to its foreign markets, the company may charge higher prices in home markets to maximize its profits. Promotional dumping occurs when an exporter charges consumers a lower introductory price in new foreign markets to create market for the product (Boltuck 1991). Exports at low price might be aimed at developing trade connections/increasing market share in new markets. Price discrimination in this case may be motivated by steep learning curve for the product (Vermulst 1999). Cyclical dumping involves producers selling below full or even marginal cost during a recession in order to keep plant in business. It is profitable for the firms to cut prices in order to generate profits than to hold process up (Willig 1998, p. 62). Predatory dumping has already been described above. Strategic dumping occurs when governments campaign to develop export advantages in targeted sectors to gain market shares in global oligopoly industries. The scope for strategic dumping however is limited to certain countries or groups of countries and to certain industries. This is a relatively new concept, which has appeared in recent writings in industrial economics. There is more discussion of strategic dumping later in this chapter. Table 5.1 describes the various forms of dumping and summarizes their impacts. These forms of dumping are then reclassified into two categories: non monopolizing and monopolizing.

Non-monopolizing dumping: Of the various forms of dumping described above, first three, namely, the market-expansion-based, promotional, and cyclical are distinguished as non-monopolizing in nature. These forms of dumping involve rational business strategies and can be entirely consistent with robustly competitive conditions in the importing country's markets. They may have adverse effects on domestic producers of competing goods (Willig 1998, Boltuck 1991) but domestic consumers benefit from the low prices. If the importing market is competitive, the benefits to consumers outweigh the losses of domestic producers and there are net welfare gains to the economy (Willig 1998, Boltuck 1991).

Monopolizing dumping: Dumping is stated to be harmful when it is monopolizing in nature. Economists thus argue that 'it is monopolizing dumping that ought to be actionable'. The traditional form of monopolizing dumping is predatory pricing. Most economists focus on this form of dumping and argue that dumping constitutes an unfair trade practice only when it is carried out with predatory intents (Palmeter 1991, Tharakan 1995, Trebilcock and Howse 1999, and many others). The anti-dumping law is a bulwark against such anti-competitive practices of foreign exporters. New developments in the industrial economics, however, indicate that there is a scope for strategic dumping which may also result in monopolization. Prevention of this form of dumping is another economic rationale of anti-dumping measures. We shall now focus on these two forms of dumping and examine why prevention of these forms of dumping is economic rationale of anti-dumping measures.

TABLE 5.1: Forms of dumping—Description, driving force, and impact

	Description	Driving force	Impact
Non-monopolizing dumping			
Market expansion	Expansion of sales by price discrimination if the lower price the lower price elasticities of demand occur in the company's home market relative to its foreign markets.	Difference in price elasticities	Induces competition, benefits consumers but harms producers.
Promotional	Introduction of a product in a new market to create market for the product using price discrimination strategy (Boltuck 1991).	Steep learning curve for the product Vermulst (1999)	Society benefits from the low prices and increases in productivity efficiency and the industry learns more about the product.
Cyclical	Exporting at a low price in the presence of excess capacity due to depressed demand. A rational business strategy whereby the exporter may be acting in an economically efficient manner.	Maintaining full capacity	May reduce capacity of less efficient (domestic) producers, improve global resource allocation increase global welfare, harm producers.
State	Exporting at low prices by state-owned enterprises in countries with inconvertible currencies.	Need for hard currency	Earns hard currency for the non market economy, benefits consumers in importing countries, harms producers.

Contd

Table 5.1 Contd

	Description	Driving force	Impact
Monopolizing dumping			
Predatory	Exporting at low prices to drive out rivals and establish monopoly power in the importing market.	Elimination of competition in the importing markets with the intent of recouping the loss at a later date	Eliminates competition, creates monopolies damages productive capacity in the importing country. Harms consumers and producers in the long run.
Strategic	low export prices with a protected home market to give exporters an advantage in industries with static (fixed R&D and capital expenses) or dynamic learning by doing) economies of scale.	Market dominance	Elimination of competition, injury to domestic firms.

Source: Willig (1998).

The concept of predatory pricing is borrowed from the domestic competition policy (Hutton and Trebilcock 1990). It is defined (see Ordover 1998 for survey) as the situation where a domestic firm prices below cost so as to drive competitors out of the market and acquire or maintain a position of dominance. Predation involves efforts to achieve or exploit monopoly power, restricts competition in domestic markets, and injures consumers through monopoly pricing in the long run. Economists argue that while competition policies deter predatory pricing by domestic firms to preserve the process of competition and protect the interests of the consumer, anti-dumping policy, if used appropriately, curbs anti-competitive practices by foreign firms. Most economists thus view anti-dumping as an international counterpart of domestic competition policy. Protecting the competitive processes and consumer welfare from predatory practices of foreign exporters has thus emerged as the primary justification of the tool. While probing the origins of anti-trust and anti-dumping rules, Sykes (1998) finds that the justification[4] for both sets of laws at the outset was to protect the competitive process and the consumer from monopoly power. The first anti-dumping law, passed in Canada in 1904, was surrounded by anti-predation rhetoric. In the United States, the 1916 Anti-dumping Act was aimed at predatory pricing by foreign exporters but was superseded by the 1921 Anti-dumping Act, which closely resembled the Canada's anti-dumping law. Its supporters, Sykes observed, presented their anti-dumping rules as anti-monopoly legislation to combat predatory pricing (see Chapter 2).

The economic approach was reinforced with the rise of the Chicago school. The proponents of this school emphasize that economic law and policy should only be about economic efficiency. They reject 'any legal doctrines that entrench any economic rights at all on grounds of fairness rather than efficiency' (Holmes and Kempton 1997). According to them the whole purpose of competition and competition policies is to help enhance 'consumer welfare'. They are concerned about the welfare of consumers as opposed to producers as protecting inefficient producers leads to sheltering inefficiencies. Preventing predation therefore seems to be the only justification of anti-dumping in this framework. However, these scholars (McGee 1958, Bork 1978, Easterbrook 1981 among others) argue that predation is unlikely to exist and that it is vacuous in reality. The theoretical literature suggests there are stringent prerequisites of predatory dumping which are never fulfilled. Even for a simple form of price discrimination to take place certain necessary conditions have to be fulfilled. One such necessary condition is the international segmentation of markets and/or a market structure characterized by imperfect competition in the country of the firm carrying out the price discrimination (Tharakan 1995, p. 190). If there were no barriers to market access anywhere then price differences with other markets would be leveled out because of import competition (Vermulst 1999). Mastel (1998, p. 43) argues 'if a company engages in foreign markets and its home markets is open, the price differential will induce re-exports of dumped products to the dumper's home markets'. Another necessary condition for dumping to take place is the presence of imperfect home country markets characterized by high degree of concentration, asymmetric distribution of financial resources, and substantial barriers to entry. The imperfect competitive markets make foreign competition difficult. This allows firms to charge higher prices in domestic markets. The rents thus created can be used to price discriminate internationally.

The two conditions described above are necessary for any form of price discrimination. For price discrimination to be predatory more stringent conditions have to be met. For instance, for successful predation at the international level, firms need to have capacity not only for domestic dominance, as suggested above, but also for global dominance in their industry. If the predatory firms do not have the capacity for global dominance, third country competitors will move in and bring down the prices again during the hypothesised post-predation price-hike period. The position of dominance also implies that the predator has substantial resources and that he can sustain losses for a longer period of time to drive away the competitors. However for this argument to hold, there must be imperfections in the capital market. The potential victim may be located in a country with less developed markets and/ or his capability to raise the capital must be limited. Further it has to be assumed that outside financing is costlier than internal financing. Finally, the threat of predation needs to be credible. Credibility of the threat in fact is central to the issue of successful predation (Tharakan et al. 2001). If the threat is not credible then it cannot be used as an effective signal to competitors and potential entrants in other markets not to enter or compete rigorously. It is therefore important that the predator builds a reputation as a predator. In sum, the possibility of successful predation depends on a set of crucial assumptions. The most important among them is that the predator has dominance not only in domestic market but also in international market. Other important conditions include market segmentation, imperfect capital markets, and credibility of the threat. Even if the predator meets all these stringent conditions, there is no way to rule out (re) entry during the post-predation period. In the context of this literature the Chicago school argues that predatory pricing is rare and questions the role of the government interference in ensuring competition whether it is in domestic markets (competition policies) or in trade (anti-dumping).

The Chicago school came under attack by the new industrial organization based on game theory. The game theorists created a host of models showing that under certain assumptions about information and strategy, a threat to use predatory pricing could be profitable. Though there have been counterattacks from the Chicago school (Peltzman 1991, Lott 1999), most economists do not rule out the possibility of predation. They argue that predation attempts whether of national or foreign origin must be detected and countered because it leads to welfare loss. In international trade anti-dumping serves as a tool to counter such attempts.

Strategic dumping approach is embedded in the 'Strategic Trade Theory' (Katrak 1977, Svedberg 1979, and Brander and Spencer 1981) framework. It explains how a nation can create comparative advantage through activist trade policies in industries characterized by increasing economies of scale, high knowledge intensity, and imperfectly competitive markets, which confer beneficial spillovers on the rest of the economy. In these markets, firms set prices in excess of the marginal cost of production, which results in firms typically making excess returns. There is an international competition over who gets these profits. In such cases, a government, by protecting its companies from international competition, can shift rents from foreign rivals to domestic corporations. Direct or indirect assistance or an additional tariff would increase the domestic firm's market power in its own market and allow it to drop prices in export markets. This would provide artificial advantage to the domestic firm over its foreign rivals. With access to both home and foreign markets, they gain a cost advantage over the importing countries' firms. Assuming that other governments do not retaliate, ADD in its domestic markets by the exporting country government can shift rents from foreigners to domestic companies.

In such industries, if the exporters' home market is foreclosed to foreign rivals and if each independent exporter's share of their home market is of significant size relative to their scale economies, the exporters will be able to have a significant cost advantage over foreign rivals. This advantage, which is obviously contingent on the home market being sufficiently large, eventually gives the exporting firms market power. This would allow a firm to dump its products across borders. This dumping also known as strategic dumping is likely to damage the importing country by reducing the ability of domestic firms to take full advantage of scale economies. If domestic firms are unable to compete effectively, over time domestic consumers may be injured by the exercise of market power by exporting firms (Hindley and Messerlin 1996, Schone 1996, Deardorff 1989). ADD in this case therefore is a rational trade policy for the importing country government.

This approach implies that if anti-dumping cases are concentrated in strategic industries then trade is benefited and national welfare improves. One must however note that strategic dumping is applicable only to those home markets that are sufficiently large in relation to the rest of the world so that protection in the home markets has significant impact on their ability to compete with foreign rivals (Willig 1998). Small economies are unlikely to favour strategic dumping. Furthermore, it is likely only in a few sectors such as electronic and communications where scale and knowledge economics are important (Tyson 1992).

In some recent writings (see, for instance, Holmes and Kempton 1997) however it is emphasized that there is a wide spectrum of behaviour that can be termed strategic competition. Strategic behaviour is a common phenomenon that occurs all the time. Behaviour is strategic if it is undertaken to influence the rivals' behaviour. It may not be profit maximizing given the behaviour of competitors but becomes profit maximimizing when the reaction of competitors is taken into account. The scope of strategic dumping therefore may be much wider than what is described by the state-led strategic trade policy. For instance, exporters may cut prices sharply, perhaps to 'punish' firms who have broken price agreements in order to enforce collusion: not to drive the rivals out of business but to invite them to put up prices again. They may build more capacity than is needed for various reasons. It could be deliberate with the desire to enhance the relative position in export markets. It could also be due to uncertainty in international trade or to ensure stabilization of production over business cycles (Ethier 1982) or due to overestimation of global demands (Hindley 1991). Whatever may be the reason, it translates into surpluses, which are dumped in the export markets. But not all forms of strategic behaviour are harmful or actionable. It is actionable when it intends to exploit asymmetric advantages or a 'long purse' to enlarge market share at the expense of others and thereby reducing the intensity of competition without necessarily monopolizing the market completely. One must however note that it is not easy to identify what kinds of strategic behaviour are harmful. This approach thus requires a case by case analysis to establish whether dumping is indeed intended to use asymmetric market power to enhance the market share.

In sum, economic justification of anti-dumping is not to prevent predatory dumping alone as has been highlighted by many experts. It has a much broader framework. It includes dumping with monopolizing intents that may not involve complete monopolization through predation but rather domination of the foreign markets.

Empirical evidence

While examining the economic rationale of anti-dumping use most studies address the question: Was predatory behaviour actually present when protection was granted? This research (Aggarwal 2002 for India; Hutton and Trebilcock 1990, Dutz 1998, and Leclerc 1999 for Canada; Hyun Ja Shin 1998 for the United States; Bourgeois and Messerlin 1998 and Nicolaides and Wijngaarden 1993 for the EC, Dijk for Mexico, and Holden 1998 for South Africa) focuses on the evaluation of anti-dumping measures in terms of the criteria required for predatory dumping. Predation in domestic cases means pricing below marginal costs. In the event that marginal cost data are not available, average variable cost is used. In practice, however, competition authorities follow the methodology developed by Joskow and Klevorick (1979). Under this methodology, before applying the predation test, there is assessment of structural characteristics of the markets to ascertain whether the alleged predator has market power in order to be successful and whether entry barriers are high so that he will recoup his losses through monopolistic profits in the post predation period. As discussed above, four basic prerequisites are considered necessary for predatory dumping to take place successfully. First, the alleged predator must possess a large market share at home that is protected or serves as a 'sanctuary market.' Second, there must be an opportunity to invade another market to obtain larger market shares. Third, if there are several producers in the domestic market, they must collude in order to maintain the long-term price hike that is possible after the foreign market firms have been driven out of business. Finally, significant barriers to entry must exist in the industry. If not, the price hike would create strong incentives for competitors to enter the market and undermine the monopolistic position (Schone 1996, Willig 1998). In practice, emphasis has been on the market dominance test.

Most studies while examining if predation was a likely explanation of dumping in the anti-dumping cases used the above approach followed in establishing predation in domestic markets. The central premise is that for predatory dumping in international markets, the predator must have dominance not only in domestic markets but also in international markets. These studies adopted certain criteria to analyse market power of exporters. These criteria are:

- Import penetration should be high, to indicate that domestic firms might be driven out of business.
- The large suppliers have to be dominant at the world level, otherwise predation attempt will not succeed.

- Export markets should be concentrated/the number of foreign sellers should be small, so that they can exercise monopoly power in the future.
- Exporters should be dominant producers in their domestic markets.

They evaluated the anti-dumping cases in terms of these criteria. Cases that failed to meet any of these criteria probably did not involve predatory dumping. Interestingly, all the studies have shown that predatory behaviour was not the prime target of anti-dumping policies. An extensive review by the OECD of anti-dumping cases in Australia, Canada, the EU, and the United States found that around 90 per cent of the instances of import sales found to be unfair under anti-dumping rules would never have been questioned under competition law used by a domestic firms in making a domestic sale. Shin (1998) showed that out of the sample of 282 US anti-dumping cases with positive outcomes only 20 cases could be considered to be consistent with the predatory behaviour. On the contrary, Hutton and Trebilcock (1990) analysed thirty anti-dumping cases in Canada and found that in none of these cases anti-dumping duty was a justified means of preventing predatory dumping. They also examined social benefits of ADD and concluded that communitarian values were not the motivation behind these cases. Holden (1998) concluded

TABLE 5.2:   Summary information of empirical studies on anti-dumping and predatory pricing

Author	Country	Period of investigation	No. of cases	No. of cases where predation could be the reason
Hutton and Trebilcock	Canada	1990	30	Nil
Hun Ja Shin	USA	1980–9	282	28
Bourgeois and Messerlin	EU	1981–92	297	4
OECD	Australia, Canada, EU and US			less than 10%
Dijk	Mexico	1987–96	80	2
Holden	South Africa	1992–8	N.A.	3%
Aggarwal	India	1992–2000	77	2

Source: OECD, Economics Department (1996), *Antitrust and Market Access:*

The Scope and Coverage of Competition Laws and Implications for Trade, Paris.

that 2 per cent of the total applications were likely to have involved predatory behaviour on the part of the foreign suppliers in South Africa. Aggarwal (2002) examined seventy-seven anti-dumping cases investigated in India and observed that two of the cases could have involved predatory dumping. Both involved China—an NME. Bourgeoise and Messerlin (1998) found that out of the 297 cases investigated in the EU, only 7 (2.4 per cent) could be considered as possible cases of predatory dumping. Of these four involved non-market economies. In a recent study on Mexico (Dijk 1997) showed that of the eighty cases between 1987 and 1996 that resulted in the imposition of a duty, only two could have involved predation.

Evidently, anti-dumping has nothing to do with economic rationale of preventing predatory dumping either in developed or in developing countries.

While most studies concentrate on the predatory dumping approach of anti-dumping, few attempts have been made to examine whether anti-dumping activities have been concentrated in strategic sectors. It could be due to several reasons. One, there could be practical problems involved in identifying 'strategic sectors'. Theoretically, sectors with high linkages that diffuse new technologies over a broad spectrum of industries have been dubbed as 'strategic sectors'. In practice however, identification of strategic industries raises serious difficulties (Tharakan 1994). An important question that comes up is: What should be the criteria for identifying strategic industries? Is it value addition, technology intensity, comparative advantage, or employment? Two, it is also difficult to establish whether imposition of an anti-dumping duty in a high-technology sector will really promote the industry or have positive spillover effects on the rest of the economy. Consider a high-technology intermediate good, such as semiconductors. Because it serves as an input into a whole range of modern producer and consumer electronics, the promotion of such an industry may be considered as a foundation for promoting high-technology activities. When domestic producers of such an input gain tariff protection against foreign suppliers, the price of this input rises and with it the costs of those allegedly desirable high-technology industries that incorporate the input. Rather than launching a whole sector, protecting an input can raise the costs of domestic users and cause them to cede the market to imported finished products. In 1991, when the United States imposed a 62 per cent tariff on screens for laptop computers imported from Japan, the computer makers began moving their production overseas to escape the elevated cost.[5] Three, evidence also suggests that contrary to general beliefs, under some circumstances, firms of exporting country not only might not be hurt by the anti-dumping policy in such cases of international oligopoly, but also can gain from it. It depends crucially on the firms' strategies (Chen and

Chen 2003), the form of the anti-dumping regulations and the influence of strategic behavior of both exporting (domestic) firms and competing foreign firms in the criterion used to determine dumping and on the procedures used to enforce the regulation. Kiyono (1995) found that the firms, by taking the rules of the regulation into account, can strategically distort the regulatory process itself. Finally, this form of dumping is not a widespread phenomenon. It is applicable only to certain industries and certain countries. These problems, notwithstanding there are some studies that have attempted to examine whether anti-dumping actions were in response to strategic dumping. Two studies were based on global test of the cases investigated during 1981–92 in the EU (Bourgeoise and Messerlin 1993) and during 1980–9 in the United States (Shin 1992). They used a crude test in which they eliminated exporters who operated from small economies. Only 10 per cent cases in the EU and 12.6 per cent cases in the United States could qualify the test. These studies also revealed that Japan might be the only country where such dumping was prevalent. There are a few case based studies as well. These involved steel (Crandall 1993), semiconductors (Irwing 1995) and consumer electronics (Messerlin and Noguchi 1993). These studies showed no signs of strategic dumping.

THE POLITICAL ECONOMY PERSPECTIVE

There is huge literature, both theoretical and empirical, on the political economy approach (see Blonigen and Prusa 2001, Tharakan 1995, and Nelson 2006 for an excellent survey of literature and references). The political economy approach argues that anti-dumping use is not motivated by anything other than protectionism. This argument begins with the premise that free trade does not bring unambiguous gains to all sections of the society. It implies gains for some while loses for others. Since those who gain are not capable of compensating those who lose, there are protectionist pressures in the economy. Pressure groups constitute domestic producers in import competing industries who are likely to lose from free trade. These producers lobby (see Rodrik 1995, Blonigen and Prusa 2001, and Nelson 2006 for references and survey) to strive for protection. In doing so, they find anti-dumping the most potent tool of protection. Once an application is made domestic firms face a high probability of obtaining protection. Theoretical and empirical literature suggests that even if no dumping is finally found, the initiation of investigations itself results in imports fall.[6] This has therefore become a tool of choice for them.

Government constitutes another pressure group in this game. It provides the adjudicatory framework for investigating the complaints and decides whether to initiate the case. The Government's choices are usually mercantilist

(Caves 1976, Baldwin 1984, O'Rourke and Sinnott 2001). There could be several reasons for this such as political concerns, that is voting concerns and political pressures (see Magee et al. 1989, Mayer 1998, and Nelson 2006 for useful literature), equity concerns (Baldwin 1984), or trade patriotism (O'Rourke and Sinnott 2001). Oligopolists, by lobbying effectively, may convince them to grant protection from import competition (Tharakan and Waelbroeck 1994). Government knows that trade protection is beneficial as long as it is not used by trade partners (Messerlin 1993,1995). Therefore it behaves differently at two levels. At the collective level (during trade negotiations) it negotiates with the trading partners to achieve trade liberalization. At the individual level (the intra-national level), it tries to benefit from the opening of its trade partners while remaining selectively closed to imports through contingent protection measures. Anti-dumping offers the best option for doing this. Anti-dumping can easily be manipulated to justify its use. Using this tool, governments can administer protection in a way that appears impartial, automatic and rule-based where many of the procedures may be biased towards a positive finding. Hence governments readily tend to support the use of the GATT compatible anti-dumping mechanism.

Consumers/downstream users who lose from protection are marginalized in the system. The WTO agreement does not require a public interest test for imposing ADD. The anti-dumping law in most countries does not define or elaborate on public interest and leaves the matter at the discretion of the authority. Even in countries which have provisions for community interest clause it has been observed that the clause rarely led to a decision not to impose duties in instances where dumping and injury was found to exist (Hoekman and Mavroidis 1996, Leclerc 1999).[7] It could be because consumers are less organized and less influential (Tharakan 1995). Moreover, their individual losses may not be great enough to induce them to organize.

This school thus focuses on the strategic interactions between the import competing domestic firms and the national authorities to use anti-dumping for protection and suggests that the higher the expected rents from such protection, the greater is the use of anti-dumping. The expected rent in turn depends on various industry specific or macroeconomic factors. Majority of research focuses on the behaviour of firms and bureaucrats and thus deals with the micro political economy of anti-dumping use.[8] There is however small body of literature on the macro-political economy as well. These macro and micro-factors impinge on the expected success of the petition and the expected benefits if successful and hence motivate the protectionist pressures to request anti-dumping investigations and governments" eagerness to accommodate them. Use of anti-dumping according to this perspective is determined by all these factors and not by the desire to ensure fair trade. As discussed in Chapter 2, evolution of anti-dumping use in the early 1920s was primarily driven by the motives of protecting the nascent industries in the then newly industrializing countries even though it was heavily surrounded by anti-monopoly rhetoric.

Empirical analysis

There have been several empirical studies that have tested whether considerations other than unfair trade practices influenced the use of anti-dumping. Two streams of literature may be distinguished. While one stream of literature is concerned with analysing micro factors affecting anti-dumping proceedings, another deals with macro-level factors.

Following the seminal work by Finger et al. (1982), several studies have analysed the micro factors that affect the decision making process in anti-dumping investigations (Tharakan 1991, Moore 1992, De Vault 1993, Hansen and Prusa 1996, 1997). Most of the studies have been made for the US and EU cases and they show that a host of non-economic factors influenced the investigations. These included: political pressures, lobbying, concentration, case size, etc. Thus, Finger et al. (1982) and Eymann and Schuknecht (1993) find that the likelihood of positive anti-dumping decisions increases with the size of the complaining industry in terms of employment or output for the United States and EU, respectively. Baldwin and Steagall (1994) suggests that injury findings in US anti-dumping and CVD cases are more likely, the less the complaining industry is 'competitive' internationally (as measured by the import penetration ratio). Tharakan and Waelbroeck (1994) find that in the EU concentrated industries have a greater chance of success when filing anti-dumping complaints. Czinkota and Kotabe (1997) show that the US International Trade Commission (ITC) supports both sunset industries and relatively concentrated industries with stable or growing markets. In a study on Mexico, Francois and Neils (2004) found that the outcome is more likely to be positive in large industries producing intermediate products. They concluded that like the traditional developed country users of administered protection, Mexico has also used its anti-dumping regime to supply protection for political reasons.

A series of papers including Finger (1981), Herander and Schwartz (1984), Feinberg and Hirsch (1989), Hansen (1990), Krupp (1994), Leichenberg and Tan (1994), and Sabry (2000) have estimated determinants of US anti-dumping filings by a 3- or 4- digit SIC industry for different time periods. Though their methodologies differed substantially, there is general consistency in results across these studies. Import penetration, industry employment, and capital intensity appear to be significant variables.

There are a few studies that have analysed the macroeconomic determinants of the contingent protection policy. While some of them focused on safeguard measures (Takacs 1981, Feigenbaum and Willett 1985, Salvatore 1987), others analysed the factors affecting anti-dumping and/or CVD (Leidy 1997, Becker and Theuringer 2001, Knetter and Prusa 2003, and Feinberg 1989). While focussing on the United States and the EU these studies have found that the use of contingent protection, whether in the form of anti-dumping or CVD or safeguard measures, is largely induced by domestic macroeconomic pressures.

In a recent study, Feinberg (2004) analysed the impact of macrovariables on the outcomes of the US anti-dumping cases. He reveals that macroeconomic phenomena can also play a role in anti-dumping outcomes. A 10 per cent increase in the real appreciation of the dollar increases the probability of a positive outcome for petitioners by about 4 percentage points and increases the probability of an affirmative US ITC decision by between 2 and 7 percentage points (depending on whether the iron and steel cases are included or not). Furthermore, an increase in the growth rate of US GDP is found to increase the likelihood of a favourable outcome. This appears to be counter intuitive but he explains that this could be because during the strong growth it becomes easier for the industry to prove that under performance of the industry is due to unfairly trade.

MACROECONOMIC ANALYSIS OF FACTORS[9]: DEVELOPED VS DEVELOPING COUNTRIES

There is thus a widespread support for the political economy perspective of anti-dumping. However, most empirical studies are directed to the developed countries (Leidy 1997 and Feinberg 1989 for the United States, Becker and Theuringer 2001 for the EU, Knetter and Prusa 2003 for four developed countries—United States, Canada, Australia, and EU). Furthermore, most these studies are narrowly focused. For instance, Feinberg (1989) concentrated on the effect of exchange rate movement on US anti-dumping filings across four import source countries: Brazil, Korea, Japan, and Mexico for twenty-four quarters from 1982 to 1987. In doing so, he employed a single-variable model. Knetter and Prusa (2003) also focused on the relationship between exchange change variations and anti-dumping filings. They used an extended model which had, apart from exchange rate, real GDP also as an explanatory variable. They ignored other macroeconomic factors. Analyses of Leidy (1997) for the United States and Becker and Theuringer (2001) for the EU are constrained to short time series which weakened the creditability of their results. Feinberg and Reynold (2005) is a probit analysis conducted on all reported member-country filings over the 1995–2003 period. It is not thus directed exclusively to the United States or the EU. But the focus of the study is narrow. It examines whether anti-dumping filings may be motivated as retaliation against similar measures imposed on a country's exporters. The effect of macroeconomic, industry-specific, and political considerations is dealt with through industry, country, and year fixed effects. They found strong evidence that retaliation was a significant motive in explaining the rise of anti-dumping filings over the past decade.

We analyse here the use of anti-dumping in developed and developing countries using a comprehensive model of various macro factors influencing aggregate anti-dumping filings across countries. In what follows, we present our hypotheses, data and methodology, and empirical results.

Hypotheses

Macroeconomic pressures

Domestic macroeconomic conditions: If the macroeconomic environment is sluggish any import competition may put further downward pressure on the capacity utilization, profit margins, and employment. Besides, under such circumstances, the probability of an affirmative material injury finding also increases. Domestic producers therefore lobby and pressurize the government to provide protection to the domestic industry. Authorities respond leniently to the emotionally compelling argument that foreigners are behaving unfairly. Thus,

Hypothesis 1: Low levels of domestic activity influence the anti-dumping use positively. Countries that have been undergoing recessionary conditions file more anti-dumping cases.

The model includes growth rate in industrial value addition (IVAGR) to test the above hypothesis.

Balance of payment conditions: Import surge and adverse trade balances increase the probability that domestic industry would seek protection and authorities would readily accept their complaints.

Hypothesis 2: The number of anti-dumping cases per year is related to a widening in the trade deficit and import surge.

Two trade-related variables namely, trade balance as a ratio of total trade (TRBAL) and import growth rate (IMGRTH) are used in the analysis. While the former is expected to be have a negative relationship with anti-dumping filings, the latter will have positive relationship.

Trade liberalization

Some trade negotiators view anti-dumping as a price paid to sustain the overall consensus in favour of an open trading system. They argue that the necessity of having an effective anti-dumping remedy increases as a country liberalizes as a matter of political necessity. Findings in a systematic analysis of individual preferences on trade and their underlying determinants by Mayda and Rodrik (2001) suggest that trade patriotism and chauvinism are strongly related with a protectionist attitude. It is reported that when asked about their views on trade, typically 60 per cent or more respondents in opinion polls expressed anti-trade views. Such preferences matter in trade policies as the politicians resist initiatives that are against public opinion. The use of anti-dumping assists governments in their efforts to continue trade liberalizing measures by ensuring relief to domestic industries in case they are injured due to an import surge. Thus, when tariff rates are reduced authorities adopt a lenient view towards initiating anti-dumping cases. A review of the anti-dumping cases initiated by the EC from 1980 to 1997 (Bourgeoise and Messerlin 1998) demonstrates that the industries most frequently involved are those that have a low MFN tariff.

Hypothesis 3: Anti-dumping initiations are inversely related with tariff rates. Countries lowering their tariff barriers are the active users of anti-dumping.

We include change in average tariff rate (TARIFF) in the model to test the above hypothesis.

Capacity building for posing a retaliation threat

Some scholars argue that one of the motives for initiating anti-dumping cases might be retaliation (Finger 1981). There are several instances of retaliatory use of anti-dumping among developed countries (Blonigen and Bown 2003). Prusa and Skeath (2002) find evidence consistent with 'tit-for-tat' retaliatory anti-dumping actions for both developed and developing countries. In general, retaliation refers to countries filing anti-dumping actions specifically against those countries that have named them in the past. In this study however, we argue that countries tend to file more anti-dumping cases if they have been subject to such investigations in general in the past. There is evidence (Prusa and Skeath 2002) that all new users with a few exceptions were subject to anti-dumping investigations before they started reporting anti-dumping cases themselves. Almost two-thirds of the new users were subject to at least ten cases. Some countries, such as Korea (forty cases) and Brazil (fifty-five cases), were named in several cases. It could be that these countries felt the need for developing capability to retaliate so as to discourage the use of anti-dumping against them.

Hypothesis 4: A larger number of anti-dumping cases are initiated by countries if they have been victimised by such initiations in the past

It is expected that the number of cases filed against a country in the past (AFF) influence their decisions to initiate case in time period t.

Data and Methodology

For testing the above hypotheses, we required data on anti-dumping initiations and macroeconomic variables in each country on an annual basis for the period from 1980 to 2000. We constructed the data set by combining the WTO data on the number of anti-dumping initiations per year by reporting country with the data on macro economic variables provided by the World Bank in World Development Indicators CD-ROM. We thus had a panel data set of ninety-nine countries over the period 1980–2000 (twenty-one years). For the empirical analysis, we reclassified reporting developing countries into two categories: low and middle income countries and upper income countries. The classification as described above was adopted from the World Bank (2000). Appropriate adjustments were made for the EU countries.

For the empirical analysis, it was important to decide the lag structure of the regressors. Normally, reporting countries analyse the pricing behaviour of foreign firms over the year prior to the filing of the case. This is termed investigation period. Injury is analysed over a period of at least three years. This period is often called the injury investigation period. However, such a relatively long period is used particularly to establish causation. As a matter of practice, the industry must be suffering material injury during the investigation period and detailed injury margin calculations are based on the data existing during this period which is one year preceding the anti-dumping application. It was therefore decided to use the regressors with one year lag.

Our model thus is

$$ADINI_{it} = f(IVAGR_{it-1}, TRBAL_{it-1}, IMGRTH_{it-1}, TARIFF_{it-1}, AFF_{it-1})$$

where

$ADINI_{it}$: The number of anti-dumping initiations in country i in the year t
$TARIFF_{it-1}$: Average tariff rate in country i in the year $t-1$
$IMGRTH_{it-1}$: Growth rate of imports in country i in the year $t-1$
$IVAGR_{it-1}$: Growth rate of industrial value addition in country i in the year $t-1$

AFF_{it-1}: The number of cases initiated against country i in the year $t-1$
$TRBAL_{it-1}$: Difference in exports and imports as a ratio of total trade in country i in the year $t-1$

For testing the above model we have used a count of the total number of anti-dumping initiations by a particular country in a given year. It varies from zero to several for some countries. Since the dependent variable is a non-negative discrete variable, we have employed count models for estimation. The Poisson regression model, a non-linear model, is widely used for such data. The distribution takes the following form:

$$\text{Prob}(Y = y_{it}) = [\exp(-\lambda_{it})\lambda_{it}^{y_{it}}]/y_{it}!, \ y_{it} = 1, 2, 3, \ldots$$

where

$$E(y_{it}) = \lambda_{it} \text{ and } V(y_{it}) = \lambda_{it}$$

Typically, the Poisson regression model is given by

$$\log \lambda = X\beta$$

Here β is estimated either by an iterative non-linear weighted least square method or by a maximum likelihood method.

The Poisson maximum likelihood estimator is consistent and efficient provided the mean is equal to the variance. However, in empirical analyses, it is not uncommon to find over dispersion where the variance of observed counts is larger than the mean. A common alternative suggested for the Poisson model in this case is the Negative Binomial model, which allows for over dispersion. It is derived by generalizing the Poisson model by introducing an individual, unobserved effect into the conditional mean μ_i such that

$$\log \mu_{it} = \log \lambda_{it} + \log u_{it}$$

The Negative Binomial takes the form

$$\log \mu_{it} = x_{it}\beta + e_{it}$$

where e_{it} reflects either a specification error or a cross-sectional heterogeneity and $\exp(e_{it})$ is gamma distributed. The distribution of y_{it} conditional on x_i and u_i remains Poisson with conditional mean and variance μ_{it}:

$$f(y_{it}|x_{it}, u_{it}) = \{[\exp(-\lambda_{it}u_{it})](\lambda_{it}u_{it})^{y_{it}}\}/y_{it}!$$

The distribution has mean λ and variance $(\lambda + 1/\theta)$.

We began by estimating the Poisson model. The goodness of fit statistics provided by the Poisson model estimates however suggested that we could reject that the data were Poisson distributed at the 1 per cent level for each model due to over dispersion of the data. Clearly, Negative Binomial specification would be more appropriate for our analysis. However, our dataset had a large number of zeros because many countries started using the anti-dumping mechanism in the 1990s while some countries never used it. Many authors argue that when a dataset contains an excessive number of zeros, the distributional assumption of even the Negative Binomial model may be invalidated. The zeros can also create computational difficulties. They suggest that the use of Zero Inflated Negative Binomial models that allow for excess zeros is more appropriate in such cases. These models make a distinction between structural zeros that occur with a probability one and hence are inevitable and sampling zeros that occur by chance and follow the model. One thus needs to model some indicators to distinguish sampling zeros from structural zeros. For their application in the present study, therefore we would need to believe that for some countries it was not possible to use the anti-dumping tool. Since this was not the case, zero inflated models were not found to be applicable in our study. We used the Negative Binomial models and captured the country-specific effects through the panel data analysis. In order to add country-specific effects to the negative binomial model we employed two methods: random effects and fixed effects. The fixed effect model truncated the sample by dropping observations for all those countries that never reported anti-dumping cases or reported them only once. We considered it appropriate to report estimates based on both random effects and fixed effect specifications to examine the sensitivity of our results to the sample and model specification.

Empirical Results

Tables 5.3 and 5.4 report empirical results based on the random and fixed effect specifications. Equations 1 and 2 are based on the data from the combined low- and lower middle-income countries while Equations 3 and 4 are estimated for the upper-income countries. Equations 5 and 6 are based on the data pooled for all groups of developing countries. Equations 7 and 8 provide results for the OECD country group. Since observations in the non-OECD country groups were very small, no separate regression was estimated for this group. However, in one of the specifications (Equation 9), the data from both OECD and non-OECD country-groups were pooled in a single regression equation to estimate the results for the developed countries. Different specifications of the model were used to avoid multicollinearity. Our results are remarkably robust to changes in the underlying model specification and sample coverage. It is important to note here that the coefficients reported are 'incidence rate ratio' (IRR). If the IRR is 1.40, then a one percentage point change in the explanatory variable would increase counts by 40 per cent. IRR exceeds one for the variables having positive relationship with the dependent variable; it is smaller than one (showing decline) for the variables with negative signs.

TABLE 5.3: Determinants of the number of anti-dumping initiations—Negative binomial regression random effect model

Equation → Determinant ↓	Low- and middle-income group countries		Upper-income group countries		All developing countries	OECD		All developed countries	
	(1)	(2)	(3)	(4)	(5)	(7)	(8)	(9)	(10)
AFF	1.167	1.141	1.051	1.05	1.110	1.011	1.009	1.010	1.008
	(5.19)[a]	(5.04)[a]	(2.393)[b]	(2.261)[b]	(6.588)[a]	(1.756)[c]	(1.81)[c]	(1.541)	(1.377)
TARIFF	0.934	0.956	0.898	0.890	0.917	1.179	1.044	1.048	0.881
	(−2.61)[a]	(−2.053)[b]	(−3.05)[a]	(−3.326)[a]	(−4.711)[a]	(1.658)[c]	(1.417)	(0.413)	(−1.505)
TRBAL	0.978		0.991	0.994	0.983	1.012	1.005	1.014	0.005
	(−1.88)[c]		(−.987)	(−0.579)	(−2.580)[b]	(0.565)	(0.225)	(0.680)	(0.448)
IMGRTH	1.017	1.018	1.015		1.018	1.026	1.014	1.024	1.014
	(1.703)[c]	(1.798)[c]	(2.653)[a]		(3.826)[a]	(2.842)[a]	(1.475)	(2.692)[a]	(1.301)
IVAGR	0.981	0.974	0.984	1.024	0.984	0.935		0.937	—
	(−1.055)	(−0.908)	(−0.608)	(1.115)	(−1.614)	(−2.98)[a]		(−2.71)[b]	
/ln_r	−0.925	−0.929	−0.456	−0.371	−0.773	−0.364	−0.583	−0.449	−0.477
/ln_s	−2.333	−2.178	−0.249	0.059	−1.555	0.036	−0.531	−0.483	−0.571
Loglikelihood	−258.90	−270.06	−315.06	−322.95	−587.26	−320.51	−449.35	−334.41	−492.45
Wald chi2	38.82	38.93	75.22	72.94	91.40	23.85	20.10	22.84	32.45
No of obs	431	431	207	219	638	126	174	156	232

Note. [a] significant at 1 per cent, [b] significant at 5 per cent, and [c] significant at 10 per cent.

TABLE 5.4: Determinants of the number of anti-dumping initiations—Negative binomial regression fixed effect model (truncated sample)

Equation → Determinant ↓	Low- and middle-income group countries		Upper-income group countries		All developing countries	OECD		All developed countries	
	(1)	(2)	(3)	(4)	(5)	(7)	(8)	(9)	(10)
AFF	1.114	1.123	1.054	1.044	1.075	1.010	1.009	1.011	1.008
	(3.041)[a]	(3.350)[a]	(2.395)[b]	(2.021)[b]	(4.274)[b]	(1.654)[c]	(1.707)[c]	(1.68)[c]	(1.332)
TARIFF	0.931	0.934	0.890	0.889	0.923	1.159	1.035	1.141	0.890
	(−2.654)[a]	(−2.573)[b]	(−3.205)[a]	(−3.318)[a]	(−4.232)[a]	(1.351)	(0.399)	(1.210)	(−1.273)
TRBAL	0.980	0.979	0.987	0.994	0.986	1.022	1.005	1.019	1.005
	(−1.652)[c]	(−1.85)[c]	(−1.399)	(−0.579)	(−2.071)[b]	(0.972)	(.344)	(0.843)	(0.359)
IMGRTH	1.017		1.017	1.017		1.026	1.014	1.026	1.014
	(1.603)		(2.845)[a]	(2.893)[a]		(2.772)[a]	(1.834)[c]	(2.815)[a]	(1.384)
IVAGR	0.971	0.992	0.968	0.975	1.001	0.952		0.954	—
	(−0.934)	(−0.294)	(−1.170)	(−0.929)	(0.101)	(−1.89)[b]		(−2.69)[a]	
Log likelihood	−188.85	−270.06	−250.46	−251.48	−453.26	−263.51	−386.58	−269.39	−417.45
Wald chi2	64.40	38.93	70.80	72.39	136.40	20.59	18.10	20.84	28.45
No of obs	149	157	169	169	318	109	143	130	183

Note: [a] significant at 1 per cent, [b] significant at 5 per cent, and [c] significant at 10 per cent.

Our findings for the developing countries pooled in one group suggest that anti-dumping initiations increase substantially when there are trade balance pressures. It is found that a one percentage-point decline in trade balance (TRBAL) leads to a 2 per cent increase in the number of anti-dumping filing. Import growth rate has similar effects. Once we distinguish between the upper- and low-income country groups, however, we find that results differ across two groups of countries. For the upper-income country group, IMGRTH emerges significant at 1 per cent while TRBAL is insignificant. Even when IMGRTH was dropped TRBAL did not become significant. In low- and lower middle-income countries however, both trade-related variables appear to have significant impact on anti-dumping filings. Trade-related pressures therefore seem to be a major concern for low- and lower middle-income countries in using anti-dumping measures. In OECD countries, external pressures approximated by the international trade position (TRBAL) were insignificant in all specifications. Import variables IMGRTH emerged at 1 per cent in the presence of IVAGR. It could also be observed that 1 per cent increase in IMGRTH was associated with 2–3 per cent increase in anti-dumping filings. However, once IVAGR is dropped its significance reduced considerably. Evidently, the impact of import surge becomes significant after controlling the effect of IVAGR. It could be that in developed countries, import competition is more readily accommodated when the market is expanding but producers tend to guard their market share when the rate of expansion slows. When economic growth is sluggish, returns from investing resources in seeking protection are seen to be higher than in investing in production activities. External pressures are shown to be unimportant for developed countries (Leidy 1997, Becker and Theuringer 2001). Knetter and Prusa (2003) used larger database and found exchange rate appreciation to affect anti-dumping filings positively in the presence of the growth rate in GDP. Our results also suggest that import surge has a positive impact on anti-dumping filings. But it weakens once the growth rate in industrial value addition is dropped.

For developed countries, anti-dumping initiations appear to be largely motivated by domestic macroeconomic pressures. anti-dumping initiations are inversely related with the industrial growth for all specifications for the OECD/developed countries. A one percentage point decline in the industrial growth rate leads to a 6–7 per cent increase in the number of anti-dumping initiations. This variable did not turn out to be significant for developing countries. The existing empirical literature documents a significant influence of domestic macroeconomic pressures on the use of anti-dumping in OECD countries (Leidy 1997, Becker and Theuringer 2001, Knetter and Prusa 2003).

Turning to the tariff rates (TARIFF), the results indicate quite a robust negative significance for both developing country groups and hence for the pooled group. A one percentage point decline in tariff rates leads to 10–12 per cent, 5–7 per cent, and 8 per cent increase in anti-dumping initiations in upper middle-income, low- and lower middle-income countries, and all developing countries, respectively. Results are quite expected. Till recently, companies in most developing countries had been operating in highly protected markets. Overprotection over a long period of time bred inefficiency. Therefore, the shift in favour of competition-enhancing policies in these countries in the 1990s appear to have resulted in pressures from the domestic industry to provide protection to be able to face international competition. Authorities also seem to adopt a lenient view in granting contingent protection in order to avoid some of the adverse effects of liberalization and in order to reassure domestic political interests that some form of 'safety net' remains in place. TARIFF is insignificant in all specifications for OECD/developed countries.

Finally, our results support the capacity creation hypothesis for the anti-dumping initiations in developing countries. AFF is significant at 1 per cent significance level in all specification for the developing country groups. For low- and lower middle-income countries this seems to be the most important variable resulting in 14–16 per cent increase in anti-dumping initiations with every 1 per cent increase in anti-dumping cases reported against them. The results are less pronounced for upper middle-income countries while for OECD (developed) countries, it is insignificant in all equations. Prusa and Skeath (2002) carried out non-parametric tests and observed that new users' (mainly developing countries) anti-dumping initiations are more often consistent with the retaliation motive than those of traditional users. Apparently, the use of anti-dumping measures against developing countries motivates them to use similar policies against other countries. This helps them in creating capacity to use these measures and pose retaliations threats that may dampen such activity against them. In an important study Blonigen and Bown (2003) have argued that the capacity to retaliate may have dampening effects on anti-dumping activities of trading partners. Perhaps the use of anti-dumping helps them in acquiring anti-dumping capabilities and posing retaliation threat to counter such activities against them. One may thus suggest that increased anti-dumping familiarity and ability across developing countries may ultimately help put the brakes on anti-dumping use by traditional users. However, this may also result in anti-dumping wars reversing trade liberalisation gains. This may therefore prove to be a costly strategy to restrain the anti-dumping use.

This study found that the use of anti-dumping measures is significantly explained by macrovariables. In developed countries, anti-dumping is primarily used as an import-deterrent device during business downswing. It appears that when on the upturn of business cycles firms in these countries are not significantly concerned with import competition. However, when on the downswing they strive for anti-dumping protection from import competition. In developing countries that are evolving from a controlled to a more liberal trading regime, anti-dumping appears to serve as a tool in enabling governments to open up their economies. However, it does not fully explain the use of anti-dumping measures. The rise in the number of anti-dumping initiations by developing countries may partly be an expression of retaliation. Using the anti-dumping law enables them to create ability to counter such actions targeted against them. External pressures such as import penetration and balance of payment deficits also exert considerable influence on the use of anti-dumping in these countries.

In sum, trade pressures, tariff rate reductions, and creating retaliatory capabilities seem to motivate the use of anti-dumping in developing countries while domestic macroeconomic pressures influence anti-dumping initiations in developed countries. There are a few studies on the determinants of the use of safeguard measures in developed countries. It is important to note that the same set of factors that affect anti-dumping use are found to influence the use of safeguard measures also in developed countries (Takacs 1981, Feigenbaum and Willet 1985, Salvatore 1987, Coughlin et al. 1989).

IMPLICATIONS FOR FUTURE REFORMS

The WTO ADA has no basic principles and objectives. The political rhetoric is that it is needed to ensure fair trade. Popular economic rhetoric is that its objective is to ensure economic efficiency and prevent predatory dumping. However, there is no mechanism built in the agreement that ensures that the law is used to achieve what is claimed to achieve. It does not ensure that anti-dumping is used to level the playing field. It has no real antitrust analogue either. Evidence suggests that the use of anti-dumping is not influenced by efficiency considerations or even fairness of trade, it is a tool of unilateral protection within the framework of the multilateral trade agreement of trade liberalization for both developed and developing countries. Empirical evidence presented in the study reinforces the view that the primary jurisdiction for the anti-dumping laws is really more political than economic. Clearly, anti-dumping measures have gone beyond punishing unfair trade practices and creating a level playing field as has been claimed by the national anti-dumping authorities. Domestic firms use anti-dumping in order to become a strategic shelter from foreign competitors. But the objective of safeguard measures is also to provide protection to domestic firms. Much of the contingent protection that is handled under anti-dumping laws could have been dealt with under safeguard measures. Then why two trade remedy measures to serve the same purpose? Apparently, safeguard mechanism does not have the anti-dumping's unique combination of economic and political manipulability.

Furthermore our findings suggest that while anti-dumping has been used as a tool of protection in both developed and developing countries, the broad factors that influence its use differ across the two sets of countries. Developed countries are likely to invoke its use to provide shelter to the domestic producers from internal business cycles; developing countries on the other hand are more concerned with the balance of payment consideration. Developing countries have recently started opening up their economies. Due to the low levels of competitiveness, they are vulnerable to destabilizing effects of trade liberalization. Therefore, to sustain the process of liberalization in these economies, it is important that the national industry has a safety net to protect it from foreign competition during the initial stages and the country does not have balance of payment crisis. The industry should be able to gain a significant market share within the domestic market, before this cover is taken off. The WTO also recognizes this infant industry argument to make concessions in various agreements. As described in Chapter 2, existing developed countries adopted anti-dumping legislations during the early phase of industrial growth in the early 1920s for protecting their infant industries from competition and this explains the spread of its use in the early 1920s. Once again, after the Tokyo Round negotiations, which resulted in substantial trade liberalization, the use of this mechanism increased sharply in developed countries. Developed countries, however, have no valid reasons now to provide safety valves to protect the industry from internal business cycles.

Finally, our findings suggest that once the WTO is fully enforced, the use of anti-dumping will spread among developing countries not only due to greater liberalization pressures but also due to the fact that more and more countries would like to create anti-dumping ability to counter the anti-dumping use against them. This may have chain effect on the use of anti-dumping and may reverse the trade gains that liberalization may ensure to developing countries. It is therefore important to restrain the use of anti-dumping against developing countries. WTO records show that around 65 per cent of the cases initiated during 1995–2004 were directed against the developing countries. An analysis of the number of anti-dumping duties currently in force in the United States and the EU against developed and developing countries indicates that a majority of duties are against the developing countries. By restraining the anti-dumping use against developing countries, developed countries will help in controlling the further spread in anti-dumping use. And this will benefit the developed and the developing countries both. Clearly, there is need to reform the agreement to close the gap between what anti-dumping is supposed/claimed to do and what in reality it is used for. This would prevent the misuse of the tool for protection purposes. The following chapters will focus on the reform proposals.

APPENDIX

TABLE A5.1:   List of variables

Variable	Description
TARIFF	Average tariff rate
IMGRTH	Growth rate of imports in period $t-1$
IVAGR	Growth rate of industrial value addition in period $t-1$
AFF	No. of cases initiated against a country in period $t-1$
TRBAL	Trade balance

Notes

1 Stiglitz (1997, p. 418) argued that 'anti-dumping imposes substantial burden on consumers and on most efficient exporters while protecting the least efficient import competing firms'. In Finger's view 'AD is a trouble making diplomacy, stupid economics and unprincipled law' (Finger 1993, p. 56). He has characterized anti-dumping as 'the fox put in charge of the henhouse: trade restrictions certified by the GATT. The fox', he argues, 'is clever enough not only to eat the hens, but also to convince the farmer that that is the way things ought to be' (Finger 1991).

2 These countries include all reporting and targeted countries.

3 It is based on the Clinton administration papers and the Bush administration papers on the trade remedy laws.

4 In reality, however, the objective of anti-dumping legislations was to protect the domestic industry (Chapter 3).

5 Business Week, 2 December 1991, pp. 38–9. Restricting imports of machine tools had different but equally adverse consequences. See The New York Times, 7 October 1991.

6 In an econometric analysis, Prusa (2001) found that imports fell on average by 15–20 per cent where investigations were dismissed.

7 Leclerc (1999) revealed that in Canada, between 1992 and 1997, only five public interest inquiries were held but none of them resulted in the tribunal reversing its initial decision to impose ADDs. In the EU, by the year 2000, there were two cases where the authority had concluded that community interest did not justify the imposition of duty. In Australia, however, there have cases where ADDs could have been imposed but since taking action was not in the interest of the public, exporters were given only warning.

8 Nelson (2006) has provided a detailed survey of literature on this topic.

9 Reprinted from: Aggarwal, A. (2004), *Macro Economic Determinants of Anti-dumping: A Comparative Analysis of Developed and Developing Countries*, World Development, 32(6), 1043–57, copyright (2004), with permission from Elsevier.

6 Proposals for Reforming the Anti-dumping Agreement
A Critical Review

The spate of arbitrary and excessively protectionist anti-dumping measures imposed, in particular against developing countries, in recent years has become an issue of intense and widespread concern. Analysis provided in the previous chapters indicate that the enormous potential of misuse of the tool can have destabilizing impact on the developing countries that have recently started opening up their economies. Evidence (Gallaway et al. 1999, Anserson 1993, De Vault 1996 among others) suggests that anti-dumping may almost always be welfare reducing. Indiscriminate use of anti-dumping may result in increased producers' welfare but it may be smaller than the consumers' loss. There has been an increasing recognition therefore that the WTO anti-dumping rules are in need of reform.

Several proposals have been made to reform the Agreement. These proposals can be classified into two broad categories depending on the underlying objective that they seek to achieve. One set of proposals reinforces anti-dumping as a practical and effective instrument to deal with only unfair trading practices. These proposals focus on establishing a theoretical framework within which anti-dumping might be justified and tailoring the code to fit into this underlying framework. The other set of proposals however is based on the assumption that the ideal solution to the evil of anti-dumping lies in seeking tighter rules on anti-dumping. While the reform proposals in the first category advocate fundamental changes in the existing agreement, those in the second category seek to clarify and improve the existing provisions to rule out the abusive interpretation of the agreement. We call the proposals in the first category 'hard reform proposals'. Reform proposals in the second category, on the other hand, are soft in nature and are called 'soft proposals'. This chapter presents a critical review of some of the major proposals. While doing so, it also examines the treatment of anti-dumping in Regional Trading Agreements. The chapter is organized into two broad parts. While Part I deals with hard proposals, Part II focuses on soft reform proposals.

PART I: HARD REFORM PROPOSALS

The central premise of hard proposals is that the fundamental flaw of the ADA is that it does not require a country to investigate whether the behaviour of exporters is consistent or inconsistent with normal business practices. These proposals emphasize that the agreement must be changed to incorporate the basic conditions for the use of anti-dumping. This part reviews these proposals. Even though these proposals are considered abstract or of theoretical interest, we strongly believe that only these reforms in the agreement can resolve the conflict between what the law is meant to serve and what it is serving. As discussed in the previous chapter, there are three major perspectives on anti-dumping: the political perspective, the economic perspective, and the political economy perspective. These three perspectives have motivated three sets of hard reform proposals. We discuss them here one by one in the first three sections. The next section discusses the proposal that anti-dumping should altogether be abolished. Several experts argue that anti-dumping serves no useful purpose. In today's trade environment characterized by increasing liberalization and increasing competition among a variety of export suppliers from different countries, market domination or monopolistic pricing is not attainable. This law allows the producers to use anti-dumping measures to batter the competition and create artificial monopolies. It should therefore be abolished altogether.

OPTION I: ADOPTION OF THE POLITICAL PERSPECTIVE

The justification for using anti-dumping actions from the political perspective is that pricing the product in export markets at a level lower than the home markets reflects the existence of underlying market-distorting government policies. The current anti-dumping practice however includes no mechanism for distinguishing between those instances of targeted pricing practices that actually reflect underlying market distortions and those that may have other reasons. Apparently, under present rules, all sales at less than normal value are simply assumed to be dumping if injury to the domestic industry is proved. This assumption is unsupportable and results in the frequent imposition of anti-dumping remedies on exporters who are engaged in normal commercial conduct that has nothing at all to do with unfair trade or an uneven playing field. If the basic objective of the ADA is to counter the market-distorting policies of the foreign country government, which put the domestic producers at disadvantage, then the it must require direct evidence of fundamental market distortions. Lindsey and Ikenson (2002b) propose two-tier test to address this problem.

Level 1: The authorities should investigate whether underlying market distortions are existing in the foreign markets.

Level 2: Once the authorities are satisfied that such distortions indeed characterize the foreign markets, they should initiate the process of finding dumping, injury, and causal relationship.

The objective of this is to filter the genuine cases of unfair trade from the innocent cases. For introducing the two-tier analysis, the following reforms are proposed by Lindsey and Ikenson (2002b).

Amendment in Article 2 to ensure that dumping investigation follows the first level test

Article 2 of the ADA should be amended to provide that authorities may initiate dumping investigation only if they determine, on the basis of credible evidence provided by the domestic industry, that the price discrimination during the investigation reflects the existence of underlying market distortions as alleged in the petition.

Inclusion of the 'market distortion' evidence in the application

Currently, the domestic industry is required to provide evidence of dumping, injury, and causal relationship in its application for initiating the investigation. It is proposed that the domestic industries should be required to present evidence of underlying market distortions also in their anti-dumping petitions. Article 5.2 of the ADA should be amended to require domestic industries to provide credible evidence of underlying market distortions in the anti-dumping petition. Now the question is: What are the indicators of market distortions? The US report (WTO 1998, p. 7) provides guidance in this matter. This report assembled a set of government policies and 'differences in national economic systems' that, in its view, lead to injurious dumping. Included in this list is a diverse set of examples: high tariffs; government subsidies; price controls; government limitations on investment; limitations on the number of producers in a particular sector; anti-competitive sanitary and phytosanitary standards; a range of services barriers including restrictions of provision of financial services, regulation of international data flows, and data processing; misuse of standards, testing and certification procedures; permissive policies towards vertical and horizontal restraints of competition; cross subsidization in multiproduct firms; employment and social policies that result in 'artificial' advantages for domestic firms; and contrasting business practices that give rise to differing debt/equity structures between domestic and foreign firms. In short, if dumping is alleged, the evidence must indicate the existence of (i) tariffs significantly higher than those in the export market under investigation, (ii) NTB significantly higher than those in the export market under investigation, (iii) government restrictions on competition in the home market, or (iv) government acquiescence in private anti-competitive conduct.

Inclusion of a requirement of investigating evidence of market distortion

National anti-dumping authorities should be required to verify the underlying market distortion evidence before initiating an investigation. Article 5.3 of the ADA should be revised to require anti-dumping authorities, before they initiate an investigation, to verify that the domestic industry has provided credible evidence of underlying market distortions.

Inclusion of a provision to provide right to defend

To ensure transparency in the system, information provided by the domestic industry should be disclosed to the exporters and they should be allowed to refute such information or any causal connection between market distortions in the home market and the pricing practices under investigation. Article 6 of the ADA should be revised to give respondents the right to present evidence that (i) the pricing practices under investigation are normal and are due to normal commercial factors; (ii) notwithstanding the existence of high prices, the respondent does not enjoy unusually high home-market profits on sales of the subject merchandise (and thus does not enjoy any artificial competitive advantage); or (iii) the respondent's home market is too small for high profits in that market to confer an artificial competitive advantage in the export market under investigation.

The above reform proposals, if adopted, would ensure that only those cases that pass the first stage would be subject to detailed anti-dumping investigations. This would go a long way in closing the gap between political rhetoric on anti-dumping and its actual use.

OPTION II: ADOPTION OF THE ECONOMIC PERSPECTIVE

As discussed in the preceding chapter, economic justification of anti-dumping is to prevent monopolizing dumping. Economists identify two categories of actions that could constitute anti-competitive dumping onto a market. The first type of market-power dumping is known as 'predatory dumping' that leads to complete monopolization of foreign markets, while the second form of dumping is referred to as 'strategic dumping' that relates to the expansion of market power in foreign markets. From this perspective, anti-dumping serves to deter these forms of monopolizing practices and protects competition. Any attempt to thwart the process of competition by foreign exporters calls for government intervention and anti-dumping policy is the trade policy instrument to deal with such practices.

The reform literature following the economic viewpoint therefore largely focuses on the interface between anti-dumping and competition policies. Economists argue that there is natural affinity between anti-dumping and competition policy. They have the common goal and justification. The core objective of competition policy is to deter monopolistic practices by domestic firms while the justification for anti-dumping is to counter such practices by foreign exporters. Competition policy and anti-dumping policy are therefore mutually reinforcing in that they share the objective of increasing efficiencies and enhancing consumer welfare.

Even though in principle 'the two sets of instruments are soul mate, in practice they are total strangers' (Guash and Rajapatirana 1998). While competition policies strive to protect the process of competition, anti-dumping policies are regarded as trade policy instruments to protect the competitors. Taking note of the original common anti-monopoly rhetoric of both antitrust and anti-dumping laws, Alan Sykes of the University of Chicago has described the evolved attributes of the two systems, as follows:

Antitrust and antidumping law come from the same family tree, but the two branches have diverged widely.... [I]n the modern era, antitrust concentrated on the pursuit of economic efficiency ... address[ing] problems associated with concentrated economic power, primarily through a common law process that left to the courts much of the task of delineating the practices that violate antitrust law.... By contrast, antidumping law was intended to create a politically popular form of contingent protection that bears little, if any connection to the prevention of monopoly.... Likewise, the political constituency for antidumping law is not an antimonopoly constituency, but one for the protection of industries facing weak markets or long-term decline. (Sykes 1998, pp. 1–2).

Competition authorities do not regard price discrimination between different markets as anti-competitive unless it involves some form of monopolization. The only threat to competition is when a firm sets prices below cost in order to drive out competitors and subsequently dominate the markets. Thus the competition laws require in some form or the other that price discrimination be monopolizing in nature and that the monopolist has substantial market power to get involved in such practices. Market power is dependent upon the relative size and structure of the market (for instance, number of competitors, entry barriers, market contestability, and availability of substitutes). A firm is considered to be dominant if it has a substantial market share (Canada for instance uses 35 per cent threshold). On the contrary, any price discrimination in international markets that injures the domestic producers is considered unfair by anti-dumping laws. Clearly, in practice, the two policies have no link. Bulk of what is considered unfair according to anti-dumping always could be fair within the framework of competition policies.

The reform proposals following this school of thought are based on the presumption that the only way to curb the spread of anti-dumping is to recognize the scope of convergence between the two policies and reform the anti-dumping agreement to make it more consistent with competition policies. Following two sets of proposals have been made in the literature.

- Eliminate anti-dumping laws in favour of competition laws.
- Modify them to be consistent with competition policy principles.

These proposals are discussed below one by one.

Replacing Anti-dumping with Antitrust Principles

According to this proposal, the competitive merits of any anti-dumping petition may be evaluated by the competition agency using the same standard and framework of competition policies and not discriminate against the source from which competition arises whether it be domestic industry or from abroad. This will result in the adoption of stricter criteria for determining predation in such cases and will prevent its misuse. Moreover, the injury standard for antidumping cases will also be brought closer to the antitrust standard, which takes into account the effect of dumping on the competitive structure of the industry as a whole, rather than the material injury it causes to domestic firms.

However, replacing anti-dumping with the antitrust laws globally requires harmonization of competition laws and policies across nations which in turns calls for a common competition laws under the multilateral framework. While anti-dumping has a common multilateral framework for all member countries, there is no such multilateral competition policy framework. Since the laws differ widely across countries, extra territorial application of national competition laws to such behaviour will turn out to be highly controversial.

This could however be achieved at the regional level. Preferential trade agreements that complement the multilateral trade regime under the WTO have been actively utilized. Initiatives have already been taken to use competition policy in lieu of anti-dumping in some of these preferential trading arrangements. These developments are based on three alternative systems. At one extreme of the spectrum, the EU has replaced anti-dumping with competition laws for intra-union trade and created supranational competition law and institutional arrangement. At the other extreme, EFTA–Singapore free trade agreement (FTA) allows for a consultation scheme to deal with anti competitive activities of the partner country firms. ANZCERTA free trade treaty between Australia and New Zealand takes a middle course. It involves harmonization of competition rules between trading partners and extension of the harmonized domestic competition laws to prohibit anti-competitive activities by firms in the partner country/bloc. There are thus three different arrangements adopted for replacing anti-dumping by competition policies. In what follows we discuss them in detail.

Creation of supranational institutional arrangement

The Treaty of Rome excludes the application of anti-dumping actions between member states of the EU. It has replaced intra-region anti-dumping laws by the extensive common rules on competition. Articles 81[1] and 82 of the Treaty of Rome, as well as related regulations, stipulate the common competition rules. These rules are enforced by the EC, which is a supranational authority. It addresses all problems between trade partners derived from anti-competitive conduct in one country that negatively affects the other. Anti-dumping law is relevant only to imports from outside the Union and is also enforced by the EC. A noteworthy feature of the EU regime is that no efforts were made to harmonize national antitrust regimes, which differed very substantially across countries (Hoekman 1998, Wooton and Zanardi 2002).

A similar approach was taken in the creation of the European Economic Area (EEA) between the European Free Trade Association (EFTA)[2] states (minus Switzerland) and the EU in 1992. Article 26 and new Article 36 eliminate the possibility to use these measures, respectively. It should be noted, however, that EEA members retain the right to apply these measures for agricultural products—defined as products falling within Chapters 1–25 of the Harmonized Commodity Description and Coding System—as these products are completely excluded from the agreement. Although anti-dumping has been abolished in EEA without any reference to competition policies, in practice it is replaced by the competition laws (Sagara 2002). Thus trading across countries is subject to competition law replacing anti-dumping laws. Enforcement of the EU competition disciplines is similar as in the EU proper, though the latter task is shared between two institutions: the EC and the EFTA Surveillance Body (the EFTA analogue of the Commission). It was agreed that the latter has jurisdiction where at least one-third of the turnover of the firm(s) subject to complaint is in EFTA states and where trade between EFTA countries is affected (EEA Agreement). The EEA between the EFTA and the EU is not a Custom Union (CU) but an FTA. The two, however, share the common motivation to realize a single market and political, social, and economic stability in Europe.

In 1999, the EFTA had a major amendment itself under which the EFTA explicitly abolished anti-dumping and countervailing measures for intra-trade. (Articles 36 and 16 of the EFTA Convention.)

Harmonization of competition laws

This arrangement is adopted in ANZCERTA (Australia–New Zealand Closer Economic Relations Trade Agreement), which came into effect in 1983. Both countries had a major review of the Agreement in 1988 and signed a new Protocol ('Protocol to ANZCERTA on Acceleration of Free Trade in Goods'). Article 4 of the Protocol stipulated the abolition of anti-dumping measures after July 1990, when free trade was achieved. The Protocol, also, extended the application of both countries' respective competition law prohibitions on the misuse of market power to trans-Tasman markets.

Thus legislative amendments were introduced in both countries to allow development of symmetric jurisdictional and procedural provisions relating to competition law and its enforcement. The new legal framework ensures that:

- Australian firms can challenge dominant firms from New Zealand before an Australian court and vice versa;
- each country's enforcement agency has certain investigative powers in the other country; and
- each country's court may sit in the other country and can serve orders, which in turn are enforceable.

The laws are thus harmonized though the application of antitrust remedies remains strictly national. Ahdar (1991) argues that competition policy harmonization played a role in the decision to abolish anti-dumping.

Consultation scheme

In June 2002, the EFTA and Singapore agreed on an FTA. The parties to the EFTA–Singapore FTA agreed on the abolition of anti-dumping measures. In order to prevent dumping, they decided to make use of the necessary measures provided in Chapter V on 'Competition' (Article 16). In Chapter V both parties recognized that certain business practices, such as anti-competitive agreements or concerted practices and abuse of a dominant position, might restrict trade between the parties. They agreed to establish a consultation scheme with a view to eliminating such practices under which

A Party shall, at the request of another Party, enter into consultations with a view to eliminating practices referred to in paragraph. The Party addressed shall accord full and sympathetic consideration to such a request and shall co-operate through the supply of publicly available non-confidential information of relevance to the matter in question. Subject to its domestic law and the conclusion of a satisfactory agreement safeguarding confidentiality of information, the Party addressed shall also provide any other information available to the requesting Party.

The above instances suggest that regional agreements provide a forum for replacement of anti-dumping laws by competition policies across member states but such instances are very few. Similar competition laws and institutional arrangements, which could be achieved due to shared heritage, similar judicial system and special relationship between the Australia and New Zealand made it possible to implement far reaching reforms to replace anti-dumping by competition laws (Ahdar 1991). Agreeing to supranational laws in the case of EU could also be attributed to similarities in various economic and non-economic factors across member states. Differences in such factors might have affected the outcome. In this context, it is noteworthy that there are instances where even the formation of the CU and the entailed elimination of all tariff duties could not lead to anti-dumping abolition and its replacement with competition laws. The EU for instance refused to abolish anti-dumping and countervailing measures in the case of EU–Turkey custom union. It explicitly urged Turkey to adopt and effectively enforce acquis communautaire for a guarantee against unfair competition. The EFTA–Singapore Agreement, which is based on the bilateral cooperation, appears to be the most realistic way to replace anti-dumping laws by competition policies from a practical point of view by far. However, this also requires the trading partners to have competition policies and legal apparatus which should be tolerably harmonized. Many developing countries do not have such legal system in place and hence are not likely to benefit from such arrangements.

In sum, replacing anti-dumping by competition laws may be the first best solution from an economic point of view but not much progress can be made in this direction in the absence of a multilateral framework of competition. The second best solution would be to incorporate such provisions in regional trading agreements. Past experience suggests that governments did agree to replace anti-dumping by competition policy in regional agreements but in a very few cases. In all such cases, enforcement of common competition laws replacing anti-dumping was motivated by a broader agenda of deeper economic integration (Hoekman 1998) and were facilitated by similar economic and non-economic conditions across member countries. Even the EFTA–Singapore model of cooperation requires some degree of harmonization of competition laws.

Modifying Anti-dumping Laws to be Competition Friendlier: Introduction of the Two-tier Approach

Several economists suggest that a more practical approach would be to modify anti-dumping laws to make them 'competition friendlier' (Hoekman and Mavroidis 1996, Tharakan 2000, Messerlin and Tharakan 1999 among many other). This can be achieved if anti-dumping cases are confined only to monopolizing cases through a 'two-tier approach' to anti-dumping investigations. This would involve a first phase aimed at confirming that the accused company has sufficient market power to be able to involve in unfair practices. Only in those cases where a positive finding is made would the anti-dumping investigation move to its subsequent phase.

This literature focuses mainly on predatory price-dumping. Strategic dumping is by and large ignored in this literature. This could be because the focus has been on the 'strategic trade policy approach' the applicability of which is considered to be very limited (Chapter 5). Recent writings on strategic dumping argue that the scope of strategic dumping is much wider than what is described by the state led strategic trade policy. It involves any form of dumping with intents of dominating the foreign markets. This requires case-by-case analysis and the 'two-tier approach' can very well be used for identifying such cases. We shall here discuss a two-tier approach both for predatory dumping and strategic dumping.

Two-tier approach: Predatory dumping

Predation means pricing below average cost (total or variable) with the intent of driving out rivals (presumably with shallower pockets), thence raising price above average cost to recoup losses and enjoy market power. It is not merely pricing below cost, but is a strategic behaviour and requires assessment of the possibility of this behaviour. Establishing predation therefore is based on a two-tier approach developed by Joskow and Klevorick (1979). Competition legislation in almost all the countries requires the authorities to establish that the alleged predator have substantial market power before applying the cost-based test. Thus, it has two stages of investigation. These are as follows:

Stage 1: Investigation of the market structure to determine whether the alleged predator has market power in order to be successful and whether entry barriers are high so that he will recoup his losses through monopolistic profits in the post-predation period.

Stage 2: Establishing pricing below cost using the Areeda Turner test (1975): $P < AVC$.

Following this practice in competition legislation, one school of economists (Palmeter 1991, Tharakan 1995, 2000, Trebilcock and Howse 1999 among many others) proposes to introduce this approach in anti-dumping legislation also. They argue that anti-dumping actions need to be limited to cases where predation is proved. They propose to include two stages of investigation. The first step involves the decision as to whether predation was feasible in the market under investigation. Once an affirmative finding is made, the second step takes into account appropriate price-cost comparisons and other relevant factors.

Certain criteria have been evolved based on the structural characteristics of the industries to establish predation in international trade. Even though there is no unanimity about the factors that need to be considered in the first step, emphasis has been on the market dominance test. The criteria is based on the assumption that the predator has dominance not only in domestic markets but also in international markets. As discussed in Chapter 5, these are as follows.

- Import penetration should be high to indicate that domestic firms are being driven out of business.
- Exports should be dominated by large suppliers so that they are in a position to drive out other exporters.
- Export markets should be concentrated/the number of foreign sellers should be small, so that they can exercise monopoly power in the future.
- Exporters should be dominant producers in their domestic markets.

It is proposed that anti-dumping cases should be evaluated in terms of these criteria in order to judge whether there was a likelihood of predatory dumping. Cases that meet these criteria may then be subjected to price-cost comparisons. This would eliminate harassment suits (Norman and Thisse 2001) and target only anti-competitive practices without requiring harmonization of competition policies across countries.

Two-tier approach: Strategic dumping

As described in the previous chapter, a few studies have attempted to develop the criteria for determining whether anti-dumping actions are in response to strategic dumping. Using this criteria, the two-tier test can be applied to identify the cases of strategic dumping also. The existing literature indicates that the presence of strategic dumping can be detected if all of the following are present:

- protected home market for the dumping firm;
- large home markets;
- presence of economies of scale;
- little competition internationally.

If dumping is due to strategic behaviour (Chapter 5 for details), it may be punished if the following conditions hold:

- rivalrous behaviour of foreign firms damages the domestic firms;
- excess capacities are created by foreign firms to increase share in foreign markets.

Two-tier approach: The Hoekman–Mavroidis proposal

In the 1990s, the notion of contestable markets became widely accepted as the ultimate goal of competition policy (see, *inter alia*, Hoekman and Mavroidis 1994, Lawrence 1995, Sauvé and Zampetti 1995). It was argued that international trade liberalization and competition policy share the common objective of promoting open ('contestable') markets and undistorted competition (OECD 1994, p. 3). Following this approach, some economists argued that the first stage should concentrate on investigating the contestability of the relevant markets in both exporting and importing countries (Hoekman and Mavroidis 1996). It would require the investigating authorities to examine market access restrictions and market structures in exporting countries also. Under the current international laws however this may not be possible. Under the present system of laws, domestic courts have jurisdiction to judge actions of foreign parties to the extent that the latter have a direct, immediate, and substantial effect on the market of the importing country. Investigating the foreign market structures however is not under the jurisdiction of the importing country authorities. This problem according to Hoekman and Mavroidis (1996) may be solved if each country can apply its own competition rule to the actions of firms located in their respective jurisdiction when an anti-dumping investigation is initiated. In cases where the investigating authority in the exporting countries finds that no competition law is violated and where their counterparts in the importing country agree to this finding, the case should be closed. If the importing country (investigating) authority does not accept the criteria, rules and the methodologies of the exporting country's authority, it can investigate whether competition legislation would have been violated had the exporting firm been located in its territory. Break it into two: This kind of cooperation is not likely to be effective at the multilateral level and may lead to controversial results affecting bilateral relationship between countries. But it is feasible in bilateral agreements.

In short, two-tier tests have wide application. They can eliminate arbitrary anti-dumping use by targeting only those cases where the intent is to monopolize the foreign markets either through predatory dumping or strategic dumping. This can considerably reduce the administrative burden by restricting the number of actual anti-dumping proceedings. Only those cases that are cleared in the first stage would require detailed investigation. Their appeal also lies in the fact they are practical and do not require any harmonization of competition laws or any multilateral agreement on competition policies.

OPTION III: ADOPTION OF THE POLITICAL ECONOMY PERSPECTIVE

As discussed in previous chapters, both historical and empirical evidence seem to suggest that the use of anti-dumping is not aimed at stemming dumping, but rather, at addressing the market disruptions that result from an import surge. This means that anti-dumping measures have become a substitute for safeguard measures. Indeed, highly flexible criteria for proving dumping and consequent injury induce firms around the world to seek (and obtain) protection from the anti-dumping procedures rather than from safeguard measures. In principle, both of them serve the same objective. While the former are targeted against the sources countries of import surge, the latter are indiscriminatory in nature. This difference is also narrowing down over the years. In the past, most anti-dumping complaints were targeted against one country at a time. Of late, there has been rise in multiple petitions in anti-dumping cases that means that each anti-dumping petition targets imports from multiple country sources (Irwing 2005). Imports are thus more broadly shut out of the market when duties are imposed. While single petitions give rise to substantial trade diversion, as countries not facing the ADDs increase their exports significantly after the imposition of duties, such diversion is less likely when multiple petitions are the norm. Furthermore, there are several instances where countries do not stop after imposing duties against a country/ a group of countries. Once they find that trade diversion is taking place, they open investigations in the imports of the same product against other countries as well charging them of dumping. This has resulted in multiple cases against the same product. The objective therefore is to protect the industry from all the major sources of exports. In that sense, anti-dumping is serving primarily as safeguard measures now.

Several economists ((Nicolaides and Van Wijngaarden 1993; Messerlin, 1996; Tavares, Macario, and Steinfatt 2001; Finger et al. 2001; Roitinger 2003 among many others) argue that if anti-dumping is also a protectionist tool then there is no logic of having two tools serving the same objective. Of them, only one tool could be selected. Safeguard in this context is the most obvious candidate for selection by economists for several reasons. First, as has already been discussed in Chapter 1, safeguard measures are more transparent, less belligerent, and better focused than anti-dumping. Instead of blaming foreigners for the country's trading problems, safeguards direct the government's attention to the domestic factors that may be limiting the competitiveness of local firms. Second, safeguard measures are subject to more stringent conditions in terms of prerequisites and compensation than anti-dumping. This would restrain the use of trade remedy measures. Third, use of safeguard measures would eliminate the questionable practice of finding dumping. Fourth, the duties would be temporary. Finally, from an economic perspective safeguard measures are found to be superior to anti-dumping. An open trading system can best be maintained when the protection costs arising from the use of such measures are kept within national boundaries (Tavares 1995) and safeguard measures offer countries this possibility of keeping protection costs within national boundaries.

One proposal along this line is to abolish anti-dumping and use only safeguard measures where increased imports are harming the domestic industry. Since safeguard measures are less attractive, this would reduce the petitions considerably. Economists (Roinitger 2002, Hoekman and Leidy 1989) however argue that higher prerequisites and compensation requirements for temporary import restrictions impair the government's trade policy flexibility and governments are not ready to sacrifice such flexibility by means of an international trade agreement. Replacing anti-dumping by the existing safeguard agreement would therefore be difficult to realize. This can be achieved if safeguard measures are made more attractive by lowering either prerequisites or compensation requirement before replacing anti-dumping with them. Hoekman and Leidy (1989) proposed to suspend the compensation requirement for a stipulated period of time or completely get rid of this without tinkering with the pre requisites to allow the industry to undergo the process of structural adjustment without imposing extra cost on the economy. The Uruguay Round negotiations also softened the compensation requirement by allowing a three years' grace period. Article 8(3) reads:

The right of suspension referred to in paragraph 2 shall not be exercised for the first three years that a safeguard measure is in effect, provided that...

Evidence suggests that this did not change the situation. Anti-dumping remains the preferred tool where safeguard measures could very well have been used.

Rointinger (2002) however argues that these are prerequisites that should be eliminated. There is no need to give any concession in the compensation requirement. His argument is that governments do not want to compromise with their ability to restrict trade when they feel that it is important to do so.

This is because promoting efficiency is not the only objective of trade policy per se. The objectives of trade policy are varied. Governments therefore require flexibility in the trade policy. Anti-dumping provides a high degree of flexibility to the national authorities in initiating and determining anti-dumping charges to ensure that the decisions are based on the trade policy objectives of the government. Lowering safeguard prerequisites would provide the same flexibility to the governments to use this tool and replacing anti-dumping with this new safeguard mechanism would perhaps be acceptable to both the politicians or negotiators. For instance, establishing 'serious injury' should be done away with altogether. Removing this requirement would remove the 'producer bias' inherent in the measure. Safeguard investigations should not focus solely on the effect of the proposed restriction on domestic producers of like or competing goods; but rather, should focus on the national economic interest of the restricting country (Finger 2002). If injury to import-competing industries is not a prerequisite, other interest groups (such as consumers or environmentalists) may also be able to apply for temporary import restrictions. Furthermore, the Preamble of the Agreement highlights the importance of structural adjustment and the need to enhance rather than limit competition in international markets in the use of the safeguard clause. Rointinger (2002) argues that this does not have merits on economic efficiency grounds. There is no guarantee that the safeguard measure actually promotes adjustment. This may happen only if the need for adjustment arises because of an increasingly liberalized world trade. But this need could also be attributed to changing consumer tastes, technology bringing about new production methods, or environmental concerns causing more stringent national regulation. In all these cases, temporary import restrictions might just ease the pressure on import-competing industries. Once the prerequisites are lowered the requirement of full compensation should be strictly imposed. The exception to the full compensation requirement in case of absolutely rising imports should cease to exist. Lowering prerequisites with full compensation would ensure trade policy flexibility without creating temptations to the interest groups to use the tool excessively. Under the revised safeguard clause, the Dispute Settlement Mechanism does not intend to deter import restrictions per se. Instead, its primary task would be to ensure that any temporary import restriction comes along with full compensation.

Above arguments notwithstanding, one must note that the presence of either compensation requirement or prerequisites in the revised safeguard agreement would still make it less attractive than anti-dumping. Anti-dumping involves neither. It is therefore doubtful that supporters of anti-dumping would accept it.

ABOLISHING ANTI-DUMPING

Proponents of this view (Knoll 1991, Niels and Kate 1997, Finger 1981, 1991–3, 1998 among others) suggest that anti-dumping should be eliminated altogether. Three major arguments are as follows.

- The anti-dumping agreement is fundamentally flawed. It has no underlying principle. Its objective is to counter unfair trade practices but it fails to define what unfair trade practices are. In the absence of any basic underlying principle, it does not take account of whether price discrimination is fair or unfair.
- Fundamental reforms propose to restrict the use of anti-dumping only to unfair trade practices. But these proposals have invited hostile reactions from anti-dumping supporters.
- Furthermore, even if such reforms are applied to dumping cases, it would lead to nowhere. This is because government sponsored/predatory/strategic dumping occurs very seldom. All efforts involved in creating elaborate institutional arrangements and capacities would be futile.

While abolishing anti-dumping is preferable, it is not feasible due to lack of political consensus. The two largest economies of the world namely the United States and the EU will not accept any substantive reform even in the current framework of Doha mandate fearing backlash from the domestic industry and domestic political segments. These countries which are the strong defenders of the law are not willing to give up their right to impose anti-dumping against trading partners even in preferential trading agreements that they enter into. Though they have been very active in extending preferential trade agreements, not only with the countries in proximity but also with key countries in different regions, their approach towards the treatment of anti-dumping remains highly conservative. It is noteworthy that even the formation of the EU and the entailed elimination of all tariff duties were not enough for the EU to abolish anti-dumping and countervailing measures in the case of Turkey. Similarly, the United States did not agree to abolition of anti-dumping in North American Free Trade Agreement (NAFTA) although Canada had been eager to abolish anti-dumping measures for intra-regional trade (Hoekman 1998, Sagara 2002). Only a replacement option of a judicial review for final anti-dumping or countervailing duty determinations with a binational panel review could be achieved. Thus, in NAFTA, each party reserves the right to apply its anti-dumping law to goods imported from the territory of any other party. A distinctive point about the treatment of anti-dumping and countervailing measures is that Article 1904 provides each party with the right to replace judicial review of final ADD or CVD determinations by a binational panel review. However, the jurisdiction of the binational panel review is limited to looking into whether the final determinations of an investigating authority were in accordance with the importing party's anti-dumping or countervailing duties laws, using the same standard of review that a reviewing court would apply. The final determinations, providing there are no flaws in the lawful process of investigation, cannot be reversed by the binational panel review.

In 1998, the WTO Secretariat issued a report titled 'Inventory of Non-Tariff Provisions in Regional Trade Agreements (RTAs)'. It compiled the data for sixty-nine RTAs reported to the WTO by that time. According to the data in the report, of the sixty-nine RTAs, sixty-two allow member countries to impose anti-dumping measures on each other. A breakdown of the sixty-two RTAs shows six CUs out of ten and fifty-six Free Trade Agreements (FTAs) out of fifty-nine. Currently, the RTAs that have abolished the application of anti-dumping laws include: the EU, the EU–EEA FTA, ANZCERTA, and Canada–Chile FTA. Even those countries that engage in more than one RTA do not necessarily adopt the same treatments for trade remedy measures all the time. In fact, they have chosen different types of treatments on a case-by-case basis, depending on trade relations with the other party.

There is a proposal that member countries willing to participate in the process of globalization should abolish it unilaterally. This proposal is not operational. There appears to be prisoner's dilemma in the case of anti-dumping and free trade whereby all countries would be better off only if they cooperate and abolish anti-dumping. Once someone defects from the group the defector would gain the most benefits. As a results, others will follow until finally everyone loses. Thus, abolishing the law unilaterally is constrained as governments are concerned about the potential for their partners to engage in unfair trade practices in the absence of any trade defence instrument. They may consider anti-dumping a useful defensive instrument in this connection.

PART II: SOFT PROPOSALS—A PLAUSIBLE APPROACH

Most soft proposals focus on improving clarity, transparency, and predictability by incorporating additional procedures and tests and providing elaborations to specific requirements. The argument is: keep the basic text of the Agreement intact but raise the investigation standards to prevent the misuse of the instrument. Several such reform proposals have been offered by legal experts and economists. In addition, a large number of submissions have been made to the Rules Negotiating Group. The largest number of submissions have been made by a group of countries that call themselves 'Friends of Anti-dumping' but are severe critic of this policy. These countries are mainly developing countries with a few exceptions (for instance, Japan, Norway, and Switzerland). Other developing countries that made significant contributions include Egypt (six submissions), India and China (three submissions each), Brazil[3] (three submissions). In addition, Venezuela, Argentina, and Korea have also made their submissions. Among the traditional users, Australia and the United States have been the most active participants in terms of the number of submissions made. EU and Canada have made three and two submissions, respectively. While going through these proposals, two observations may be made. One, while developed countries (traditional users of anti-developed) focus on transparency, procedural fairness, disclosure of information, and public hearings, developing countries (in particular FANs) have made far-reaching proposals covering almost every aspect of the Agreement. Two, developed countries seem to resist any significant change in the current Agreement. The objective of this part of the chapter is to critically review some of the major proposals towards reforming the Agreement. The analysis would be done largely from the perspective of the developing countries. We conclude that any effort to fine tune the agreement will add to complexities to an already complex mechanism and may place a higher burden on the national administrators of this remedy and on the targets. This may prove to be counterproductive for the developing countries, which lack resources and capacities to effectively implement the remedy and counter the use of it against them. Developing countries therefore need to be selective in pushing these proposals.

This part starts with issues concerning dumping determination, goes on to injury-related provisions, followed by establishing causation. The fourth section discusses provisions related with other procedural aspects of the ADA. The last section concludes the analysis.

ISSUES CONCERNING DUMPING

Like Product

Chapter 3 discussed in detail how within the existing ADA framework the authorities enjoy wide discretion to define the scope of product under investigation. This means that the authorities often compare dissimilar products. In the interest of legal certainty, therefore, the scope of manipulation should be limited. Rules need to provide a more rational and disciplined framework to define the scope of product under investigation.

One proposal in this regard is that the market based approach taken by the Panels and AB in the Liquor Taxes cases to the determination of like products in the context of Article III.2 could be useful for the determination of like product in the anti-dumping field (Bronckers and McNeils 1999).

The Liquor Taxes cases[4] emphasized that what counts in defining like products is competition in the market place which is determined from the consumer's perspective. Products that are not substitutable cannot be like products simply because they do not compete. According to this view, showing that directly competitive and substitutable products are like products should be a starting point in the determination of like product. Products that are not in direct competition should be excluded from the definition of like products even though they might be physically similar. Thus the focus needs to be on substitutability.

Treating market factors as the starting point could provide a way for the anti-dumping authorities to address the problem of high-quality, high-priced imports that also fall into the same category as dumped imports. The famous Bed Linen case against India may illustrate this point. In this case, an exporter of luxury bed linen was also covered in the investigation along with producers of standard bed linen. This was despite the fact that the bed linen he exported was at the top of the range and was many times more expensive than the standard bed sheets, so much so that consumers could not easily substitute between them. The use of market factors could, therefore, result in an altogether different decision. Thus when quality differences translate to large price differences it will be possible to argue that the two products are not in direct competition with each other, which means that they are not substitutable. It is, therefore, suggested that the definition of 'like products' needs to be reconsidered. A mere reference to similarities in physical characteristics or even 'uses' is not enough. What is crucial is whether from a consumer's perspective, 'like products' are substitutable (or sufficiently competitive). Showing the products to be directly competitive/substitutable could be a starting point for the 'like product' determination in anti-dumping.[5] In that regard, the use of economic analysis and concepts, including basic actors such as cross-price demand elasticities, could prove to be useful (see Hoekman and Mavroidis 1996).

The above suggestion is in compliance with Article 15.2(b) of Rules on Custom Valuation. It defines 'similar goods' as goods that although not alike in all respects have like characteristics and like component materials which enable them to perform the same functions and to be commercially interchangeable. It should not, therefore, be difficult to amend the WTO Anti-dumping Agreement also along similar lines.

It is therefore proposed that adding 'substitutable (or directly competitive) product' to the definition of 'like product' would be a welcome modification in the agreement.

According to a proposal (TN/RL/W/158, 28 May 2004) submitted by the 'Friends of Anti-dumping (FANs)[6] Club' on 'model matching', for purposes of identifying the 'identical' and 'most closely resembling' models ('model matching'), the authorities must use all characteristics that have a significant effect on the commercial value or the end use of the product. Moreover, the authorities must put priority on those characteristics which affect the product's commercial value or its end use more than the others.

This is a very soft proposal. Instead of proposing to focus only on 'directly competitive' product it requires the authorities to put priority on the end use after examining all characteristics of the product. This will add one more vague provision to the plethora of other such provisions. How to place priority on the end use? Should there be a weightage system? If yes, how much weightage should be given to the end use vis-à-vis other characteristics? The proposal also requires authorities to give respondents opportunities to comment on model matching. As discussed in Chapter 3, it is impossible for respondents to convince authorities even when they have proper evidence to do so. It is therefore not clear how these changes provide 'clearer rules' to benefit both authorities and respondents.

Conditions for Constructing the Normal Value

Article 2.2 lists three situations in which the investigating authorities may reject the use of sales in the domestic market of the exporter in the calculation of normal value. These conditions need to be reviewed and refined to prevent their misuse. In what follows proposals relating to these conditions are reviewed. In addition, we also argue that legal provisions need to be incorporated to instruct the authorities to construct the normal value when sales are made to related producers. We review reform proposals in this regard.

Low volume of sales

One situation in which normal values are constructed is when there is a low volume of sales in the domestic markets of the exporting country. A quantitative criterion is also provided to define the term 'low volume of sale'. However, the agreement does not specify whether viability of the domestic sales needs to be assessed at the like product level only or for each particular model or type. Since different countries follow different practices, it is proposed (Didier 2001, FANs, TN/RL/W/150)[7] that the agreement must make it clear that the check needs to be performed at the product level. In this context, the Report of the AB in the Bed Linen case from India has important implications. The AB noted that

... from the wording of Article 2.1, it is clear to us that the Anti-Dumping Agreement concerns the dumping of a *product* ...

While commenting on the calculation of dumping margins by the EC, the AB argued:

The European Commission clearly identified cotton-type bed linen as the product under investigation in this case. Having defined the product as it did, the European Commission was bound to treat that product consistently thereafter in accordance with that definition. We see nothing in Article 2.4.2 or in any other provision of the Anti-Dumping Agreement that provides for the establishment of 'the existence of margins of dumping' for types or models of the product under investigation; to the contrary, all references to the establishment of 'the existence of margins of dumping' are references to the product that is subject of the investigation.

This judgement has important implications for other anti-dumping provisions, as well, including the 5 per cent viability test. For instance, footnote 2 under Article 2.2 of the ADA states

Sales of the like product destined for consumption ... shall normally be considered a sufficient quantity ... if such sales constitute 5 per cent or more of the sales of the *product* under consideration ... (emphasis added)

There is thus nothing in this provision to support the notion that in an anti-dumping investigation two different stages are envisaged or distinguished in any way by this provision of the ADA, nor to justify the distinctions made among types or models of the same product on the basis of these 'two stages'. Clearly, viability of the domestic market ought to be assessed at the like product level only.

In the light of the above Appellate Body (AB) judgement, it is important to review footnote 2 under Article 2.2 of the Anti-dumping Agreement and amend it to provide that the 5 per cent domestic sales shall be calculated against export sales of the like product (not model/type/category).

The proposal submitted by FANs (TN/RL/W/150, 16 April 2004) also proposes that the test should be applied to all sales and not just those deemed to be in the ordinary course of trade. This is because the objective of this test is to determine whether the domestic market is sufficiently large to enable domestic sales prices to serve as a legitimate measure of normal value.

Finally, a careful reading of footnote 2 under Article 2.2 suggests that it is not rigid about the 5 per cent viability test (Chaper 3). Nevertheless, in practice the 5 per cent viability rule is applied mechanically by the investigating authorities. This is because the provision is open ended. It leaves it entirely to the discretion of the authorities to decide on when and under what conditions a lower ratio could be used as the basis for sufficient sales. Since this is a major issue from the developing countries' perspective as discussed in Chapter 3, it is proposed that the agreement needs to elaborate on the conditions under which lower ratio could be considered of sufficient magnitude to provide for proper comparison. The more far reaching reform would be if the agreement is amended to provide that in the absence of sufficient domestic market sales there is no basis for dumping charges (Lindsey and Ikenson 2002a). But this proposal will not be accepted due to resistance from the developed countries.

Sales in the ordinary course of trade

Another situation when the investigating authorities may choose to construct the normal value is where there are no sales of the like product in the ordinary course of trade in the domestic market of the exporting country. However as discussed in Chapter 3, this is one of the most ambiguous provisions in the current ADA and is particularly harmful for the developing countries.[8] It is in direct contradiction with the political perspective of anti-dumping itself. According to this perspective, countering artificial comparative advantages enjoyed by the foreign producers because of a sanctuary market at home is the primary objective of anti-dumping. The existence of below-cost sales in the home market is actually affirmative evidence of the absence of a sanctuary market (Lindsey and Ikenson 2002b). This is because a sanctuary market is supposed to be characterized by artificially high prices and profits. If home market sales at a loss are found in significant quantities, it is an indication by itself that there is no sanctuary market.

Several submissions made to the Rules Group have highlighted the need to clarify the ADA provisions to this effect.[9] One would however propose to exclude this test altogether and rewrite the wordings to exclude only specified aberrational sales such as obsolete inventory or damaged goods (Lindsey and Ikenson 2002b). The proposals submitted to the WTO by FANs widens the scope of such sales by including: sales of samples, sales to employees, barter sales; sales of the like products to a toller or subcontractor for further-manufacture, upon the condition that the further-manufactured product will be returned to the responding party. But at the same time, it also proposes to include sales below cost with some refinement of the concept. Such refinements may again provide room for maneuverability and should be clearly rejected. Besides, there are a few proposals to add a provision or footnote to clarify that the below-cost test must be performed for all sales of the like product as a whole, and not any sub-group of these sales. But, this may widen the scope of sales 'not in ordinary course of trade' (FANs, TN/RL/W/150).

The above proposal will not be acceptable to the developed countries. The second best proposal therefore is to amend the wordings of the existing provision. The wordings of the provision provide discretionary powers to the authorities to discard all price data on domestic sales where the volume of sales above unit cost represents less than certain percentage of the total sales volume. This practice is contrary to the spirit of Article 2.2.1 that clearly states that only those sales that are not in the ordinary course of trade should be disregarded provided they constitute more than 20 per cent of domestic sales. The wording of Article 2.2.1 needs to be tightened to restrain such practices that result into the use of constructed normal value.

Footnote 5 to Article 2.2.1 may further be clarified by adding '... only sales not in ordinary course of trade are to be disregarded ...'. However, this reform will not make any significant impact. One proposal is to define 'reasonable period of time' for prices which do not provide for recovery of all costs (FANs, TN/RL/W/6). But it may be difficult to come to any consensus on the length of the reasonable period and it will itself be discretionary.

The 'particular market situation'

The agreement instructs the authorities to construct the normal value when there is 'the particular market situation' without elaboration on what this means. This gives wide discretionary powers to the authorities to reject the actual data. It is therefore important to elaborate on this provision. Scholars argue that hyperinflation in the domestic markets of the exporters or restriction on foreign competitors' entry into domestic markets or the presence of high tariff and non-tariff barriers may be the instances in which the particular market situation can prevent proper comparisons between the normal value and export prices (Stanbrook and Bentley 1996, China, TN/RL/W/66). A footnote may be added to specify these situations as the 'particular market situation'. However, FANs (TN/RN/W/150) submission argues that the term is unnecessary and the first best option is to delete it altogether. There should not be any resistance in accepting this proposal.

Sales to domestic related customers

The current anti-dumping agreement does not specifically address the issue of whether home market sales to affiliates may be included in or excluded from the calculation of normal value. Article 2.3 directs investigating authorities to construct export prices at ex-factory level when exports take place via related importers. However, the agreement has no provision for adjustments in normal value when sales are made through affiliates (as discussed above). As a result, export prices constructed at the ex-factory level are generally compared with domestic sales prices to the first unrelated buyer without effective adjustments. This gives an upward bias to the normal value as further downstream in the domestic distribution chain the reference price is taken the higher it is and creates asymmetry between the level of trade of the constructed export price and that of the normal value.[10] Therefore, it is proposed that Article 2.2 should have a provision on the normal value of sales that are made through affiliated parties.[11] The proposed provision needs to be applicable only where authorities demonstrate that prices to related parties are affected by the relationship. Generally, it is assumed that prices charged to related parties are lower than the prices to unaffiliated customers. The USDOC carries out a test termed 'arm's length test' or 99.5 per cent test on the basis of this assumption to determine whether home market sales to affiliates are made in the ordinary course of trade. If prices to the affiliated party are on average 99.5 per cent or less of the price to the unaffiliated parties, the USDOC determines that sales made to the affiliated party are affected by the relationship. In that case it rejects it as 'sales not made in the ordinary course of trade'. In the 'Certain Hot-rolled Steel Products' case, Japan questioned this practice in the DSB. Their argument was: This law treats low prices as abnormal but ignores that high prices can also be abnormal, skewing the normal value upwards. The AB agreed with this argument and found the application of the 99.5 per cent test inconsistent with the term 'ordinary course of trade' due to the distortion that it is likely to introduce in the calculation of the normal value. It argued that Article 2.1 applies to any sales not in the ordinary course of trade and not just sales that lower normal value. In view of the rulings given by the AB, it is proposed (Didier 2001, TN/RL/W/150) that a provision may be appended stating that

when domestic sales are not in ordinary course of trade because of association or a compensatory arrangement between the manufacturer and the domestic distributor or a third party, and the domestic price is *demonstrated* (emphasis added) to be affected by the relationship (resulting in high/low prices) (*by 'x' percent*), the normal value shall be constructed on the basis of the price at which the products are first resold to an independent buyer by adjusting that for costs (including taxes and duties) incurred between manufacturer's sales to distributors and resale and distributor's profits accrued'.

The above suggestion is in agreement with Article 1(2) of Rules on Custom Valuation and should be acceptable. It states:

In determining whether the transaction value is acceptable for the purpose of paragraph 1, the fact that the buyer and seller are related ... shall not be the ground for regarding the transaction value as unacceptable.... provided that the relationship did not influence the price.

This provision will be effective only if authorities have a well-defined criteria to interpret the term 'related parties'. Unfortunately, however, there is no clear definition of 'affiliation' in the ADA. Footnote 11 provides the definition of affiliation in the context of determining the domestic industry. The concept of related producers in the agreement depends on control. While defining 'control' the agreement stipulates that 'one shall be deemed to control another when the former is legally or operationally in a position to exercise restraint or direction over the latter'. Legally, this means that one of them holds 50 per cent or more (majority share) of the outstanding voting stock of the other. In practice, however, investigating authorities interpret this concept using their discretion. For instance, the EC continues to deem the existence of control even in the case of minimal shareholding of 1–5 per cent. It is, therefore, important to provide a clear definition of affiliation for all practical purposes. Here again Article 15.4 of the 'Rules on Custom Valuation' provides a comparatively more elaborate definition of affiliation for the purpose of these rules. It states that persons shall be deemed to be related only if

- they are officers of one another's business;
- they are legally recognised partners in their business;
- they are employer and employee;
- any person directly/indirectly owns, controls, or holds 5 per cent or more of the outstanding voting stock or shares of both of them;
- one of them directly/indirectly controls the other;
- both of them are directly controlled by a third person;
- together they directly or indirectly control a third person; and
- they are members of the same family.

These criteria could be adopted in the ADA. However, the criteria of control is based on 5 per cent ownership and is not likely to have any significant impact on the (mis)use of the law. One of the proposals is to define control based on more than 50 per cent ownership (FANs TN/RL/W/146). However, any significant change in the disciplines of the ADA will be resisted.

Construction of the Normal Value

Alternative methods for constructing normal value have been provided in the ADA. These are: the cost of production method, export price to the third country-based method, and the use of best available information method. All these methods are fraught with ambiguities and need reconsideration.

Use of the cost of production methodology

For constructing the normal value, the investigating authorities adjust the cost data by a reasonable amount for administrative, selling, and general costs and for profits. When the amounts for administrative, selling, and general costs and for profits cannot be determined on the basis of actual information, the investigating authorities have full discretion to choose (i) profits and administrative, selling, and general costs of the exporter in question in respect of production and sales in the same general category of product, or (ii) profits and administrative, selling, and general costs of any other exporter/producer subject to investigation in respect of production and sales of the like product in the domestic market of the country of origin, or (iii) any other reasonable method. Clearly, the current agreement under which the authorities have complete discretion may lead to substantial bias in the calculation of normal values.

It is, therefore, important to impose an obligation to apply a separate reasonability test to the methodologies set forth in Articles 2.2.2 (i)–(iii). One suggestion (Lindsey and Ikenson 2002b) is that Article 2(6) as a whole would need to be safeguarded by a general reasonability test such as has been foreseen only for Article 2(6) (iii) now. The definition of reasonable could be the same as that which has been implied in Article 2(6) (iii) itself, that is profits should not exceed the profits normally realized by sales of other producers in the same general category of products on the domestic markets. More specifically profit rates should be the average industry-wide profit rates derived from public sources. It may be worthwhile to consider both these proposals but they are not adequate to remove the ambiguities in this provision. If the methodologies set forth in Articles 2.2.2 (i)–(iii) are by definition reasonable, at most there is a rebuttable presumption that the results generated by these methodologies are reasonable.

Another suggestion is that Article 2.2.2 of the ADA should be amended to set out an order of preference among different methodologies of approximating profits (India, TN/RL/W/26, FANs, TN/RL/W/150). The use of Article 2.2.2 (iii) that provides for 'any other reasonable method' without specifying such method needs to be given the last priority while Article 2(6) (i) should be given the first priority. But leaving 'any other reasonable method' in Article 2.2.2 (iii), even with the status of last priority, will continue to cause problems. Its presence will also induce the authorities to use this method; justification poses little problem.

It is also proposed that only Article 2.2.2 (i) yields justifiable methodology. Articles 2.2.2 (ii) and (iii) should be deleted (FANs, TN/RL/W/150). However, according to scholars, it would pose problems when the respondent has no sales of any product in its domestic market.

Finally, it is proposed (TN/RL/W/150) to delete the 'general' and 'administrative' costs to clarify that expenses related only to sales of the like products may be added to the cost of production for the purposes of the below-cost test and the constructed value. It is argued that even though Article 2.2 of the ADA provides for 'a reasonable amount for administrative, selling, and general costs and for profits' the basic principle which is reflected in GATT Article VI provides that constructed value shall include 'a reasonable addition for selling cost and profit'. However, this proposal will not be acceptable to supporters of anti-dumping.

Use of the appropriate third country method

The agreement stipulates that the authorities may also use the price of goods exported to appropriate third countries to construct normal values by adjusting it for the differences relating to price comparability between the goods sold to the importing countries and the like goods sold by the exporter to importers in the third country, in a prescribed manner. The agreement does not define the criteria for selecting the appropriate third country. It is usually the 'third country' suggested by the complainants or the investigating country itself. One suggestion is to refine the agreement so that the possibility of the choosing itself as the third country is ruled out. The second suggestion in this regard is to have a well-defined criteria for choosing 'appropriate third country'. Specific criteria in terms of economic parameters may be a welcome precision. This will require the authorities to consider the level of income, export shares, presence of viable domestic industry, and competition conditions among other factors in choosing appropriate third country. But there will be a huge scope of changing the focus depending on the suitability, on a case-by-case basis.

Best available information

Article 6.8 that permits the use of best facts available for making preliminary and final determinations also needs refinement. Chapter 3 discussed how the use of this method not only increases the probability of affirmative finding but also results in higher dumping margins. A review of the anti-dumping cases suggests that any failure by the foreign firms to respond to the authorities' onerous reporting requirements allows the authority to disregard all its data and instead use the best information available, which typically means data reported in the domestic firm's petition. It states

In cases in which any interested party refuses access to, or otherwise does not provide, necessary information *within a reasonable period* or *significantly impedes the investigation*, preliminary and final determinations, affirmative or negative, may be made on the basis of the facts available. The provisions of Annex II shall be observed in the application of this paragraph.

In view of the fact that this article is particularly harmful for developing countries and that it has been referred repeatedly at the WTO level, several submissions have been seeking clarifications in various provisions under this agreement (FANs, TN/RL/6; Argentina, TN/RL/81; India, TN/RL/26).

However, detailed proposals have been submitted by FANs in their submission TN/RL/93 (see also Dutta 2004). Some of these proposals are listed here.

- Suitably amend the agreement to clarify that the authorities would use facts available with respect to that element of information that has not been provided.
- Append a footnote clarifying criteria for the term 'reasonable period of time'. However, actual time period should be determined on a case-by-case basis.
- Discard the concept of 'significant impediment' since it has been used by authorities as a catch all excuse to use facts available.
- Amend Annex II.1 to provide that authorities must make 'reasonable efforts' to obtain necessary information by:
  - notifying the respondent in detail of the information which was insufficient in response to authorities' questionnaires and
  - permit the respondent to submit the required information within a 'reasonable period of time', which must be determined on a 'case to case basis' in the light of the special circumstances of each investigation.

Annex II.7 clarifies that 'if an interested party does not cooperate and thus relevant information is being withheld from the authorities, this situation could lead to a result which is less favourable to the party than if the party did cooperate'. It does not lay down the conditions under which respondent will be regarded as co-operative. The proposal is that Annex II.7 may be amended to clarify that a party shall be regarded as being cooperative, *inter alia*, if the party provided a substantial portion of the entire information requested by authorities and substantially all of that information could be verified, or if the party made reasonable efforts to submit the requested information in the light of its ability to submit the information and its ability to fulfil the instructions provided by the authorities.

One proposal is that Annex II.6 should instruct the authorities to provide a sufficient explanation of the reasons why submitted information has been totally or partially rejected and specifically identify the information that the authorities intend to substitute for the rejected information. The current provision reads 'If evidence or information is not accepted, the supplying party should be informed forthwith of the reasons thereof ...'.

It is not clear how these amendments will mitigate the arbitrariness surrounding the use of 'fact available'. The first proposal is one of the key proposals in this regard. It requires the authorities to use 'facts available' only to substitute for information that is not submitted or is not rejected. But the authorities can easily reject the available information on the plea that information is interconnected. Rejection of one information may lead to rejection of other related information. Proposal requiring authorities to make reasonably efforts to obtain necessary information and to provide explanation why submitted information was rejected do not involve substantive amendment either. These involve only procedural upgradation. Other proposals are too technical. Remedy perhaps lies in simplifying the questionnaires and providing technical assistance to the developing countries in data maintenance system. We shall discuss these proposals in Chapter 7.

Construction of Export Prices

In cases where there is no export price or where it appears to the authorities concerned that the export price is unreliable because of association or a compensatory arrangement between the exporter and the importer or a third party, the agreement permits the authorities to construct the export prices (ADA, Article 2.3). It is discussed in Chapter 3 how this provision penalises exports via related importers. This issue needs to be addressed,[12] as with increasing globalization more and more exports are being undertaken via trading houses. Article 2.3 could thus be suitably amended along the lines proposed in the case of normal value (Didier 2001, FANs, TN/RL/W/150).

When export price is unreliable because of association or a compensatory arrangement between the exporter and the importer/a third party, and the export price is *demonstrated* (emphasis added) to be affected by the relationship (resulting in high/low prices) (by 'x' per cent), the export price shall be constructed on the basis of the price at which the products are first resold to an independent buyer by adjusting that for costs (including taxes and duties) incurred between manufacturer's sales to distributors and resale and distributor's profits accrued.

The proposed amendment requires the authorities to verify whether the export price is affected by the relationship before its construction.

Fair Comparison

The Agreement does not provide for symmetrical adjustments in normal value sales and exports. Authorities exploit this loophole by giving upward bias to the normal value and downward bias to the export price. This asymmetry, which is totally arbitrary, skews the dumping margins in upward direction. Chapter 3 discusses some of the issues relating to fair comparison. In what follows we present and explain some proposals made in this regard.

Symmetrical adjustment[13]

Following proposals have been made by FANs (TN/RL/W/158, 28 May 2004),

- The agreement must incorporate the basic requirement of 'symmetrical adjustments' in Article 2.4 by adding 'with symmetrical adjustments thereof'. Thus the article should read:

  'A fair comparison shall be made between the export price or constructed export price and the normal value, with symmetrical adjustments thereof.'

- A definition of symmetrical adjustments needs to be added: 'Where a category of adjustment (e.g., due allowance for differences in selling or other expenses, and profits) is applicable both to the export or constructed export price and to the prices used for normal value, authorities must make comparable adjustments to both prices. Moreover, the adjustment to both prices must fully reflect the actual amount of the expense incurred'.

It is argued that for eliminating manipulative practices of the authorities, it is important to incorporate the requirement of symmetrical adjustments explicitly in the agreement. Some scholars[14] feel that the existing provisions need no tinkering. The proposed elaborations would add further complexities to an already complex agreement. Furthermore, to seek such adjustments, exporters will need to maintain detailed disaggregated data on various expenses. Exporters from developed countries will have an edge over the developing countries exporters in asking for such adjustments bringing little benefit to developing countries.

Allowance for duty drawback

Another problem relating to fair comparison is that the investigating authorities at times do not permit the required allowances on unreasonable grounds. One such allowance is duty drawback claims. This problem is particularly serious for developing countries where import duties are higher than in developed countries (Chapter 3). Several instances are given in Chapter 3, which indicate the importance of addressing this issue. However, no specific proposal has been made in this regard.

We argue that it is important to have case-based information on the experience of exporters regarding certain allowances and to examine how the law can be modified in the light of such experiences. Our suggestion[15] is that the requirement of establishing that import charges are borne by the like product and by materials physically incorporated therein (or import duty and rebates are linked) must go on the presumption that if an exporter is importing raw materials, the domestic prices that he is faced with are either equal to the landed value (export price plus custom duty) or are higher. Since domestic prices in such cases are inclusive of the custom element, it is immaterial whether the imported material is physically incorporated in the exported product. So long as the exporter avails of duty drawback, he should be granted this adjustment. This adjustment may be calculated by discounting the domestic price by custom duty. In no case will this result in excess revision. This is an important proposal and developing countries should pursue it in the current Round negotiations.

Exclusion of certain types of export sales from the calculation of export prices

The AD provides for the exclusion of low priced sales from normal value. However, the treatment of such sales with respect to export price and constructed export price is not explicitly addressed in the ADA. This problem is also discussed in Chapter 3. For ensuring fair comparison therefore, Article 2.1 may be refined to provide that low priced sales shall be excluded from the calculation of export price and constructed export price. These include sales of samples, sales to employees, barter sales, sales of the like products to a toller or subcontractor for further-manufacture, upon the condition that the further-manufactured products will be returned to the responding party, and certain sales to affiliated parties (FANs, TN/RL/150). But the problem of asymmetrical adjustments cannot be resolved by incorporating such provisions unless the wordings of the 'ordinary course of trade' are also changed to exclude only 'aberrational sales'. In the absence of such change, this provision may increase the complexities without really solving the main problem.

Burden of proof

Article 2.4 places the burden of ensuring fair comparison on the authorities. In this regard it is noted that certain traditional users of anti-dumping measures in practice place the burden of proof squarely on the respondent with respect to demonstrating that differences in terms of levels of trade or other trade conditions in fact affect price comparability. The provisions of Article 2.4 leave too much leeway to authorities to reject claims regarding such differences. There are proposals (FANs, TN/RL/W/158, see also Bhansali 2004a) that the authorities should have the responsibility to ensure that due allowances have been made. It is not clear how this can be implemented. In view of the fact that the agreement already instructs the authorities to make due allowances for fair comparison, any efforts to push this amendment would perhaps be waste of time.

Dumping Margin

Article 2.4.2 provides three alternative methods of calculating dumping margins.

- A comparison of a weighted average normal value with a weighted average of prices of all comparable export transactions.
- A comparison of normal value and export prices on a transaction-to-transaction basis.
- A comparison of weighted average normal value with prices of individual export transactions if the authorities find a pattern of export prices, which differ significantly among different purchasers, regions or time periods.

Major problems noted in this stage of the calculation of dumping margin relate to zeroing of dumping margins and the possibility of upward bias in the margins when the second and/or third method of comparison is used (Chapter 4).

Zeroing of dumping margins

Zeroing is one of the worst forms of distortions in the dumping margin calculations. It eliminates all negative dumping margins and creates artificial dumping margins. The panel rulings in the EU Bed Linen case against India and the US–Stainless Steel from Korea Case notwithstanding, the use of zeroing continues by the US and to a limited extent by the EU (Bhansali 2004a, Lindsey and Ikenson 2002a, 2002b). Given this blatant non-compliance of the panel rulings, experts are of the view that zeroing needs to be prohibited at all levels explicitly. Article 2.4.2 needs to be redrafted so as to provide that dumping margins should be based on comparisons that fully reflect all comparable export prices.

Article 2.4.2 of the ADA should be revised to clarify that when calculating dumping margins, negative dumping amounts should be treated as such and given their full weight in the calculation of the foreign producer's overall dumping margin. Several submissions have made proposals to eliminate this practice (FANs, TN/RL/W/113 and TN/RL/W/6, India TN/RL/W/26, China TN/RL/W/66). It needs to be pushed hard.

Comparison of weighted normal value with individual export prices

When a normal value established on a weighted average basis is compared to prices of individual export transactions, the probability of finding dumping increases (Chapter 3). The use of this practice, therefore, needs to be restricted by agreement. The best proposal in this regard is to disallow the use of this average to individual method of calculating dumping margins.[16] This would discourage the practice of zeroing also. Some countries such as the United States use this method in administrative reviews.

In their submission (TN/RL/W/158 28 May 2004) FANs are of the view that only the first yields a fair comparison. The second method provides authorities with unpredictably broad discretion to choose among the transactions to be used as the basis for normal value. The third method is objectionable because the concept of 'targeted dumping' lacks any theoretical or empirical basis.

Their proposal is to amend Article 2.4.2 of the ADA to require that, in both original investigations and administrative reviews, dumping margins must be calculated on the basis of comparing average export prices to average normal values or transaction-specific export prices to transaction-specific normal values. Comparisons of individual export prices to average normal values are never allowed.

INJURY: SOME PROPOSALS

Discussion on injury-related issues in Chapter 3 indicates that the following disciplines need be addressed: the support criterion, the injury indicators, the cumulation and the determination of injury margin.

In what follows, we have reviewed and also offered some proposals and explained their practicality.

The Support Criterion

Investigating authorities for determining injury must begin by determining the set of domestic producers who compete with the imports under investigation. Domestic industry for the purpose of injury means 'the domestic producers whose collective output of the products constitutes a major proportion of the total domestic production of those products'. The agreement does not provide any quantitative criterion for 'a major proportion'. This leads to wide variation in the practice. In some countries (Mexico and Trinidad and Tobago) the term 'domestic industry' may mean only 25 per cent of the domestic production of the goods in question. Several member countries have proposed to clarify the definition of domestic industry. These include: India (TN/RL/W/26), FANs (TN/RL/W/10), Australia (TN/RL/W/86), United States (TN/RL/W/98), China (TN/RL/W/66), Canada (TN/RL/W/47), and Egypt (TN/RL/W/105). The United States also proposes (TN/RL/W/72) to clarify the definition of domestic industry to address the special circumstances raised when domestic and foreign producers have limited selling seasons.

First, a footnote clarifying the quantitative criterion of 'domestic industry' may be appended. For the purpose of injury analysis, we propose that the domestic industry should be defined to include at least 50 per cent of domestic production where the domestic industry means the producers producing like product (see also FANs, TN/RL/W/150).

While most proposals focus on defining 'major proportion', no specific proposals have been received on what should be included in the definition of 'domestic industry'. We propose that the laws should restrict the scope of omissions from the domestic industry. For instance, it is not desirable to exclude all companies related to exporters. It is important to develop some criteria to restrict the term 'related parties'. Here some guidance may be provided by the anti-dumping legislation in different countries. In Korea, for instance, producers who imported six months prior to the date of receipt of the application and those whose import quantity is insignificant are included in the definition of domestic producers. Furthermore, the Agreement must be amended to categorically mention the treatment of captive production and exports so that in future cases this loophole is not exploited in the injury analysis.

Injury Indicators

There is no scientific method of determining injury. It is always possible for the authorities to focus on the indicators that suggest that the industry is performing poorly and make an affirmative determination. Though the need for reforms of injury-related provisions is recognized,[17] there are no specific proposals to deal with this issue. Some of the scholars have however made some suggestions which are provided below.

The agreement describes a wide array of economic factors without giving a proper framework as to how the authorities need to evaluate them. Some factors are systematically related while others are applicable to the business enterprise as a whole and cannot be examined product-wise in multi-product corporations making it difficult to evaluate them consistently. Even though EU claims to adopt high standards of anti-dumping investigations, we found (Chapter 4) that injury assessment for the EC means confirming that employment and profits are down. It is long proposed that the number of admissible indicators for injury need be reduced dramatically (Hoekman and Leidy 1989). Only those factors that have direct implications on material injury should be included. These are for instance: volume of dumped imports, share of dumped imports in total domestic availability, prices, profits, capacity utilization, employment, and investment. This would not only reduce the administrative burden of going through various indicators which are not factored into the analysis finally but would also make it more focused.

Another issue that was raised in the context of injury in Chapter 3 is whether initiating anti-dumping investigations on the basis of threat of injury alone should be permissible (Sykes 2005). Any investigation based on threat of material injury will necessarily be speculative because it involves analysis of events that have not yet happened. It is therefore suggested that the agreement should be clearly amended to instruct the authorities that that 'no injury decision should be based on the threat of injury alone'. There are proposals from the developing countries to refine the provisions on 'threat of injury' (India, TN/RL/W/26; Egypt, TN/RL/W/110; China, TN/RL/W/66; FANs, TN/RL/W/6). Egypt (TN/RL/W/105) also emphasized the need to clarify disciplines on material retardation. However, these details may hardly help. These are based on subjective judgement and any further fine-tuning may bring little gain to the developing countries.

A widely criticized provision in injury determination is that of cumulation. The WTO ADA permits an investigating authority to accumulate dumped imports of a product from more than one country that are simultaneously subject to anti-dumping investigations. Chapter 3 has presented some data to show how harmful this practice has been for developing countries. It is proposed that for elaborating on the conditions provided in Article 3.3, a sentence could be added stating that 'significant differences in market share/export volume trends over the past years of different exporting countries indicate a difference in the conditions of the competition and the inappropriateness of cumulation'. How effective will it be? Experience suggests 'not much'. It leaves the term 'significant difference' open ended and hence vague. The USITC generally considers four factors when deciding whether to cumulate: (i) interchangeability between imports from different countries and between imports and domestic product, (ii) overlap between the domestic product and the imported product in four geographical markets of the United States, (iii) similar distribution channels, and (iv) simultaneous presence of imports. Despite these conditions, cumulation has become a profitatble strategy for the developed countries.

Several proposals have been made to clarify this provision to restrict its use (FANs, TN/RL/W/6 and /29; TN/RL/W/7; China, TN/RL/W/66, TN/RL/W/86; Argentina, TN/RL/W/81, TN/RL/W/98). However most of them seek to set an appropriate parameter for the definition of negligible volume of imports or clarify the conditions in which cumulation is permitted. FANs (TN/RL/W/199) propose that in the event that named (targeted) countries individually account for less than 3 per cent of the domestic consumption of the like product in the importing, their volume of imports should be arranged in descending order and those that make up 7 per cent should only be subjected to anti-dumping initiations.

We argue that developing countries should be exempted from this provision altogether. We shall discuss this proposal in Chapter 7 that focuses on the special and differential treatment to developing countries.

Lesser Duty Rule

The agreement requires the authorities to preferably apply a lesser duty rule in accordance with Articles 6.1 and 9.1. The agreement however does not give any guidance on such calculation and arguably leaves its members with substantial discretion. Several proposals related to the 'lesser duty rule' have been already submitted to the Negotiating Group on Rules.[18] Developing countries including India (TN/RL/W/170) seem to be pushing it very hard. Following amendments are proposed in the ADA in this regard.

- Make the 'Lesser Duty Rule' mandatory under Article 9.
- Codify methodologies for determination of injury margin for proper and transparent application of the 'Lesser Duty Rule'.

It is proposed (India, TN/RL/W/170 and FANs, TN/RL/W/119) that wordings of Article 9.1 need rewriting to instruct the authorities that the amount of the ADD shall not exceed the margin of dumping established or the injury margin, whichever is lower. The principles of calculating 'injury margin' need to be set out in an appendix. Injury margin should be based on a fair comparison of the import price of the dumped goods with the selling price of like product produced by the domestic industry (price undercutting), or the difference between the target price and the import price of the dumped goods (price underselling). The methodology of calculating this should be developed along the lines of dumping margin calculations (Bhansali 2004b). While calculating price undercutting, zeroing practice on injury should also be prohibited explicitly. A recent paper (Tharakan et al. 2006) argues that one improvement in the calculations of injury margin would be to use 'counter factual' analysis.[19] They have investigated 354 EU anti-dumping cases using the counter factual analysis and found the reported injury margins from the Commission were inflated because of a flawed estimation procedure. However, as discussed in the next section, this methodology requires elaborate information on demand elasticities as we shall discuss later, which are generally not available in the developing countries.

It is believed that this rule will have a significant impact on ADDs. One must however note that these proposals may increase the complexities without being effective in reducing average duties unless the methodologies of calculating dumping margins and injury margins are made fully unbiased (Chapter 3). Furthermore, evidence suggests that the lesser duty rule has not been very effective. We examined the EU ADD patterns during 1995–2004 for 1485 firms provided in the Global Anti-dumping Database prepared by Bown. We could compare the final ADD with final dumping margin for 431 firms. Two observations followed. One, dumping margin was greater than the duty only for 173 (40 per cent) of 431 firms. Two, the difference between final dumping margin and the final duty had been greater than 20 percentage points in only 52 cases. In the rest 121 cases, it had been inconsequential. Finally, incorporation of such laws may affect the developing countries asymmetrically. Due to lack of resources and understaffed authorities, it may make it difficult for them to follow these detailed procedures first to establish dumping margins and then injury margins. In view of this, it is strange that developing countries are pursuing this proposal very hard. Furthermore, the United States already opposed this proposal. It submitted a document focusing on some perceived methodological and practical difficulties with the mandatory application of the lesser duty rule

CAUSATION

One of the major problems with the agreement is the absence of clear cut standards to judge whether there is causal link between dumped imports and injury. Article 3.5 contains the non-attribution test for determining the causal relationship. Using this test, the authorities need to disentangle the effects of dumped imports from those caused by other factors. The effects caused by factors other than dumping need to be excluded from the determination of material injury so as to ensure that these effects are not attributed to the dumped imports. For ascertaining the effects of various factors on the domestic industry, however a relatively long period is needed. While the industry must be suffering material injury during the regular investigation period and detailed injury margin calculations in the case of application of a lesser duty rule will be based on the data existing during the regular investigation period, the analysis of injury and causation needs a longer period in order to examine trend factors. The WTO Committee on ADP therefore adopted a 'Recommendation Concerning the Periods of Data Collection for Anti-Dumping Investigations G/ADP/6' (adopted on 5 May 2000), which states that the period of data collection for injury investigation should be at least three years. Thus the analysis is based on 3 yearly trends. The Agreement however does not specify any methodology to separate the injurious effects of various causal factors. Developing countries have been highlighting the need to develop the procedures and criteria utilized to analyse the causal relationship, with a view to ensure that even in the presence of other factors, a causal relationship will be found only when there is a clear and substantial link between the dumped imports and the injury (FANs, TN/RL/W/6; India, TN/RL/W/26; China, TN/RL/W/66). Experts propose that the authorities should use basic tools of quantitative economic analysis (Lindsey and Ikenson 2002b; Boltuck 1991,

1993).[20] In this context, they refer to the unitary causation analysis used by the USITC.

Near the end of the 1980s, the USITC designed a comparative static price-theoretic economic model known as the Comparative Analysis of the Domestic Industry's Condition (CADIC) model to determine whether anti-dumping actions would improve the industry materially. It is based on the unitary injury analysis, which does not address the question whether there is injury but instead simply asks whether the domestic industry will be better off without injury. In other words, they use a counter factual model of injury.

The underlying framework of the CADIC model is a generalized imperfect substitute model usually known as an Armington model. Boltuck (1993) stated that an Armington assumption made in this model is that products are differentiated by country of origin. Therefore, consumers are more likely to distinguish those products by regarding the place where they were produced. The model takes into consideration three imperfect substitute products, which account for the demand in a domestic market. These are: (i) the domestic product, (ii) the subject imports, and, (iii) the non-subject fairly traded imports. The approach used in the CADIC model is elasticity based. In estimating the effects of dumped imports on the price and production of domestic products, the demand for the three goods in the domestic market as well as the supply of domestic products must be considered simultaneously. By equating the supply and demand functions, the competitive market equilibrium condition for the domestic product, the subject imports, and the fairly traded non-subject country imports is as follows:

$$E_i \ln(p_i) = \ln(c_i) + S_{ii} \ln(p_i) + \sum S_{ij} \ln(p_j) i$$

where

E_i is the price elasticity of supply for ith product

p_i is the price of the ith product

c_i is the intercept term of the ith demand equation

S_{ii} is the own price elasticity of demand for the ith product

S_{ij} are the price elasticities of demand for the ith product with respect to the price of the jth product.

An important feature of this kind of elasticity based model is that much depends on the elasticities. The values for the elasticities are derived not only from the actual data but also from market specific qualitative information or from previous economic studies that may seem to be applicable. If the cross elasticities between subject and non-subject imports are high, the effects of anti-dumping will be limited. If cross elasticities between subject goods and domestic production are high then anti-dumping would address the injurious effects effectively.

This methodology is considered WTO consistent. In the US-Korea (DRAM) dispute case (WT/DS296/R), panel ruled that the methodology was WTO consistent as it was based on a comprehensive analysis of all those factors set forth in the WTO provisions. It is however subject to certain limitations. A major problem with this methodology is that it is based on 'unitary analysis' of injury. 'Bifurcated' analysis first asks whether the domestic industry is suffering 'material injury'. Only if the answer to that question is yes does the analysis proceed to the second stage and inquire into the cause of the material injury. 'Unitary' analysis does not ask the first question, but instead simply asks whether the domestic industry would be materially better off without the dumping (or dumped imports). Hence, unitary analysis is based on a relative analysis of the industry and may result in anti-dumping even if in absolute terms there is no injury.

Some experts argue that the key is to create a system where you can tell whether the authorities are doing the right thing or not and in that context, the unitary analysis is more appropriate than the bifurcated analysis. However, while analysing the methodology critically, one finds that even though the system was strictly based on economic analysis, much depended on the approach used for calculating elasticities. Thus the use of this method does not fully eliminate the controversy surrounding the causation analysis. While reviewing the US–Mexico Food Systems and The Tomato case, Almonte-Alvarez and Conley (2003) revealed how the USITC manipulated the findings by using the elasticities from the previous studies even when the actual data could be used for the purpose.

Apparently, it is not possible to devise any unambiguous methodology to examine the causal relationship between dumping and injury. Any attempt to introduce changes in the existing provisions would lead to more complexities without eliminating arbitrariness (Nedumpara 2003).

OTHER PROCEDURAL ISSUES

Conditions for Initiating an Anti-dumping Case

It is generally proposed that in view of the harassment effect that anti-dumping investigations have, initiation standards of anti-dumping investigations must be raised. The agreement requires the petitioners to provide evidence on dumping, injury, and causal relationship but it does not require them to submit credible evidentiary documents to the authorities and there is no obligation on the authorities to verify the information submitted by the domestic industry.

Under the current system initiating an anti-dumping investigation is rather easy. For instance, in Guatemala-Mexico case of grey Portland cement, Guatemala authorities initiated the case on the basis of two invoices submitted by the domestic industry. Articles 5.2 and 5.3 must be amended to require the petitioners to supply documentation on company-wise representative price, export price, injury trends, and causal link and instruct the authorities to verify them before initiating a case.[21] This would filter a number of bogus cases at the initiation stage and at the same time reduce the burden of investigating the case also.

The EC has proposed a Swift Dispute Control Mechanism (TN/RL/W/67) to ensure that unjustified initiations are not allowed to continue. The EC's proposal includes three models: (i) fast track panels, (ii) arbitration, and (iii) a standing advisory body. The first model allows a member to request for expedited consultations and in the case of failure thereof, for establishment of a panel as soon as a violation on initiation standards is noticed. The second model offers arbitration as an alternative to panel process. The third model suggests that a standing advisory body may be constituted to give non-binding advisory opinion on the WTO legality of the initiation of an anti-dumping/CVD investigation. We shall not discuss these proposals in detail here. Nedumpara (2004) provides an excellent commentary on these models from a legal perspective. He argues that these models present a variety of issues, which often lead to lack of internal consistency with the provisions and functioning of the dispute settlement system and that a better way of dealing with this issue would be to strengthen the existing provisions on initiation under the ADA and to improve the effectiveness of judicial review by domestic courts/tribunals of such initiation decisions. Without going into legal details, we believe that this swift dispute control mechanism to deal with unjustified initiations would complicate the already very complicated system. This would lead to excessive legalization of the system. There are studies that have shown that the increasing legalization of the system has adversely affected the developing countries. Developing countries should not allow such proposals to be discussed.

Another problem relating to initiation procedures with the agreement is that it stipulates that an application must be supported by 50 per cent of the industry expressing opinion and 25 per cent of the total domestic production. The current agreement may be abused where the non-complaining firms do not express their opinion). Developed countries including Canada (TN/RL/W/47) and Australia (TN/RL/W/86) have also underscored the need to clarify the rules. It is proposed that Article 5.4 may be modified (Didier 2001) by clarifying that the application shall be considered to have been made 'by or on behalf of the domestic industry ... if the domestic industry expressing either support or opposition to the application represents more than 50 per cent of the total domestic production' (see also, FANs TN/RL/W/10). It must however also be clarified that 'domestic industry includes captive production, production for exports, and production by parties related to exporters'.

Repeated/back-to-back anti-dumping investigations in some countries on the same product originating in the same countries is an important issue particularly from a developing country point of view and warrants attention. India raised this issue in its submission (TN/RL/W/26) to the Rules Group. China (TN/RL/W/66) also supported this proposal. The EC is ready to agree to a separate provision in the draft implementation decision for making it harder for industry to bring back-to-back cases in a period of 365 days. However, we propose that there should be a separate provision in the Agreement to preclude the initiation of any investigation for a period of 365 days from the date of termination of a previous investigation on the same product from the same country.

Replying to questionnaires, some of which extend to hundreds of pages, constitutes a major burden, particularly for small and medium-sized exporters from developing countries. Hence the use of simple questionnaires is recommended. The questionnaires should be as simple as possible, focusing only on the necessary information.

Sunset Reviews

Under Article 11.3 of the WTO Agreement all anti-dumping orders are to be terminated five years after their initiation unless the authorities determine in a review that the expiry would be likely to lead to a continuation of dumping and injury. In practice however anti-dumping measures can be extended almost indefinitely. In order to demonstrate fairness and massively reduce the anti-dumping cases in force in which developing countries are mainly the targets, it is important to make this code effective. Article 11.2 states:

... Interested parties shall have the right to request ... to examine whether the continued imposition of the duty is necessary to offset dumping, whether the injury would be likely to continue or recur if the duty were removed ...

Under the current system the subject matter of the review investigation is only the likeliness of recurrence of dumping and injury. However, a WTO Panel in the US-DRAMS' from Korea case ruled,

If the only injury under examination is future injury ... the authority must necessarily be examining whether that future injury would be caused by dumping with a commensurately prospective timeframe.

Thus the panel indirectly upheld that the current system should be replaced by a requirement of a new proceeding all over again. But a new proceeding will be based on the threat of injury and can easily be manipulated. It seems important to make Article 11.3 effective. The sun should be allowed to set; only one sunset review should be permitted and the initiation of any new proceeding should be precluded for a period of 365 days. Developing countries have underlined the need for strengthening the provisions of this clause.[22] Australia in one of its submissions states that 'it does not necessarily consider that it is abuse of the sunset review system where measures have existed for long periods. Such a situation may not indicate abuses but may merely show, amongst other possibilities, that there may have been little change in circumstances and that dumping could still cause or be causing material injury'. This shows that any proposal to strengthen may face stiff competition. However it needs to be refined.

We argue that Article 11.3 could be amended by adding the following: 'the continuation of AD measures is however admissible only once, without complicating the procedures. The duty may remain in force for a maximum of 10 years. No review shall be carried out after that. If an anti-dumping duty order is terminated after completing 10 years a new application concerning the same product and country shall only be admissible after the lapse of one year'. This proposal may considerably reduce the number of measures currently in force in major industrialized countries against the developing countries.

In addition to above proposals, there have also been proposals for strengthening the panel's role by abolishing Article 17.6 (ii),[23] streamlining the procedures of various reviews,[24] dealing with circumvention,[25] abolishing non-market regime methodologies,[26] Public notices and evidence,[27] price undertaking,[28] inclusion of a public interest test,[29] and operationalization of the special and differential treatment.[30] The last two of them are discussed in detail in Chapter 7. In other word, almost every aspect of the Agreement is covered. However, these incremental improvements mare not expected to enhance the provisions of the anti-dumping and achieve the objective of restricting its use. Implementation of many of these proposed reforms would be extremely burdensome and render the resources spent on the investing a massive waste.

Some of the reforms proposed above have already been introduced in the regional context. In Interim Agreement between Slovenia and the European Communities agreed upon in 1996 for forming an FTA for future accession to the EU, both parties decided to keep the right to impose anti-dumping measures, while the following stricter conditions were added: prompt notification before initiating an investigation, prior consultations to provisional or definitive measures, and preference of price undertakings and price monitoring to anti-dumping duties.

The Agreement between New Zealand and Singapore on a Closer Economic Partnership was signed in 2000. Although both parties kept their rights to impose anti-dumping measures for intra-trade, they agreed to strengthen the rule to implement the WTO ADA in order 'to bring greater discipline to anti-dumping investigations and to minimize the opportunities to use anti-dumping in an arbitrary or protectionist manner'. (Article 9.1). The *de minimis* dumping margin is raised to 5 per cent. The maximum volume of dumped imports from the exporting party, which shall normally be regarded as negligible is increased from 3 per cent to 5 per cent of imports of the like product by the importing party. Existing cumulation provisions under Article 5.8 continue to apply. The period for review and/or termination of ADDs provided for in Article 11.3 of the WTO ADA is reduced from five to three years. The notification procedures are also strengthened (Article 9.2 of the Agreement); each party is required to inform the other party immediately following the acceptance of a properly documented application from its domestic industry for the initiation of an anti-dumping investigation.

Most of the reforms are however peripheral in nature and are not expected to have far reaching implications for restraining anti-dumping use.

CONCLUSION

What really needs to be done is to evolve fundamental principles and objectives of the tool and restrict the circumstances in which anti-dumping can be used. Numerous proposals have been offered along this line of thought. These can easily be operationalized also. This would not only reduce the number of unwarranted anti-dumping cases but would also substantially reduce the administrative burden of the investigating authorities. Unfortunately however these proposals have failed in mustering support from politicians or politically influential business houses. The reason for this lies in the political economy of reforms. The political process of formulating anti-dumping policies is influenced not just by notions of economic efficiency or fairness. Rather, it is the necessity pressures of imparting flexibility to trade policy that has driven the governments to use and support this policy. In order to be able to restrict imports under exceptional circumstances (due to political or non-political factors), governments need trade policy flexibility. Anti-dumping which is not contingent on specific circumstances, does not involve compensation and which provides ample opportunity to manipulate the investigation imparts this flexibility to trade policy. Governments are not expected to sacrifice this easily available option to regulate trade. It is therefore not surprising that these hard reform proposals have attracted severe criticism and remained unrealistic from a practical point of view. Interestingly, such resistance comes from the developed countries which are also the champions of the 'free and fair trade argument' and are policing the trade policies and their implementation in the developing countries.

Apparently, hard reforms in the ADA are unlikely to happen. Reforms of the agreement cannot wait for the member countries (in particular the United States and the EU) to agree to such proposals. Even if a hypothetical assumption that the countries agree to it is made, it would require institutional changes at the multilateral changes which would have a long-term implication. As Messerlin puts it

anti-dumping is out of control, competition policy is out of sight, and safeguard policy is out of use. But maintaining the status quo would greatly erode the GATT disciplines. Estimating correctly antidumping measures cover a substantial proportion of trade-reaching 5% of the total manufacturing trade in the case of the EU. (Messerlin 1996)

Furthermore, it seems that, at least on political grounds, anti-dumping cannot be abandoned, despite a compelling case for its elimination (except in the case of predation). The experience shows that countries are generally reluctant in relinquishing their rights to impose anti-dumping even at the regional level.

In this scenario, it is probably more realistic to acknowledge that the practical solution lies in refining the existing provisions. The broad objective of the soft proposals is that the provisions that are of a general nature should be clarified and made more precise and action oriented. Whenever possible, measurable criteria for the evaluation of the implementation of these commitments are proposed. It is believed that strengthening the disciplines of the ADA will prevent the imposition of anti-dumping measures, and will thus ensure market access improvements. While negotiating on technical details and procedural requirements however the developing countries need to be very selective. Given the difference in the level of development, it is not justifiable to make an attempt to harmonize the standards by overloading the mechanism with regulatory details. Developing countries are likely to lose in this game. Technical details and procedural requirements cannot deter developed countries from using it while developing countries would find themselves severely constrained in its use. The United States has more elaborate legal statutes than the WTO Agreement. In addition, country-level courts of appeal rulings and legislative amendments have further clarified implementation procedures over time. However this has not deterred the country from using this tool frequently. In an extensive study on the evolution of discretionary anti-dumping practices in the United States, Blonigen (2002) has shown that the rule changes due to implementation of 1995 Uruguay

Round agreements reduced the US baseline dumping margin by 20 percentage points, but greater extensive and intensive use of discretionary practices evolved in later years compensated for these Uruguay Round effects by the end of the sample in year 2000. This clearly establishes how discretionary practices can evolve substantially in a relatively short time period in these countries due to their legal expertise. Unfortunately however, most developing countries (including FANs) in their proposals are seeking finer details and elaborate procedures. They do not seem to have clear vision as to what their goals should be and how they should achieve them. Their principal objective should be to restrict the use of anti-dumping against them and not to facilitate it. They should focus on those reforms, which are likely to directly benefit them. This can be achieved through adopting appropriate decisions in regard to various proposals. Furthermore, if developing countries really want substantial gains in this round then they must press for more fundamental changes within the existing framework. Two of such proposals relate to inclusion of a public interest test and strengthening of the S&D treatment provisions. The desirability of these reforms are discussed and critically examined in Chapter 7.

Notes

1 Due to Article 12 of the Treaty of Amsterdam that came into effect in 1999, the article numbers were amended. The former Articles 85, 86, 92, and 93 were modified to the new Articles 81, 82, 87, and 88, respectively.

2 Member countries at present are Iceland, Liechtenstein, Norway, and Switzerland. The original members in 1960 were the following seven countries: Austria, Denmark, Norway, Portugal, Sweden, Switzerland, and England. Afterwards, Iceland, Finland, and Liechtenstein also joined the Association. On the other hand, England, Denmark, Portugal, Austria, Finland, and Sweden gradually withdrew to join EU.

3 * Brazil and China are also members of the FAN club.

4 Japanese Liquor Case II (1996) and Korean Liquor Taxes (1998).

5 It may be observed that Australia in its submission (TN/RL/W/44) was not convinced that any such proposal would improve the definition of like product.

6 The 'Friends of Anti-dumping Negotiations' include Brazil, Canada, Japan, Korea, Taiwan, Thailand, Singapore, Hong Kong, Mexico, Chile, Costa Rica, Israel, Norway, Switzerland, India, and Colombia,

7 See also proposals submitted by FANs (TN/RL/W/29).

8 FANs proposal (TN/RL/W/150, 16 April 2004), Canadian Proposal to The WTO (TN/RL/W/1, 28 January 2003).

9 (TN/RL/W/7) Canada (TN/RL/W/47), FANs (TN/RL/W/6, TN/W/150), Australia (TN/RL/W/86).

10 These issues have been identified in the submissions by FANs (TN/RL/W/10), China (TN/RL/W/66), Argentina (TN/RL/W/81), Australia (TN/RL/W/86), and the United States (TN/RL/W/130).

11 Detailed proposals on 'Sales to affiliated parties' are presented in document TN/RL/W/146 by FANs.

12 Several submissions emphasized reform in the provisions relating to construction of export prices. See for instance proposals submitted by FANs (TN/RL/W/10, TN/RL/W/29), China (TN/RL/W/66), Argentina (TN/RL/W/81), Australia (TN/RL/W/86).

13 The need for symmetrical adjustment was highlighted in the proposals submitted by FANs (TN/RL/W/10) and China (TN/RL/W/66).

14 Bhansali (2004a) presented at the national seminar organised by the Ministry of Commerce 22–23 September 2004.

15 My thanks to Parthasarthy (Lakshmikumaran and Shridharan firm) for making this useful point.

16 See FANs (RL/TN/W/158). The United States also seeks clarification on this matter in its submission (TN/RL/W/72).

17 Proposals from China (TN/RL/W/66), India (TN/RL/W/26), Canada (TN/RL/W/1), EU and Japan (TN/RL/W/138), FANs (TN/RL/W/10), US (TN/RL/W/130) highlighted the need to reform provisions of injury determination.

18 The mose recent ones include those submitted by the FANs: TN/RL/W/119 (16 June 2003), TN/RL/GEN/1 (14 July 2004); the US: TN/RL/GEN/43 (13 May 2005), TN/RL/GEN/43 (13 May 2005); India: TN/RL/W/170 (9 February 2005), TN/RL/GEN/32 (22 March 2005); and Brazil: TN/RL/GEN/58 (13 July 2005) and (TN/RL/W/189).

19 Details are provided in the next section.

20 Need for reforms has been highlighted in various proposals from FANs (TN/RL/W/6), India (TN/RL/W/26), and China (TN/RL/W/66), but no specific proposals have been made.

21 Proposals that seek to introduce these reforms include: TN/RL/W/10, TN/RL/W/48, TN/RL/W/1, TN/RL/W/86, TN/RL/W/47.

22 The proposals include those by Korea (TN/RL/W/111), India (TN/RL/W/26), China (TN/RL/W/66), Egypt (TN/RL/W/110), FANs (TN/RL/W/83).

23 TN/RL/W/130. Surprisingly very few proposals have addressed the issue of Article 17.6 (ii).

24 TN/RL/W/10, TN/RL/W/7, TN/RL/W/1, TN/RL/W/86, TN/RL/W/138, TN/RL/W/156.

25 TN/RL/W/205/Rev1, TN/RL/W/205, TN/RL/W/50, TN/RL/W/110.

26 Despite an intense debate in the literature on the issue of Non-market Economy Treatment Provisions, few proposals cover this issue. China has touched upon this issue in its submission TN/RL/W/66.

27 TN/RL/W/29, TN/RL/W/46, TN/RL/W/35, TN/RL/W/132, TN/RL/W/47.

28 TN/RL/W/118.

29 TN/RL/W/174, TN/RL/W/194, TN/RL/W/47, TN/RL/W/13, TN/RL/W/47.

30 TN/RL/W/13, TN/RL/W/26, TN/RL/W/36, TN/RL/W/46.

7 Effectual Reforms for Reining in Anti-dumping Use

A Perspective

One possible reform in the ADA while preserving the basic concepts and principles lies in making the assessment of public interest mandatory. Anti-dumping decisions should be based on an evaluation of the potential future impact of adopting or not adopting measures not only on producers but also on final consumers, and related industries. At present, the consideration of producer interests dominates the rationale for anti-dumping laws and there is nothing to indicate that there is an interface between import-competing interests and the interests of wider society. Many believe that a significant progress in strengthening the agreement can be made by including a genuine public interest clause. A number of negotiating proposals on anti-dumping submitted to the WTO have covered the 'public interest' issue and have advocated the inclusion of a public interest test in this Agreement. However few have suggested the modalities to do so.[1] Part I of this chapter addresses the question: Should this clause be introduced in the ADA, and if yes, in what form? Analysis in this chapter suggests that although there is a strong case for a public interest clause and modalities of incorporating such a test are also possible, yet developing countries need not focus on this proposal during this round of negotiations.

Part II of the chapter focuses on another substantive legal provision, that is S&D Treatment. The term S&D treatment refers to GATT rights and privileges given to developing countries but not extended to developed countries. The concept of S&D treatment in the GATT evolved from debates in the 1960s as to how the growth and development of developing countries was best facilitated by trade rules. The term itself derived from a reference in the 1973 Tokyo Round Declaration, which recognized the importance of the application of differential measures in developing countries in ways that will provide special and more favourable treatment for them in areas of negotiation where this is feasible. Its inclusion in GATT reflects a long history of calls by developing countries for special treatment in global trade arrangements. This chapter looks at the S&D treatment from a historical perspective, discusses the rationale of operationalizing its provisions in this Agreement, and finally offers proposals to operationalize it.

PART I: ADDING A PUBLIC INTEREST CLAUSE

This part has five sections. The first section outlines the theoretical justification for including public interest clause in the ADA. The second section describes the current status. The third section provides methodologies to incorporate this clause within the ADA. The fourth section discusses whether a public interest clause will make any difference to anti-dumping decisions while the penultimate section addresses a question whether it is appropriate for the developing countries to push for this amendment.

Theoretical Justification for Inclusion of a Public Interest Clause in the ADA

Dumping affects the interest of domestic producers adversely. They therefore make an appeal to the government for protecting them from the 'unfair trade practices' of foreign firms. Although it is not stated, the primary objective of the anti-dumping legislation is to protect these producers from injury caused by imports of the dumped goods (Chapter 5). However, there is no one-to-one relationship between dumping and the welfare of the importing economy. Even if domestic producers are harmed by allegedly dumped imports, other domestic interests, namely, downstream import-using industries and consumers, are benefited by them. This latter group has a conflict of interest with the former in this regard. The overall effects of an anti-dumping measure is therefore ambiguous. If it benefits some segments of the economy, it may have adverse effects on others. It may in fact impose a number of costs on the domestic economy by adversely affecting its price structure and creating difficulty for downstream industries to obtain the supplies they need. USITC (1995) and Gallaway et al. (1999) examined the net aggregate effects of all US anti-dumping/CVD orders for 1991 and 1993 respectively using a computable general equilibrium model. While the USITC estimated the loss at $1.6 billion, the latter found that the welfare loss ranged from $2 to $4 billion annually. An anti-dumping law with no public-interest provision fails to take account of the costs resulting from conflicting interests of different segments of the economy. The objective of a public-interest clause is to ensure that investigating authorities consider anti-dumping complaints in a wider context, taking into account not the interests of the affected domestic industry, but also the costs of the anti-dumping intervention to the national economy.

There is thus, a clear justification for imposing duties only when there is a net gain, that is when producer gain from such duties exceeds consumer loss.

According to Finger and Zlate (2003) the national economic interest is the simple sum of all the private economic interests in the national economy. A country's anti-dumping policy can therefore be reconciled with its larger national interests only when all economic interests are taken into account. Here a properly devised and effectively implemented public-interest test would help. Incorporation of a public interest test could serve as a filter that will distinguish those where the consequences of action are more favourable than not acting from those where the net benefits are negative.

Adding a public interest clause would also lead to compromise between the political and the economic perspective. Economists stress efficiency and are reluctant to acknowledge that producers have rights other than those associated with maximizing efficiency. Economic theory that is built up around the notion of efficiency as an objective, views it as the key to protect competition. Through defining efficiency in terms of consumer welfare, the economic justification for anti-dumping laws that they offer is that these laws protect the competitive process and the consumer from monopoly power of the foreign exporters. They rule out the protection of domestic producer interests *per se* as a primary economic justification for the anti-dumping remedies. This theory argues that the central goal of any competition policy is the promotion of consumer welfare. On the other hand, politicians would argue that the domestic industry is legally entitled to protection against 'unfair' behaviour by foreign firms that results due to an asymmetric market position created artificially by government policies giving them an unfairly deep pocket and puts domestic players at a disadvantage. The central goal of the anti-dumping policy according to them is the protection of producers' interests. Inclusion of a public interest clause would bring about reconciliation between the two approaches and would make promotion of national interests as the main goal of the anti-dumping policy. The objective of both the approaches is to ensure that the economy is affected positively as a result of interventionist policy. The ultimate debate in anti-dumping therefore is whether the overall benefits to the economy of applying measures outweigh the effects of not doing so. Even though much of the literature focuses on the circumstances that lead to dumping, in spirits, it is concerned with the overall effects on the economy. This was the approach that was adopted by Viner in early economic writings (Chapter 5). Instead of ensuring that anti-dumping is response to certain types of dumping, one may therefore analyse the overall effects of anti-dumping. Adding a public interest clause could thus be a major step towards reforming the agreement.

In addition to the economic theory/political perspective, there is an ethical perspective to anti-dumping also. Ethical perspective of anti-dumping actions is generally ignored. From this perspective, a policy is good if the majority benefits, even if someone's rights are violated along the way. Anti-dumping actions address the interests of the domestic producers only. If the requisite findings of dumping and injury are made, anti-dumping remedies for the import-competing producers follow automatically—regardless of the consequences for the other interested parties. The parties who lose from the anti-dumping protection are marginalized in the system. This is not a rational policymaking. If major affected interests are systematically ignored in the decision-making process, the policy will result in protecting the interests of import-competing domestic producers at the expense of all other interested parties. A public interest clause in a revised ADA could serve as a means of access to socio-economic justice for these adversely affected parties. It is thought to be a way of balancing producer interests with consumer (consumers of the product) interests.

Furthermore, adding a public interest clause would also impose due restraint in the application of anti-dumping measures. Such restrictions on anti-dumping rules are extremely important because the impact of anti-dumping measures on trade is significant and because these measures are likely to spread with increases in trade volume and direct investment. Expanding the power of multiple stakeholders to affect the outcome of anti-dumping investigation proceedings may exert some discipline over the application of this agreement.

Finally, incorporating a public-interest test is also consistent from the legal perspective. Though the present agreement does not require any kind of explicit public-interest test, it does indicate that it is desirable. In that regard, Article 7.1 of the current agreement states 'It is desirable that the imposition [of duties] be permissive in the territory of all Members'. This clearly captures the essence of the Agreement.

One may therefore suggest that there is a strong case to establish a 'Public Interest Clause' in the strengthened anti-dumping rules. Even if discretionary in nature, it provides for a wider and more complete analysis of the situation in the domestic importing market. It can help in reconciling a country's anti-dumping policy with its larger national interests. This is necessary not only as a matter of sound economics but also as a matter of justice. A properly devised public interest test with appropriate substantive provisions could prove to be useful in reforming this highly criticized (see for instance Lindsey and Dan Ikenson 2002a) trade defensive measure.

The public interest clause is not a completely new concept because it exists in some National Anti-dumping Legislations. It should not therefore be difficult to address various elements of a 'public interest' test and translate the concept into concrete anti-dumping rules.

PUBLIC INTEREST CLAUSE: THE CURRENT STATUS

The current ADA imposes no substantive obligation on the authorities to take the broader public interest into account. Article 6.1 of the ADA requires that notice of an investigation be given to all interested parties. It reads as follows:

All interested parties in an antidumping investigation shall be given notice of the information which the authorities require and ample opportunity to present in writing all evidence which they consider relevant in respect of the investigation in the question.

Article 6.11 defines the term ' interested parties' for the purpose of this Agreement. It speaks for the inclusion of

(i) an exporter or foreign producer or the importer of a product subject to investigation, or a trade or business association a majority of the members of which are producers, exporters or importers of such product. The Government of the exporting Member; and
(ii) a producer of the like product in the importing Member or a trade or business association a majority of the members of which produce the like product in the territory of the importing Member

in 'interested parties'. The term thus includes not only the exporters and domestic producers but also the importers of the product under investigation who are likely to be adversely affected by anti-dumping actions. Article 6.11 goes on to state:

This list does not preclude Members from allowing domestic or foreign parties other than those mentioned above to be included as interested parties.

The Agreement thus allows member states to add to the list. Furthermore, Article 6.2 of the Agreement provides that throughout an anti-dumping investigation, all 'interested parties' shall have a full opportunity to defend their interests. It states:

Throughout the anti-dumping investigation all interested parties shall have a full opportunity for the defence of their interests. To this end, the authorities shall on request provide opportunities for all interested parties to meet those parties with adverse interests so that opposing views may be presented and rebuttal arguments offered.....

Nonetheless, the Agreement does not contain any provision that requires that this input be given any weight in actually making determinations or assessing duties.

The Agreement also requires national authorities to provide opportunities for industrial users of the good subject to investigation and representative consumer organizations to provide relevant information during investigations. But this is limited to the cases where the product is commonly sold at the retail level. Article 6.12 of the Agreement reads as follows.

The authorities shall provide opportunity for industrial users of the product under investigation and for representative consumer organisations in cases where the product is commonly sold at the retail level to provide information, which is relevant to the investigation regarding dumping, injury and causality.

There is no provision in the agreement that places an obligation on the national investigating authority to act in accordance with the information so supplied.

Clearly, the adversely affected parties (including importers, downstream and upstream industrial users, and consumers) have no rights but merely privileges and investigating authorities conducting an anti-dumping action are not obliged to take their views seriously. Thus, anti-dumping duties may be imposed even if they are contrary to the public interest. Indeed, some countries including the EU, Canada, Brazil, Paraguay, Singapore, Thailand, and Malaysia have 'public interest test' provisions.[2] China has also introduced the concept of the public interest as a basis for imposing anti-dumping measures in its new anti-dumping legislation, which has become effective on 1 June 2004. Most other countries however impose duties without consideration of the public interest whenever the investigation finds the presence of dumping and injury.

SUGGESTIONS

There is no doubt that anti-dumping policy around the world would be greatly improved by mandating the inclusion of a public-interest test. The inclusion of provisions on public interest in the ADA was raised in several papers submitted by the developing countries.[3] For incorporating this clause in the current Agreement, the following are the principal changes to anti-dumping disciplines that we suggest for future negotiations.

Amend the Agreement to Make Public Interest Considerations Mandatory

The Agreement needs to be amended to require that members consider the public interest in initiating anti-dumping cases and in assessing final duties in cases where interested parties make submissions to this effect. In other words, this test should be applied both at the beginning of the procedure before initiation of an AD case, and also at the end of a case before duties are applied for the domestic industry. Procedures can be established to provide that investigating authorities take into account the views of these said groups before reaching a decision to initiate an anti-dumping investigation and imposing the duty.

In practice, public interest investigations (wherever mandatory) are generally *post hoc*. These are held only after ADDs are applied. The point is to determine whether there are public interest considerations that, as a matter of policy, warrant a reduction or elimination of those duties. However, as suggested in the previous chapters, anti-dumping investigations have the 'harassment' effect. It is therefore important to discourage the initiation of anti-dumping cases in the first place by making the filing conditions more stringent. Articles 5 of the ADA may therefore be revised to require the application of a public-interest test before anti-dumping investigations are initiated. Furthermore, Article 5.8 may require the authorities to reject the application and terminate investigations if there is evidence that it would not be in the public interest. Article 5.8 in the current Agreement states;

An application ... shall be rejected and an investigation shall be terminated promptly as soon as the authorities concerned are satisfied that there is not sufficient evidence of either dumping or injury....

Add to this a new line,

An investigation shall not be initiated if the authorities are satisfied that it is not in the public interest to impose such measures.

In Singapore, the anti-dumping legislation requires the authority (The Minister of Trade and Industry) to consider the 'public interest' factor before initiating an investigation (see Hsu 1998 also). Once a petition is received, the authority (the Minister of Trade and Industry) is directed to see if there is sufficient evidence to warrant an investigation into whether the elements necessary for the imposition of an anti-dumping duty ... under Section 14(1) exists' and whether *such an investigation is in the public interest*. If the minister determines that there is such evidence and that an investigation is in the public interest, Section 19(5) requires that he publish a notice of initiation of investigation. A unique feature of this Act therefore is the inclusion of 'public interest' as a criterion for making decision whether to initiate an investigation.

A public interest clause may also be made applicable at the end of a case before imposing the measures by adding to Article 9 a new paragraph:

In deciding on whether or not to apply definitive anti-dumping measures and on the extent and level of such measures the investigating authority shall consider whether anti-dumping measures would be in the public interest.

Extend the Definition of Interested Parties

The class of persons defined by the ADA as interested parties with rights to defend their interests in anti-dumping hearings, to present oral evidence, receive oral information given during a hearing, and see all non-confidential information relevant to the presentation of their cases, may be expanded to include industrial users and representatives of consumer organizations. Under the current rules, representatives of consumer organizations and industrial users can be defined as 'interested parties' only if the authority conducting an investigation extends this privilege to them and they are to provide information only in cases where the product under investigation is 'commonly sold at the retail level'. Widening the access to anti-dumping investigations so as to allow consumer organizations to influence decision-making, irrespective of the nature of the product, will most probably serve to restrain national authorities from disregarding citizen's interests. This would also encourage more active participation by downstream users and consumers who would be hurt by the dumping duties.

Regulations developed under the 'Special Import Measures Act' (SIMA) in Canada already define 'interested parties' to include all industrial users and consumer organizations. In the 'EU anti-dumping legislation' however the scope of their participation is limited in only those anti-dumping cases, which involve finished consumer products. The 'Bureau of the Consumers of the EU' protests about the restrictive nature of the Commission's guidelines, which limit the scope of its participation (Tharakan et al. 1998). Since such investigations are few and far in between, this discourages capacity building in these organizations to face such investigations and discourages them to participate even in those cases where they are invited. Since the scope of participation in the anti-dumping cases is limited in the EU, these cases are a low priority for the consumer organizations. These organizations also have constraints in terms of material and human resources. Such problems however may be sorted out if they build up some capacity due to participation pressures in the anti-dumping investigations.

Widening the coverage of 'interested parties' may also encourage lobbyists/lawyers to organize the users/consumers into an effective political force. There is an untapped client base here. Trade lawyers will recognize the business opportunity that adding users as interested parties would provide and will develop this market in a similar way as they developed a market among protection users and subsequently among foreign exporters.

Specify the Criteria for 'Public Interest'

The criteria for public interest may be articulated more clearly and in a broader sense. The term 'public interest' may receive the same treatment as does the term 'injury'. Anti-dumping provisions state that injury is caused if domestic competing interests are harmed as a result of a range of factors. The same procedure could be applied to public interest to serve as notice that protection from dumped goods should not be taken for granted. This would require inclusion of a provision of investigations into public interest that would be parallel to that already there for the 'injury' investigation. For this, a non-exhaustive list of factors be included that would guide the authorities whether and how to conduct a public interest inquiry.

The Anti-dumping Legislation of Canada, which has a unique feature of explicit public interest inquiries, may provide guidance in this context and is therefore studies in detail there. Until recently, SIMA provided no guidance to the Tribunal (CITT) about the issues that were relevant to the determination as to what constituted the public interest. Amendments introduced in SIMA in 2000 prescribed in Paragraph 40.1(3) (b) of the *Special Import Measures Regulations* factors that the Tribunal may consider in the public interest inquiries. It provides a list of factors that could be considered by the Tribunal in a public interest inquiry. It also clarifies that 'In their submissions and replies, parties should address all the factors that they consider relevant in assisting the Tribunal to arrive at its opinion.' And that, the Tribunal will take into account any factors that it considers relevant'. The list of factors is thus non-exhaustive in nature.

. Factors that form a test for public interest in Canada include:

- whether goods of the same description are readily available from countries or exporters to which the order or finding does not apply;
- whether imposition of the full duties has had or is likely to have the following effects:
  - substantially lessen competition in the domestic market in respect of like goods,
  - cause significant damage to producers in Canada that use the goods as inputs in the production of other goods and in the provision of services,
  - significantly impair competitiveness by limiting access to:
    goods that are used as inputs in the production of other goods and in the provision of services, or technology, and
  - significantly restrict the choice or availability of goods at competitive prices for consumers or otherwise cause them significant harm;

- whether a reduction or elimination of the antidumping or countervailing duty is likely to cause significant damage to domestic producers of inputs, including primary commodities, used in the domestic production of like goods; and
- any other factors that are relevant in the circumstances.

Scholars however argue that this language is not as clear as the term 'injury'. Emphasis on the words such as 'significant' and 'substantial' may severely limit the effect of the public interest provision. Far from improving consumers' lot, the wordings used in the text might actually increase the threshold needed before anti-dumping duties are reduced (Leclerc 1999). It is therefore important to place the term in a framework along the similar lines as injury. It may state that

In conducting a public interest inquiry, the authorities shall include all relevant factors including damage to downstream users, problems of access to inputs, price rise, impact on choice or availability of products to consumers, impact on short-term and long-term competition in the marketplace, effects on employment, effects on public health.... This list is not exhaustive.

The impact of the ADD on users/consumers would be measured in just the same way as 'injury test' procedures are used to measure the impact that import competition has on the protection seeker: jobs lost because of higher costs, lower profits, idled capacity, and so on. All interested parties may be given the same rights and opportunities in this part of the investigation as in the 'injury' part.

Establish Procedures for Balancing the Interests of Consumers (Including Industrial Users) and Domestic Industries

Having determined the impact of the above factors on public interest, the authorities may be required to weigh up all the positive and negative consequences for both the complainants and the rest of the economy as a whole and decide whether it is in the overall interest of the economy to use these measures. Where the costs and benefits of imposing punitive import duties are clearly and substantially out of balance, national authorities should be able to prevent real damage to the economy. In other words, they must ensure that the negative impact of the proposed duty on the Community as a whole should not be disproportionate to the objectives of giving protection to the domestic industry against unfair trade practices of the exporters. This test may be applied both before reaching a decision to initiate an anti-dumping investigation and before imposing the duty.

Procedures for pre-initiation 'public interest' review

The investigating authorities could, first of all, examine the competitive behaviour of the domestic producers who are petitioning for the anti-dumping measures and determine whether these producers were engaged in restrictive business practices and enjoying undue market domination and setting price cartels. If they were, anti-dumping petitions from such 'anti-competitive' industries should be rejected as the anti-dumping measure would only reinforce the companies' market dominance in the importing country in an undesirable manner through raising prices and limiting competition from imports. For this, the authorities may seek advice of the National Competition Boards. Investigating authorities may also invite views/arguments of the adversely affected groups on whether the initiation of an anti-dumping investigation would have a significant impact on employment, prices and supply that would affect the national welfare significantly. These views would assist the authorities in forming an opinion about whether such an investigation is in the public interest.

This procedure should not be difficult for the authorities to follow. Procedures followed in public interest inquiries in Canada may set standards for a pre-initiation public interest inquiry also. Though public interest inquiries in Canada are *post hoc,* they involve two phases: one, the *commencement phase* and two, the *investigation phase.* In the commencement phase the Tribunal decides whether there are reasonable grounds to commence a public test inquiry. It invites requests for a public interest inquiry. Such requests may be made by any party affected by the injury findings within forty-five days of the injury finding. A copy of the request is made available on the Tribunal website for getting responses. Within ten days after the deadline for responses, the Tribunal decides whether there are reasonable grounds to believe that the imposition of the duties might not be in the public interest. If it decides that these grounds exist it issues a notice of commencement of public interest inquiry. The investigation phase then follows.

The procedures followed in the commencement phase in Canada could be followed before initiating an anti-dumping investigation. This would also serve the objective of making initiation conditions more stringent.

Procedures for post-hoc public interest inquiries

The existence of a disproportionate impact in this case could be measured in a number of ways. For example, the estimated welfare gain for the petitioning industry could be compared with the estimated welfare loss for specific downstream industries or for consumers. If the loss is some designated multiple of the gain, the impact would be deemed disproportionate and duties would not be imposed. One suggestion is that the cost-benefit comparisons could be made with the use of fairly basic techniques of quantitative economic analysis. This approach involves the following steps (Homes and Kempton 1997):

- estimation of all the quantifiable impacts on prices, outputs, risk, jobs, environmental impact, etc.;
- quantification of non-quantifiable variables by assigning positive and negative values to them; and
- adding up all pluses and minuses to obtain the net affect.

These impacts are measured in whatever units they occur

The Cost Benefit Analysis (CBA) approach was used by the USITC in its 1995 report and the FTC (1994) report which shows that it is feasible at least retrospectively as a tool of policy evaluation. However, we believe that formal CBA which can produce a net benefit or cost type figure cannot easily be used prospectively for various reasons, most notably the problems of quantifying non quantifiable variables which makes it subject to manipulations.

Alternative solution therefore is that the authorities could consider whether imposing duties in certain cases would undermine the national economic interest. The calculation of public interest should be carried out by enumerating all of the potential consequences of the dumping and any measures. They may weigh the costs and benefits of imposing anti-dumping measures subjectively and where they reach the conclusion that the two are out of balance, they may reverse the decision of imposing such measures. Relatively easy to administer, such a public interest test would have real teeth while still giving wide scope for the use of antidumping measures.

WILL THE PROPOSED PROCEDURES BE EFFECTIVE?

Whether the proposed procedures will make any difference to antidumping decisions is unclear. A number of issues have been raised in that context. In what follows, we examine some of them.

First, some scholars argue that there is an in-built contradiction between the ADA in its current form and the inclusion of a public interest test. They believe that inclusion of a public interest test would require anti-dumping rules to reinforce the concept that anti-dumping systems should not operate to give protection to domestic producers against normal price competition and that dumping practices are deemed to exist only in the cases of 'unfair' pricing practices (i.e., aggressive and injurious pricing). Unless this assumption is made central to the antidumping investigations, inclusion of public interest cannot be successful. But this would require reformulation of the current WTO definition of dumping so as to cover only unfair dumping. They argue that serious objections to any such efforts will come up. Despite the urgings from economists during the Uruguay Round, the WTO ADA does not provide for a 'public interest' clause and does not even include consumers, central to any national interest inquiry, among 'interested parties' for purposes of anti-dumping investigations. Presumably, it was considered that an overly broad interpretation of the public interest rule that would give equal consideration to consumer welfare interests would make *the agreement* ineffective. Any attempt to include the provision for public interest test that would balance the consumers' interest against the producers' interest may not therefore be successful. The Canadian International Trade Tribunal (CITT) regularly turned down requests for these kinds of public interest investigations since this feature was first introduced in Canadian Law 1994 (Leclerc 1999).

During the Grain Corn 77 inquiry, the CITT held that consumer interests are not balanced against producer interests as a matter of course; for consumer interests to be considered, 'compelling or special circumstances' must exist. In subsequent public interest inquiries, CITT continued to express this view. The director of competition intervened in several cases heard by the Tribunal. However, it appears that in most cases in which the director intervened, the Tribunal still imposed anti-dumping duties. In Caps, Lids, and Jars[4] case, the CITT of Canada heard strong representations from the Competition Bureau regarding the consumer impact of reduced competition resulting from anti-dumping duties. However, the Tribunal rejected the notion that consumer interests and competition policy issues must take precedence over the protection from dumping afforded by SIMA to the domestic producers. Interestingly, while refuting any possibility of elimination of competition, the Tribunal agreed that there was no danger of the domestic company gaining a monopoly hold on the market; foreign competitors were healthy, and consumers could switch to alternative methods of canning if monopoly prices were charged. This raised an important question: why, if a domestic producer would find it difficult to establish a monopoly, would it be any less difficult for a foreign producer to do so?

In the Preformed Fibreglass Insulation public interest inquiry the Tribunal acknowledged that there were no readily available substitutes for the goods, and that there was 'little likelihood of competition from the subject goods produced in countries other than the United States [that is, the country potentially subject to the anti-dumping duties].' The Tribunal also recognized that the price of domestic goods would rise if ADDs were imposed. However, it rejected the suggestion that ADDs should not be imposed simply because it was likely to result in price rise. While reacting on the expected elimination of competition, the Tribunal took the position that it is the director's responsibility to oversee any anti-competitive conduct. Apparently, protecting consumer interests has not been the motive for using anti-dumping action. It will therefore likely be politically unacceptable (Krishna 1997).

Second, it is also argued that the public interest test is not effective even in the countries (such as the EU and Canada) that follow this test (Krishna 1997). The public interest provision in Canada was enacted in 1994 at the suggestion of the Consumers' Association of Canada and followed a House of Commons Report, which found that 'concentration on producer interests was too narrow a focus and the consumer interest must be considered.' An examination of the CITTs anti-dumping cases however shows that the provision has been used infrequently, and that when it is used, ADDs are seldom reduced. Between 1994 and 2000, 315 anti-dumping cases were initiated in Canada. Of these, 216 resulted in final measures. Over the same period however, only eleven public interest inquiries were initiated, of which four resulted in duty reduction.[5] EU experience is not convincing either. The pre-Uruguay Round EU anti-dumping regulation already contained a Community interest clause, which was strengthened after the Uruguay round. However, to the best of our knowledge, 'public interest' investigation affected the Commission's decision in only one case[6] till date. Examination of the community interest in twenty recent antidumping investigations by NBT (2005) found that in only two cases the product represented a small cost for consumers. The study revealed that the commissions investigations did not contain any calculation of the total costs for the community of imposed measure and benefits for the community industry. The argumentation follows the remarks made by those interested parties who have made themselves known during the investigation. In Singapore, the anti-dumping legislation requires the authority to consider the 'public interest' factor before initiating an investigation. Hsu (1998) did not find it effective in preventing the authority from initiating a case.

Recent developments however, are encouraging. In some recent decisions the CITT appears to have taken a more liberal approach to public interest issues and has accepted public advocacy and consumer concerns, recommending that the federal government reduce anti-dumping duties to less than the full amount. During 1999–2004, four inquiries were conducted. Two of them resulted in duty reduction. In the Prepared Baby Food Case and the Contrast media case the Tribunals could not set aside the emotionally compelling issues of public health in favour of corporate interest and reduced the original duties. In both of them, therefore, public heath concerns emerged as the main objective. In each case, the Tribunal considered a range of factors bearing on public health and welfare that it assessed as paramount. In Contrast Media, the factors included: price effects of ADDs on imaging product, availability of choice to radiologists, issues of supply to hospitals, competition factors related to the fact that there was a single Canadian producer, and availability of alternate sources of supply. The driving consideration was that the product was essential to radiographic imaging and was a case where price and availability would have a direct impact on the health and well-being of Canadians. In the Prepared Baby Food case, price was a concern of virtually every witness and submission. The Tribunal expressed concern that a lack of competition would result in prices rising unduly and that the higher prices would affect low-income families and infant health adversely. These cases appear to have expanded the public interest concept and have set certain standards for future. They indicate that the issue of contradiction may be tackled effectively by the national authorities by maintaining a balance between the two and that inclusion of a public interest test may not require full harmonization of the anti-dumping mechanism with competition policy rules but rather only a certain degree of compatibility. One may suggest here, for instance, that reduction in competition in itself may not be a sufficient condition for a public interest test. Rather, the impact of reduction in competition on the public interest may become an important consideration. In the Caps, Jars, and Lids case, the CITT was of the opinion that even if monopoly prices were charged, purchases of caps, lids and jars accounted for only a small proportion of overall consumer expenditures. Reduction in the level of competition thus was of little significance. On the other hand, in the contrast media case, the impact of increased prices, even for a relatively small volume of product, would have been significant on hospital budgets and ultimately on service to patients. This would also lead to a shift away from LOCM (low-osmolality contrast media) procedures by hospital to HOCM (high-osmolality contrast media) which have more serious side effects on patients. Thus the price rise and elimination of competition would have had serious implications for the public interest in the contrast media case.

There is thus a case of the inclusion of a public interest clause in the ADA. Theoretically it will reconcile different perspectives on anti-dumping. Operationally, it is feasible. From a practical point of view, it will raise anti-dumping standards without introducing substantive amendments in the basic principles of the agreement or undermining the fundamental intent and enforcement of the agreement.

PUBLIC INTEREST CLAUSE AND DEVELOPING COUNTRIES

From a developing country perspective, the inclusion of a 'public interest' clause in the legislation would add to the uncertainty of the proceedings and administrative complexity and would increase cost of investigation to the parties and the government (see Banks 1993 for the Australian experience). It will also be time-consuming. The length of time between the commencement of an investigation and actual relief can be rather long. ADDs apply during the entire period from the time of the preliminary determination through to the completion of the final findings. If the time for the holding of a public interest hearing is added to the issuance of the final recommendation, substantial time will have elapsed during which ADDs in one form or another are in effect and before any recommendation as to the public interest is made.

One way to sort this out would be to examine the public interest before initiating an investigation. But this would immensely increase the administrative burden perhaps with a little gain especially in developing countries. It is because a strengthened public interest clause does not necessarily mean that consumers' organizations will play an important role in anti-dumping cases. Even in the developed countries there are instances where timely response from consumer organization could prevent anti-dumping duty imposition but it could not happen (Tharakan et al. 1998). In the 'Personal Fax Machine' case, for instance, the 'Bureau of the Consumers of the EU' was invited by the Commission to participate but it did not make any submission. Tharakan (1999) argued that the refusal of the Bureau to defend the consumers' interest tilted the scale in favour of the domestic industry. In developing countries this problem may be even more serious due to lack of financial resources and capacity and more importantly due to lack of consumer movements/awareness.

Is Lesser Duty Rule an Alternative to the Public Interest Clause?

A soft option to ensure public interest is to make the lesser duty law mandatory. It is argued that the lesser duty concept appears to be a worthwhile change that will, if nothing else, at least alleviate some of the harm caused to consumers by the imposition of ADDs. This is not a mandatory provision of the WTO ADA. The current agreement states that 'it is *desirable* that the imposition of the duty be less than the margin [of dumping], if such lesser duty would be adequate to remove injury to the domestic industry'. Member countries use wide discretion in this matter as well. While in Mexico, Brazil, Argentina, and India this rule is not mandatory, the EU statue has made this rule mandatory. In the United States and Canada, on the other hand, anti-dumping duty equivalent to the dumping margin is imposed. While examining the effectiveness of the lesser duty rule, we analysed the duty structure of the United States and the EU in a comparative framework (Chapter 3). We found that the distribution of anti-dumping duty imposed against Indian exporters in the EU is more highly skewed than that in the United States. Apparently the lesser duty rule in the EU is not very effective. A part of the explanation lies in the fact that the calculation of the extent of injury itself is subject to several ambiguities. The more inefficient the domestic industry the greater is the likelihood of higher injury margins. The system thus protects inefficiency. The lesser duty rule is likely to be ineffective unless there is an unambiguous methodology of calculating injury elimination level.

In sum, inclusion of a public interest clause in the Agreement may prove to be highly effective in balancing the interests of the domestic producers and the interests of consumers. From the perspective of developing countries however, it will add to administrative complexities, cost, time involved, and uncertainty. This may worsen an already adverse position of these countries in regard to this agreement. Developing countries should therefore be cautious in pressing for this reform.

PART II: SPECIAL AND DIFFERENTIAL TREATMENT IN THE ANTI-DUMPING AGREEMENT: HOW TO MAKE IT DIFFERENTIAL

The S&D treatment was incorporated in the ADA during the Tokyo Round. In the Tokyo Round (1973–9), developing country activities were largely aimed at formalizing and codifying S&D treatment. The principal result of the Tokyo Round was the 'Enabling Clause' of 1979. The clause established the principle of differential and more favourable treatment to developing countries. It stipulates 'Notwithstanding the provisions of Article I of the General Agreement, contracting parties may accord differential and more favourable treatment to developing countries, without according such treatment to other contracting parties'.[7]

According to Fritz (2005) S&D treatment is the result of the long-standing struggle of developing countries for a more equitable world economic order. The journey from GATT 1947, which made no concession for developing countries to the enabling clause may be summarized as under.

- During the ITO negotiations (November 1947 and March 1948) the developing countries managed to introduce an additional clause in the Havana Charter which allowed them to apply national protection measures to support 'economic development and reconstruction' on industry and agriculture.
- In 1948, this clause was introduced into GATT 1947 as Article 18 via an amendment (see Chapter 3). Concessions with regard to import restrictions

due to concerns about industrial development and balance of payments were however ineffective in providing market access and stabilization of the raw materials prices.

- In 1964, developing countries lobbied to establish a new organization within the UN system: UNCTAD which is exclusively dedicated to trade and development.
- In the same year, a new Part IV dealing with trade and development and encompassing Articles 36 and 37 were introduced into GATT (Chapter 3 endnote 7).
- In 1968, at an UNCTAD conference in New Delhi, the USA followed by other industrialized countries agreed to the introduction of the generalized System of Preferences (GSP) on voluntary basis.
- In 1971, the GATT contracting parties granted the GSP a so-called waiver, an exception to the Most-Favoured-Nation Treatment, limited to ten years (Chapter 3 endnote 7).
- In 1979, finally, the enabling code was incorporated in the Tokyo Round.

Most agreements negotiated during the Tokyo Round included special provisions in favour of developing countries. Incorporation of Article 13 in the ADA in the Tokyo Round was a part of these broad developments taking place at that time.

Its wordings were as follows.

It is recognised that special regard must be given by developed country Members to the special situation of developing country Members when considering the application of AD measures under this Agreement. Possibilities of constructive remedies provided for by this agreement shall be explored before applying antidumping duties where they would affect the essential interests of developing country Members.

These wordings were general and were taken directly from Article 37C of Part IV incorporated in the GATT, the objective of which was to lay broad framework to provide differential treatment to developing country members. It did not provide any guidance as to how the developed countries could give special treatment to these members in specific agreements. Most agreements encompassed their own S&D treatment clauses with detailed provisions. The ADA was also given its own S&D treatment clause but this does not move beyond the general framework. Even though the provision was ad hoc in formalization, developing countries readily accepted it.

The declaration launching the Uruguay Round contained a clear and unequivocal reaffirmation of special and differential treatment as a principle of the trading system. It had become a part of the system of trade rules. While negotiating on complex WTO disciplines, developing countries sought comforts in this provision. The final provisions contain multiple elaborations on the earlier (Tokyo Round) notions of special and differential treatment. However, in the ADA no efforts were made to ensure that this provision is effectively implemented. There was no elaborations of the S&D treatment provisions provided in Article 13 of the Tokyo Round agreement, now enshrined in Article 15 in the WTO ADA. Its wordings remained exactly the same.

Article 15 requires developed countries to give special regard to the situation of developing countries when considering the application of anti-dumping measures but does not make any specific provision for addressing how they should do it. It is therefore not surprising that the developing country members are of the view that developed members do not comply with Article 15 when imposing anti-dumping duties (G/ADP/W/416 dated 8 November 2000, G/ADP/M/15 dated 14 March 2000, G/ADP/M/16 dated 20 September 2000, G/ADP/M/17 dated 9 April 2001, G/ADP/M/18 dated 21 November 2001). This issue was raised in the anti-dumping dispute cases also. But the panels' ruling could not provide any guidance as to how to operationalize this article.

The panel in European Communities—Anti-dumping Duties on Imports of Cotton-Type Bed Linen from India admitted that Article 15 imposes no obligation to actually provide or accept any constructive remedy that may be identified and/or offered. It also pointed out that Article 15 does not require that 'constructive remedies' must be explored but rather that the 'possibilities' of such remedies must be explored and the explorations may conclude that no such possibilities exist. The panel however suggested that the exploration of possibilities must be undertaken by the developed country members. It was thus of the view that 'Article 15 does impose an obligation to actively consider, with an open mind, *the possibility* of such a remedy prior to the imposition of an anti-dumping measure that would affect the essential interests of a developing country'. The panel however did not come to any conclusion as to what might constitute 'constructive remedies provided for under this agreement'.

The panel in the United States—Anti-dumping and Countervailing Measures on steel plates from India opined that the first sentence of Article 15 imposes 'no specific or general' obligation on developed country Members to undertake any particular action. The panel did not agree with India that this 'mandatory provision does create a general obligation, the precise parameters of which are to be determined based on the facts and circumstances of the particular case'. The panel held that 'Members cannot be expected to comply with an obligation whose parameters are entirely undefined'. The panel also disagreed with India's view that special regard must be given throughout the course of the investigation. It was of the view that it refers to the final decision whether to apply a final measure.

Apparently, Article 15 is too general to be enforceable. Interestingly, it is a mandatory S&D treatment provision within the WTO framework,[8] but the modalities for its application need clarification. Several questions remain unanswered. How can developed countries give special regard to developing countries? What are the special situations? How can the developed countries explore the possibilities of 'constructive remedies'? What are 'constructive remedies'? What is meant by 'essential interests'?

SHOULD ARTICLE 15 BE CONCRETIZED

Despite a long history of efforts by developing countries for S&D treatment, there has been an intense debate among scholars as to whether it really is worth the developing country's effort to drive towards reinvigorating S&D treatment or whether to focus negotiating efforts elsewhere. One school of thought (see for instance Michalopoulos 2000, Tortora 2003, Garcia 2004, Fritz 2005, Chang 2006) argues that so long as there is a gap in economic capacities and levels of development of WTO members S&D treatment will be required. They need greater flexibility, policy space, and preferential access to developed market access. Giving more regards to developing countries is very important for world trade and world's stability. Tortora (2003, p. 2) argues 'the more the trade agenda is expanded, the more demanding the commitments are, and the more necessary it is to accommodate the various interests and levels of development of the WTO members'. The challenge is to more carefully rationalize these provisions and to elaborate on them. Developing countries must defend their interests in the new round of multilateral trade negotiation. Leaving these provisions to the discretion of developed countries would invite skepticism to the benefits of these provisions. Fritz (2005) recommends that there is necessity to bring S&D treatment provisions in focus not only due to the continuing difficulties of many developing countries to implement the WTO agreements but also due to the fact that there is very little connection between liberalization and growth. Chang (2006, p. 631) argues that 'the notion of reciprocity cannot be discussed without some reference to the relative position of the parties involved'. He questions the use of term special treatment for the concessions given to the developing countries. His argument is that they are differential treatment for countries with differential capabilities and goals and are inevitable for the level playing field. Garcia (2004) also emphasizes that developing countries need a comprehensive agreement on S&D treatment to ensure policy space for themselves and that WTO is bound to support them in this pursuit.

Another school however argue that S&D treatment provisions are not the best way to safeguard developing countries' interests (see for instance Hoekman 2005). According to this school of scholars, S&D treatment has not been a success in promoting development (Hoekman and Ozden 2005 for literature survey). They express their doubts on the importance of these provisions and cite several studies that have examined the benefits that Generalized System of Preferences (GSP) schemes have yielded for developing countries in the support of their argument. These studies reveal that benefits of the GSP schemes have been modest in aggregate and are more important for some countries than others (see for instance Karsenty and Laird 1987, McPhee 1989, UNCTAD 2004). According to the estimates of UNCTAD (2004), the share of realized GSP preferences in the total of dutiable exports from the developing countries was only 24.2 per cent—just one quarter in 2001. The figures for the LDCs are even more modest. The share of preferred imports compared to the total imports of the industrialized countries is even smaller. In 1999, of all imports of the European Union only 5 per cent were GSP imports (WTO 2001). Fritz (2005) reviewed 155 S&D treatment provisions provided in the WTO by category and analysed their effectiveness. He concluded that these provisions have only been marginally been successful. They are too inadequate to be effective and too vague to be implemented. In an earlier study, Footer (2001) found that there had been a trend towards stricter and narrower interpretation of S&D treatment provisions making them ineffective in protecting developing countries' interests.

These studies are viewed by many as providing the ground for the argument that any drive towards strengthening these provisions would involve huge opportunity cost in terms of sacrifice of substantial gains that may be achieved by focusing on more concrete negotiations. On the basis of these findings, these scholars argue that it is a futile exercise to evolve the concept and its implementation. Instead of examining why these provisions have failed to yield substantial gains, they suggest that these provisions are of little value.

Is it not true that the reasons for their modest success lie in their limited scope, restrictive and vague character, and poor implementation due to resistance by the developed countries? Or, that these are not more than token compensation offered to developing countries for their agreeing to complex rules that are tailored to suit the needs of the developed countries? WTO Secretariat (WTO 2002) itself concedes that even the mandatory provisions are not effectively enforceable. In fact, there are strong reasons for their inclusion in the WTO and they need to be strengthened to ensure level playing field. There are special motivations for providing differential treatment to developing in some of the agreements due to built in asymmetries in them. One such agreement is ADA. This is perhaps the reason why Article 15, even though ineffective, is made mandatory in this Agreement. There are asymmetries built in the agreement, its use, and effects against the developing countries. As a result, these countries are highly vulnerable to this mechanism. Furthermore, provisions of the agreement are so vague that no reform within the same framework, howsoever radical, is likely to yield substantial gains to the developing countries. Introduction of complexities may restrict the use of the tool by developing countries while developed countries will continue to use the tool uninhibited. In what follows summarizes the asymmetries in the agreement, its implementation, and its effect. Although these arguments have already been made in various chapters of this book, from a reader's perspective it is considered appropriate to provide a summary of the arguments in the context of the S&D treatment.

Asymmetries in the Agreement

As has already been discussed earlier, a central problem for the developing countries in respect of possible anti-dumping measures against their exports is that their home market prices for domestically manufactured products are in most cases higher than those in their export markets.[9] This home market price distortion is largely due to inefficient cost structures, which result primarily from the production conditions under which firms in these countries operate.

Furthermore, even though the legal provisions are not directly discriminatory against developing countries their implication is much more severe for developing countries. Most developing countries do not have institutional capacities to counter or to use the tool. They are not equipped with the institutional requirement. In addition, legal provisions of the Agreement are highly ambiguous and complex. There are ambiguities in every step of finding dumping and establishing injury and causation. While developed countries have financial resources and legal capacity to exploit this vagueness to their advantage, enterprises from developing countries, particularly SMEs lack the technical and legal capacity or the resources to mount an effective defence. Besides, the assistance that developing countries can provide to their enterprises to defend their cases in an investigation process initiated by a developed country is very limited.

Asymmetries in the Use of the Mechanism

Though the cases reported by developing countries have increased, the use of anti-dumping among developing countries is still not widespread. Several developing countries have the law but have not yet made use of it. This is because governments in these developing countries lack the expertise, capacity, and resources to effectively use anti-dumping and countervailing measures to protect even the legitimate concerns of their domestic industries.

On the other hand, the number of cases reported against them is still large and has been increasing sharply. Thus exports from developing countries have been facing more frequent anti-dumping measures. In the early 1990s, there was a quantum jump in the number of cases initiated against low- and lower middle-income countries. While in the late 1980s, only 15 per cent of the cases were reported against them, in the early 1990s, their share doubled to 34 per cent. It rose further to 40 per cent in the early 2000s. More than 14 per cent cases were directed against upper income developing countries. Taken together, developing countries were targeted in around 65 per cent of the cases during 2000–June 2004. On the other hand, they are responsible for launching 62 per cent of the cases. With the MFA coming to an end in January 2005, there is likely to be a stupendous increase in anti-dumping cases against developing countries. Since the share of developing countries in world trade is very small (smaller than in imports), this indicates that the intensity with which anti-dumping measures are imposed against them is several times higher than that at which these measures are imposed against the developed countries. It is also of serious concern that an increasing use of such tools against developing countries may generate chain effect. To counter the attack and to pose retaliatory threat, these countries would need to institute anti-dumping capabilities by using the tool themselves. As argued in the earlier chapters, this is a double-edged sword for developing countries that would hurt them both as users and as targets.

Asymmetries in the Effects of the Anti-dumping Actions

Developing countries account for a very small proportion of exports of most countries. Therefore the impact of the anti-dumping investigations initiated by them on subject countries is not likely to be large. On the contrary, any measure initiated by the developed countries is likely to result in total destabilization of the exports of the developing countries simply due to large magnitudes. Furthermore, developing country firms are generally significantly smaller than exporting firms from developed country members and, therefore, lack resources and capacity to bear the costs of exploring new markets. Finally, any adverse impact on one export product significantly affects the overall export effort. Potential exporters of other products will also hesitate to explore export markets, as they will perceive anti-dumping duties as being one of the consequences of export success in developed country export markets. The potential benefits from trade liberalization to developing countries have thus been considerably neutralized by the use of antidumping measures against their competitive exports in a number of products.

Reforms in the Agreement and Developing Countries

Past experience suggests that reforms in the existing provisions cannot contain the use of the tool. By refining and specifying quantitative threshold, they may only facilitate its use. Several reforms have already been incorporated in various rounds. Tokyo Round negotiations focused on injury analysis while the Uruguay Round strengthened the disciplines on dumping finding and procedural requirements. However, after each round the use of the tool showed spectacular rise. The problem is that powerful trading countries defend and vigorously protect this tool in its current form. Any change accepted is peripheral and does not change the situation.

Furthermore, incorporation of complex technical details or procedural requirements are likely to harm the interests of the developing countries as these details may make it more difficult for them to meet those standards. Developed countries on the other hand would not be constrained in their use of the tool due to the expertise that they have generated over the years.

The ADA is a bad agreement in the current WTO framework to which most developing countries are signatories. There does not appear to be a realistic chance of any significant reform in the agreement. It has become a tool of convenience and powerful trading countries have been overzealous in ensuring that it remains in its current form. Perhaps the only hope in this scenario for the developing countries is to focus on S&D treatment provisions. This is a development round and developed countries will need to concede some concessions to the developing countries in this Agreement if they wish to match their rhetoric with actions. For this, Article 15 of the ADA needs to be made operative and should be strengthened and its concretion ought to be solved in the Doha Round of negotiation. Paragraph 44 of the Ministerial Declaration mandates: 'We therefore agree that all special and differential treatment provisions shall be reviewed with a view to strengthening then and making them more precise, effective and operational'. Developing countries therefore need to gear the negotiations on S&D treatment towards a meaningful evolution of the concept and its implementation.

SUGGESTIONS

The Secretariat identifies two types of S&D treatment provisions in WTO agreements. These are as follows.

- exceptions to rule to which developing countries may take recourse to and
- conduct or actions to be undertaken by developed country members for developing country members.

While the former constitutes provisions of flexibility of commitment, actions, and use of policy instruments, latter comprises of provisions under which WTO members should safeguard the interest of developing country member and provide them technical assistance. To make S&D treatment provisions effective in the antidumping regime it is important that there are negotiations on both types of provisions. Several proposals have already been submitted. In what follows we critically review these proposals under the two headings and offer some suggestions.

Exceptions to Rule to Which Developing Countries May Take Recourse

De minimis level: Dumping margin

De minimis dumping margin is fixed at 2 per cent. Many scholars have proposed to raise this margin to 5 per cent for developing countries and 8 per cent for the least developed countries. Interestingly, several proposals submitted to the Rules Group have sought to raise this level (TN/RL/W/4, TN/RL/W/6, TN/RL/W/66, TN/RL/W/27, TN/RL/W/26). To evaluate the impact of raising the *de minimis* dumping margin to 5 per cent we examined dumping margin figures provided by the US DOC and EC in final determination of anti-dumping cases investigated in recent years. For the United States, Lindsey (2000) provides a detailed database of company-specific ADD rates in all final determinations from 1995 through 1998 and it may be recalled that ADD rates imposed by the US DOC are full dumping margins. For the EC, we had information on country-specific ADDs in force as of 4 June 2003. In cases with more than one exporter, our database provided the duty range specifying the minimum and maximum duty for the exporters within the subject country. For our analysis we considered the maximum duty imposed in a given country. One must note here that in the EC lesser duty law is applicable, which means that actual dumping margins could in fact be greater than ADDs. Anti-dumping duties set lower limits for dumping margins and thus serve as a good proxy for dumping margins in this analysis. Table 7.1 summarizes the available information. It shows that even if the *de minimis* margin is raised to 10 per cent, it will not have a significant impact on the use of the anti-dumping measure. In the EC, in only 10 out of 113 country specific cases, anti-dumping duty is less than 10 per cent. In the United States, less than one-fifth of the exporters faced less than 10 per cent ADD. In the EC, more than 50 per cent of ADDs are above 25 per cent. The distribution is more highly skewed in the United States where 65 per cent of the duties are above 25 per cent.

TABLE 7.1:   Structure of anti-dumping duties—European Union and United States

Duty upper limit (%)	EU No. of country specific duties in force as of 4 June 2003	US No. of company specific duties between 1995 and 1998
2–5	2	10
5–10	8	10
10–25	46	17
Above 25	57	67
Total	113	104

Note: EC provides data on the range of anti-dumping duty levied against target companies in each country.

Source: Author's computation based on the information provided by the EC website http://www.europa.eu.int/comm/trade/policy/dumping/stats.htm and Lindsey (2000).

We also examined dumping margins calculated for Indian companies by anti-dumping authorities in the EC and the United States. Data on dumping margins was compiled from the official documents of these countries. Table 7.2 shows the distribution of company-specific dumping margins calculated by the EC and US DOC in cases investigated and found affirmative against India. In most cases, dumping margins are above 10 per cent.

TABLE 7.2:   Summary of dumping margins calculated by USDOC and EC in anti-dumping investigations against Indian companies

Dumping margins (per cent)	EC (as of 4 June 2003)	US (as of 23 October 2003)
2–5	0	0
5–10	4	1
10–25	14	7
Above 25	28	7
Total	46	15

Source: Author's computation based on *Official Journal of the European Communities*, various issues and USITC website http://www.usitc.gov/7ops/ad_cvd_orders.htm

This paper therefore argues that it is not appropriate for developing countries to spend time and energy in getting the *de minimis* dumping margin raised.

De minimis: import shares

De minimis import shares under the ADA are 3 per cent and collectively 7 per cent. Though the objective of introducing this condition is that the exporter accused of dumping should have a significant market share, experts criticize the rules for such low standards of dominance. The threshold are much lower than those used by the competition authorities for defining 'dominant position' (30 per cent or 40 per cent in general). If dominance is defined in a specific way for domestic competition, the same criterion should be applied to foreign competition as well (Hoekman and Mavroidis 1996).

Furthermore, no special or differential treatment is accorded to developing countries. As far as *de minimis* import shares under ASCM are concerned, developing countries enjoy 4 per cent and collectively 9 per cent while there is no accurate proportion for developed countries. As far as *de minimis* import shares under ASG are concerned, developing countries enjoy 3 per cent and collectively 9 per cent while no *de minimis* provision for developed countries. It raises the question why S&D treatment is not granted to developing countries in the ADA. This is simply because powerful trading countries do not want to loosen their grip over its use.

S&D treatment provision in the *de minimis* in imports may help in significantly restraining the use of anti-dumping duties against developing countries as individual shares held by exporting developing countries in developed country members' markets are very small. Various countries including FANs have submitted proposals in this regard.[10] However, few have placed it under the S&D treatment provision. Following the existing literature and the proposals under considerations, we offer two suggestions in this regard.

- The thresholds for executing negligible imports should be based on market share rather than on share of total imports.
- A sentence could be added to Article 5.8 of the WTO Agreement stating that 'no collective account will be made of dumped imports from developing country Members holding less than 3 per cent of the importing members' consumption'.

This would mean that the provision of cumulation will not be applicable to developing countries and countries with less than 3 per cent of market share will automatically be excluded from the purview of anti-dumping investigations. This raises a pertinent question as to how effective will these reforms be? For addressing this question one needs to examine the individual market share of investigated firms from developing countries in developed country markets. Blonigen (2000) has complied a unique database on US anti-dumping investigations which provides firm-level data on all foreign firms that were involved in any US anti-dumping investigation initiated from 1980 through 1995 and received at least a preliminary firm-specific anti-dumping duty. Most of the data come from *Federal Register* notices of the USITC and the ITA of the United States. This database provides information on market share of US domestic producers, subject firms, and other firms. We obtained this information and summarized in Table 7.3. It shows that in around 50 per cent cases, the share of developing country firms had been less than 3 per cent. One can therefore conclude that an introduction of this clause is likely to yield substantial benefit to developing countries.

TABLE 7.3:   Distribution of market shares held by developing countries subject to anti-dumping actions in the US: 1980–95

Market share (%)	No. of firms
0–3	54
3–9	20
Above 9	33
Total	107

Source: Blonigen (2003) and author's computation.

Pre-initiation consultations

It has been proven that anti-dumping investigations are harmful for parties affected no matter what final results are. It has already been discussed in the previous chapter that anti-dumping petitions have a profound impact on imports even if they do not result in duties. It is therefore necessary to establish a mechanism to prevent such damages to developing countries since they can not afford them. Following the existing literature, it is recommended here that consultation before anti-dumping investigation is procedurally practical. Under this system, developed countries should inform the developing country involved of the facts of violation of anti-dumping laws and request them not to continue their violation prior to the initiation of investigations. As a response to the request from the complaining developed country, the developing country may correct its violation if it believes the claim of the complaining country is reasonable. The modalities and scope of pre-initiation consultations must be elaborated so that they are applied in a consistent manner by all the developed countries. It must also be clarified that these consultations would take place before public notice of the initiation of investigation is issued to minimize the harassment effect (Goel 2004). If there is no agreement reached by two sides within a fixed period, the complaining country may set out investigation and follow what the authorities can do according to the existing procedure. This additional procedure will benefit both sides. Developing countries can get a chance to correct their aggressive conduct and possibly avoid an expensive lawsuit. Developed countries can solve dumping problems more efficiently and effectively.

Price undertakings

If a dumping investigation results in the imposition of an anti-dumping duty, the exporting firm can agree to raise its export prices (known as a price undertaking) as an alternative to the imposition of an ADD. Economists consider price undertaking to have particular competition-reducing effects. According to them price undertakings can have more inefficient outcomes than the VERs (Moore 2005). They argue that since under the rules of the WTO, governments are prohibited from negotiating VERs, they should also be prohibited to accept price undertakings. However, in practice it is preferable for the exporters from developing countries as they benefit from the increased price, rather than the importing country enjoying higher revenues. It is therefore proposed that developed countries should favourably consider price undertaking offers from developing countries. Several proposals from developing countries (FANs, TN/RL/W/10 and TN/RL/W/118; India, TN/RL/W/26; China, TN/RL/W/66; Argentina, TN/RL/W/81) have identified this an important issue from the developing country perspective.

Essential interests

Article 15 requires the developed countries to explore the possibilities of constructive remedies before applying ADDs where they would affect the essential interests of developing country members. However, the agreement does not define what the essential interests are. One could argue that, a priori, any harm to exports from developing counties affects their 'essential interests'. Furthermore, it gives the developed countries a chance to contend that the particular investigation in question does not relate to 'the essential interests' of the developing country in question (Goel 2004). The first best suggestion here is to delete the condition of essential interests imposed by the agreement. In case amendment of the text of Article 15 is not possible, then the second best solution is to define 'essential interests'.[11] This could be based on one or more of the following factors:

- trade in the product generates at least X per cent of the foreign exchange earnings of the exporter country; or
- direct and indirect employment in the 'product' manufacturing industry generates at least Y per cent of the total employment of the exporting country; or
- more than Z per cent of the product, as a percentage of the total exports of the product from the exporting country, are exported to the importing country; or
- more than P per cent of the total production of the product is exported.

The actual percentages and any other criteria could be introduced after discussions with economists and trade specialists.

Investigation period

Vermulst (1999) argues that the ADA provides no direct guidance with regard to establishing the appropriate investigation period (IP) for the purposes of dumping investigations. In this regard, where the IP established falls outside the normal accounting period in the exporting country, the added administrative burden is considerable. In the case of developing countries, these problems are often compounded by the relative lack of adequate computerization and sophisticated information management tools, which might otherwise ease the task of organizing relevant data efficiently and cost-effectively. Account should be taken of the particular need to minimize administrative difficulties encountered by developing members, where possible, and that the accounting practices of such members should be considered when setting the IP.

Conduct or Actions to Be Undertaken by Developed Country Members for Developing Country Member.

Institutional capacity

Greater emphasis needs to be placed on instruments that would strengthen developing countries institutional capacity. The main differences between developed and developing countries lie not in the trade policies they should pursue but in the capacities of their institutions to pursue them. This means that S&D treatment provisions related to technical and financial assistance as well as longer transition periods (which are linked to institutional reform and capacity building) should be emphasized. Explicit legally binding commitments regarding technical and financial assistance need to be obtained. The legal obligations assumed by developing countries in the WTO

Agreements need to be balanced by legal commitments of the developed countries to fund the assistance needed to implement them.

Financial support

The initiation of frivolous cases imposes a particularly heavy burden on developing countries, which usually lack the resources, capacity, and expertise to mount an effective defence of their interests. In this context, it must be noted that Article 27.2 of the DSU envisions the provision of additional legal advice and assistance in respect of dispute settlement to developing country members. However, the assistance currently granted is both quantitatively and qualitatively inadequate, especially given the increasing involvement of developing country members in disputes before the DSB. As a result, these members are often forced to retain private counsel to assist in cases, which can be very expensive. The level of this assistance needs to be increased.

Further, apart from the developing country members, it is the developing country exporters who need financial assistance. It is not rare to find anti-dumping investigations where the total exports by a single exporter may be only in the region of a few million USD and such exporters naturally cannot come up with the requisite 1 million USD or so to defend themselves in the ADD proceedings. Funding assistance needs to be provided to such exporters. One idea could be that a fund be set up by the WTO which is financed by a levy of a small percentage on all ADD levied by all the members, including developing country members. Developed country members should indicate the minimum costs of contesting ADD proceedings in their country and a panel of law firms/lawyers who would take on cases at these prices. Any developing country exporter whose exports to the developed country concerned are less than three times this minimum costs should be entitled to assistance from this fund to contest the anti-dumping proceedings (Goel 2004).

Legal fees should be conditionally shouldered by losing developed countries and expertise support should be available when developing countries face anti-dumping cases. Heavy financial burden is the root that developing countries have not been positively participating in anti-dumping lawsuits. If a developed country initiates an anti-dumping investigation against a developing country and finally the complaints are not justified, the legal fees in this case should be shouldered by the losing party. Generally it is fair and easy to be accepted by developed countries. If this proposal is adopted by the next round of negotiation, developing countries likely get rid of any hesitation to defend their lawful rights.

Professional training

The complex procedure of anti-dumping regime, like other regimes under the WTO, makes developing countries difficult to use it as both a complaining party and a defending party. They are in sharp shortage of human resource and financial support. Not surprisingly their response rate is very low and their anti-dumping charges are always not justified.

Providing professional expertise aid is critical for developing countries to participate in anti-dumping actions. There should be a special training program for developing countries. Especially when they face anti-dumping actions or they intend to set up their own anti-dumping institutions, expertise support should be available.

Six WTO agreements and one Ministerial Decision contain altogether fifteen provisions regarding technical assistance. These are agreements that require a high level of capacities for their implementation such as TBT, SPS, GATS, TRIPS, and the Customs Valuation Agreement. This does not however mean that no technical assistance is being provided to developing countries for the implementation of the other agreements. There are institutions that are offering technical assistance on various trade-related agreements. These include not only the WTO but also the IMF, the World Bank, UNCTAD, and UNDP. According to its Secretariat, in 2003 the WTO conducted 450 training and assistance measures while there was demand for 1000 such programmes (as reported in Fritz 2005). An assessment of the technical assistance provided in the framework of the WTO reveals that it has been of little use in promoting self-determined capacity building in the developing countries. Technical assistance follows the priorities of the donors, not the requirements of the developing countries. These programmes therefore need to be made mandatory and relevant in the context of the developing countries.

Resort to facts available

This provision and the frequent, and sometimes unwarranted use of it, causes more damage to developing country respondents and clarity and special treatment on this would benefit them more than issues such as *de minimis* and cumulation.

Given the lack of development of the industry in developing countries, in terms of the level of automation, management information systems, the data management, etc., developing country respondents find it much harder to prepare and furnish the required information in compliance with the fixed format and the strict time schedule of the investigating authority. Due to this inability that stems from the inherent lack of resources the resort to facts available by the investigative authority penalizes the developing country respondents. It is common knowledge that whenever an investigative authority resorts to facts available, there is, more often than not, a finding of dumping. This action against developing country respondents under the ADA is unfair and gives undue protection to the importing country industry, which it would otherwise not be entitled to under the ADA.

Two proposals may be offered. One, developing countries should be offered technical assistance in improving the data management systems. Since it would involve time, another proposal is that mechanisms need to be built to ensure that some special regard is given to developing country respondents in this regard.

Legal assistance and dispute settlement

Most observers (see for instance Busch 2000; Reinhardt 2001; Busch and Reinhardt 2002, 2003) note that developing countries have been more active in WTO dispute settlement. This could partly be due to the legal reforms ushered in by the DSU, notably the 'right' to a panel and automatic adoption of panel reports. However there are various other economic factors that have resulted in a greater use of the DSB for anti-dumping-related disputes. In this context, a study by Bown (2004) provides some interesting insights. He provides a first empirical investigation of the trade remedy and WTO dispute settlement interaction by focusing on determinants of WTO members' decisions of whether to formally challenge US trade remedies imposed between 1992 and 2003. His findings reveal that the size of imports lost to the trade remedy, the foreign country's capacity to retaliate, and the size of the trade remedy that was imposed are some of the important determinants of the litigation decisions. The evidence provided in his study implies that an adversely affected foreign industry may resort to a reciprocal (and retaliatory) anti-dumping measure against the protected US industry if it has the capacity to do so, in lieu of working to convince its government to file a dispute at the WTO on its behalf that would seek the removal of the US trade remedy measure. These results indicate that the more frequent use of the DSB by the developing countries could be explained by the fact that these countries lack retaliatory capacity and hence have no option but to resort to the WTO dispute settlement mechanism for the remedy.

However, empirical evidence (Chapter 3 for discussion) suggests that developing countries have not won greater concessions (more favourable outcomes) under the WTO than under GATT. Developed country complainants have become significantly more likely to secure their desired outcomes under the WTO, while poor complainants have not. It is observed (Busch and Reinhardt 2003) that the gap between developed and developing countries in winning concessions from a defendant owes to their differential rates of securing early settlement. In general, defendants tend to offer the greatest concessions in consultations or at the panel stage prior to a ruling. It is at this stage that developed countries exact concessions and developing countries do not. It is not surprising therefore that they are panel more disputes notably against developed countries. We submit that more attention needs to be directed at helping developing countries make more of consultations, as well as more of negotiations at the panel stage prior to a ruling. Since developing countries are relatively disadvantaged in this regard due to lack of their capacity, they require assistance prior to litigation. This also constitutes a constructive remedy.

CONCLUSION

While GATT has been largely successful in reducing barriers to trade, anti-dumping provisions remain a significant obstacle to liberalized trade that would benefit consumers. Numerous studies demonstrate the extent to which anti-dumping legislation does not appear to be motivated by anything other than protectionism. There is little economic argument that can support the practice of anti-dumping. Moreover, anti-dumping legislation cannot be supported on social welfare grounds, since the protection of small communities is usually not the focus of an anti-dumping investigation.

Anti-dumping actions not only defy sound principles but they also rest on a methodology that suffers from serious problems in several areas: the miscalculations of price differences, the lack of transparency and bias in proceedings, and the high cost to defendants of countering the claim along with the cost to exporting industries and importing consumers when the claim is approved. Several proposals have been made on how to improve this situation. While one school proposes to restrain its use by restricting the circumstances in which the tool can be used, the other school advocates that clarifying the rules can considerably reduce the abuse of the tool. The former approach involves fundamental changes in the agreement, which under the given political scenario are hard to be come by, the latter approach of tightening the provisions of the Agreement is not likely to restraint its use by the developed countries significantly and may in fact affect the developing countries' position adversely. One alternative is to make the public interest clause mandatory. It is administratively workable and will prove to be highly effective in balancing the interests of the domestic producers and the interests of consumers. However it may not prove to be the right solution for the developing countries. It would add to the administrative complexities and uncertainties and would also increase the cost of investigation. It would need experienced trade lawyers, more staff and would involve more resources and time but the final outcome might be same. National authorities in developing countries are already understaffed and in such scenario it may harm the interests of the developing countries.

Under such circumstances, a pertinent question is how to reduce unwarranted cases against developing countries so that they are able to gain greater benefits from their increased participation in world trade. We believe that this can be done only by strengthening the 'special and differential treatment' provision provided in the law. This argument may be old fashioned for many. But one must recognize the fact that there are gaps in the development levels of the member countries and that it is the responsibility of the international community to help bridge such gaps. Rules have to be applied in accordance to the needs and capacity of the member countries, so that the benefits accrue to all. Anti-dumping law is highly biased against the developing countries. This position can be corrected only by strengthening the provisions of the S&D treatment. Developing countries must therefore push hard to achieve meaningful reforms in this provision in the current round. The state of implementation of S&D provisions in the ADA is a source of deep concern to developing countries. There is a need to address the issue of special and differential treatment at two levels: at the broad conceptual level to examine how they can be developed to provide relief to the developing countries and at the detailed practical level to examine the actual implementation of these S&D provisions. Essentially, S&D treatment must be shifted from its currently peripheral role in which it is granted as a grudging concession to developing countries in an unequal bargaining process (Youssef 1999). It must be accorded a central and purposeful policy role intended to reduce the asymmetries in the agreement at the conceptual and the implementation level. Enforceable S&D treatment will significantly correct the in-built bias in the Agreement against developing countries. Their success in regard to negotiations on Anti-dumping Agreement will be determined by how effectively they could gear the negotiations on S&D treatment towards a meaningful evolution of the concept and its implementation.

Notes

1 Some of recent submissions (TN/RL/W/174 by FANs and TN/RL/W/174 by China and Hong Kong) have proposed some modalities.

2 National anti-dumping authorities of these countries may decide not to impose measures/reduce the duties when it is concluded that they would cause substantial injury to the domestic economy.

3 FANs (TN/RL/W/174/Rev,.17 April 2005, TN/RL/W/174, 29 March 2005, TN/RL/W/6). Canada and the EC have also made proposals for including a public interest element in the ADA—see TN/RL/W/1 and 47; TN/RL/W/13.

4 PB-95-001, 26 February 199, *supra*. This decision is reviewed in some detail in Leclerc 'Reforming Anti-dumping Law', *supra*, at pp. 133–9.

5 The cases in which a lower margin of dumping was recommended were *Grain Corn* (1997), *Re Beer* (1991), *Iodinated Contrast Media* (2000), and *Prepared Baby Food* (2000). These results were tabulated by accessing the CITT's web page and counting the number of public interest inquiry decisions available in that database.

6 Ferro-silicon originating in Brazil, China, Kazakastan, Russia, Ukraine, and Venezuela.

7 See Chapter 2 for more details.

8 The WTO Secretariat identifies the 155 provisions regarding special and differential treatment as either mandatory or non-mandatory.

9 It is discussed in detail in Chapter 3.

10 TN/RL/W/6, TN/RL/W/66, TN/RL/W/27 TN/RL/W/132, TN/RL/W/4.

References

Ackerman, F. (2005), 'The Shrinking Gains form Trade: A Critical Assessment of Doha Round Projections', *GDAE (Global Development and Environment Institute at Tuft University) Working Paper No. 05–01*, October 2005.

Aggarwal, A. (2002), 'Anti-dumping Law and Practice: An Indian Perspective', *Working Paper No. 85*, Indian Council for Research on International Economic Relations, New Delhi.

_____ (2006), 'Trade Effects of Antidumping Actions: Evidence from India', Study in Progress.

Ahdar, R. (1991), 'The Role of Antitrust Policy in the Development of Australian–New Zealand Free Trade', *Northwestern Journal of International Law & Business*, Vol. 12, pp. 317–34.

Almonte-Alvarez, J. and D.M. Conley (2003), 'US-Mexico Food System and the Tomato Trade Dispute', *International Food and Agribusiness Management Review*, Vol. 5, No. 3.

Almstedt, K.W. and P.M. Norton (2000), 'China's Antidumping Laws and the WTO Antidumping Agreement', *Journal of World Trade*, Vol. 34, No. 6, pp. 75–114.

Anderson, J.E. (1993), 'Domino Dumping II: Anti-dumping', *Journal of International Economics,* Vol. 35, Nos 1–2, pp. 133–50.

Andoh, E.K. (1992), 'Countervailing Duties in a Not Quite Perfect World: An Economic Analysis', *Stanford Law Review*, Vol. 44, No. 6, pp. 1515–39.

Araujo Jr, J.T. De, C. Macario, and K. Steinfatt (2001), 'Antidumping in the Americas', *Journal of World Trade*, Vol. 35, No. 4, pp. 555–74.

Areeda, P. and D.F. Turner (1975), 'Predatory Pricing and Related Practices Under Section 2 of the Sherman Act', *Harvard Law Review*, Vol. 88, No. 4, pp. 697–733.

Baldwin, R.E. and M.O. Moore (1991), 'Administration of the Unfair Trade Laws by the Department of Commerce: A Political Economy Analysis', in R. Boltuck and R. Litan (eds), *Down in the Dumps—Administration of U.S. Trade Remedy Law*, Brookings Institution, Washington, D.C.

Baldwin, R.E. (1984), 'Trade Policies in Developed Countries', in R.W. Jones and P.B. Kenen (eds), *Handbook of International Economics,* Vol. 1, pp. 571–619, Elsevier, Science Publishers, Boston.

Baldwin, R.E. and J.W. Steagall (1994), 'An Analysis of ITC Decisions in Anti-dumping, Countervailing Duty and Safeguard Cases', *Weltwirtschaftliches Archiv*, Vol. 130, No. 2, pp. 290–308.

Banks, G. (1993), 'The Anti-dumping Experience of a GATT Fearing Country in Anti-dumping', in J.M. Finger (ed.), *How it Works and How it Gets Hurt*, University of Michigan Press, Ann Arbor.

Barfield, C. (2005), 'Anti-dumping Reform: Time to Go Back to Basics', *The World Economy*, Vol. 28, No. 5, May, p. 719.

Becker, B. and M. Theuringer (2001), 'Macroeconomic Determinants of Contingent Protection: The Case of the EU', *Zeitschrift für Wirtschaftspolitik*, Vol. 50, No. 3.

Bekker, D. (2004), *The Determination of Dumping and The Use of Anti-dumping Measures in International Trade*, PhD Thesis, University of South Africa.

Besson, F. and R. Mehdi (2004), 'Is WTO Dispute Settlement System Biased Against Developing Countries? An Empirical Analysis', in Yiannis Stivachtis (ed.), *International Governance and International Security: Issues and Perspectives*, Published by ATINER, Athens, pp. 111–30.

Bhagwati, J. (1988), *Protectionism*, MIT Press, Cambridge, MA.

Bhansali, S. (2002), 'Anti-dumping: Some Suggestions', Paper Presented at the EU–India Network on Trade and Development (EINSTAD) Seminar held in Jaipur, Organized by Consumer Unity & Trust Society, December.

_____ (2004a), 'Note on the Proposals on Fair Price Comparison', Paper Presented at the National Seminar Organized by the Ministry of Commerce in Delhi, 21–22 September 2004.

_____ (2004b), 'Study on Injury Margins', Paper Presented at the National Seminar Organized by the Ministry of Commerce in Delhi, 21–22 September 2004.

Bierwagen, R.M. (1990), *Article VI GATT and the Protectionist Bias in Anti-dumping Laws*, Vol. 7, Studies in Transnational Economic Law, Deventer, Kluwer.

Blonigen, B.A. (2002), 'Tariff-jumping Anti-dumping Duties', *Journal of International Economics*, Vol. 57, No. 1, pp. 31–49.

_____ (2003a), 'US Anti-dumping Database and Links', *http://www.nber.org/antidump/*

_____ (2003b), 'Evolving Discretionary Practices of U.S. Antidumping', *NBER Working Paper 9625*, National Bureau of Economic Research, Inc.

Blonigen, B. and T. Prusa (2001), 'Anti-dumping', *NBER Working Paper 8398*, Cambridge, MA.

Boltuck, R. (1991), 'Assessing the Effects on the Domestic Industry of Price Dumping', in P.K.M. Tharakan (ed.), *Policy Implications of Anti-dumping Measures*, North Holland, Amsterdam.

Boltuck, R. (1993), 'The Material Injury Determination in Unfair Trade Cases: The US Experience with Competing Analytical Approach', *Trade Resources Company*, Washington, D.C., Mimeo.

Boltuck, R. and R.E. Litan (1991), *Down in the Dumps: Administration of Unfair Trade Laws*, Brookings, Washington.

Boltuck, R. and S. Kaplan (1993), 'Conflicting Entitlements: Can Antidumping and Antitrust Regulation be Reconciled?', *University of Cincinnati Law Review*, Vol. 61, No. 3, pp. 903–18.

Bork, R. (1978), *The Antitrust Paradox: A Policy at War with Itself*, Basic Books, New York.

Bourgeoise, J. and P. Messerlin (1993), *Competition and the EC Anti-dumping Regulations*, Institut d' Etudes Politique de Paris, Paris.

Bourgeoise, J. and P. Messerlin (1998), 'The European Community's Experience', in Robert Z. Lawrence (ed.), *Brookings Trade Forum*, Brookings Institution Press, Washington, D.C., pp. 127–46.

Bown, C.P. (2005), 'Trade Remedies and WTO Dispute Settlement: Why are so Few Challenged', *Journal of Legal Studies*.

Bown, C.P. and M. Crowley (2003), *Trade Deflection and Trade Depression*, Federal Reserve Bank of Chicago, Mimeo.

Bown, C.P. and R. McCulloch (2003), 'Nondiscrimination and the WTO Agreement on Safeguards', *World Trade Review*, Vol. 2, No. 3, November, pp. 327–48.

Bown, C.P., B. Hoekman and Ç. Ozden (2003), 'The Pattern of U.S. Antidumping: The Path from Initial Filing to WTO Dispute Settlement', *World Trade Review*, Vol. 2, No. 3, November, pp. 349–71.

Bown, C.P. (2002), 'Why are Safeguards under the WTO so Unpopular?', *World Trade Review*, Vol. 1, No. 11, pp. 47–62.

—— (2004), 'Developing Countries as Plaintiffs and Defendants in GATT/WTO Trade Disputes', *The World Economy*, Vol. 27, No. 1, January, pp. 59–80.

Bown, C.P. and Meredith A. Crowley (2005), 'Safeguards in the World Trade Organization', in Arthur E. Appleton, Patrick F.J. Macrory, and Michael G. Plummer (eds), *The World Trade Organization: Legal, Economic and Political Analysis*, Springer, Dordrecht.

Brander, J.A. and B.J. Spencer (1981), 'Tariffs and the Extraction of Foreign Monopoly Rents Under Potential Entry', *Canadian Journal of Economics*, Vol. 14, pp. 371–89.

Brander, J.A. and P.R. Krugonan (1983), 'A Reciprocal Dumping Model of International Trade', *Journal of International Economics*, Vol. 15, pp. 313–21.

Bronckers (1985), *Selective Safeguard Measures in Multilateral Trade Relations: Issues of Protectionism in GATT, European Community and United States Law*, Kluwer Law and Taxation Publishers the Hague.

Bronckers M. and N. Neils (1999), 'Rethinking the Like Product Definition in WTO Anti-dumping Law', *Journal of World Trade*, Vol. 33, No. 3, 73–91.

Brown, D.K., A.V. Deardorff and R.M. Stern (2003), Developing Countries' Stake in the Doha Round, Discussion Paper 495, Gerald R. Ford School of Public Policy, The University of Michigan.

Busch, M.L. (2000), 'Democracy Consultation and the Paneling of Disputes under GATT', *Journal of Conflict Resolution*, Vol. 44, No. 4, pp. 425–46.

Busch, M.L. and E. Reinhardt (2003), 'Developing Countries and General Agreement on Tariffs and Trade/World Trade Organization Dispute Settlement', *Journal of World Trade*, Vol. 37, No. 4, pp. 719–35.

Busch, M.L. and Eric Reinhart (2002), 'Testing International Trade Law: Empirical Studies of GATT/WTO Dispute Settlement', in Daniel M. Kennedy and James D. Southwick (eds), *The Political Economy of International Trade Law: Essays in Honor of Robert Hudec*, Cambridge University Press, NY and Cambridge.

Carpenter, R. (1999), *Antidumping and Counter Vailing Duty Handbook*, Publication: 3257, United States International Trade Commission, Washington, D.C.

Caves, R. (1976), 'Economic Models of Political Choice: Canada's Tariff Structure', *Canadian Journal of Economic*, Vol. 6, No. 1, pp. 187–210.

CBO (1994), 'The evolution of US laws: An Economic Perspective September 1994', *How the GATT Affects US Anti-dumping and Countervailing Duty, Policy, CBO*, Chapter 3.

―――― (2001), *Anti-dumping Actions in the US and Around the World: An Update*, Washington, D.C.

Chang, H.J. (2006), 'Policy Space in Special and Differential Treatment', *Economic and Political Weekly*, 18 February 2006.

Chen, K.M. and T.C. Chen (2003), 'Firms' Strategies and the Effects of Antidumping Policy', in Ali Bayar (ed.), *Proceedings of International Conference on Policy Modeling*, Istanbul, Turkey.

Ciuriak, D. (2005), 'Anti-dumping at 100 years and Counting: A Canadian Perspective', *World Economy*, Vol. 28, No. 5, pp. 641–9.

Coughlin, C.C., J.V. Terza, and N.A. Khalifah (1989), 'The Determinants of Escape Clause Petitions', *Review of Economics and Statistics*, Vol. 71, May, pp. 341–7.

Crandall, R.W. (1993), *The Economic Effects of Anti-dumping Policies on International Trade in Streel*, Brookings Institutions, Washington, D.C.

Czinkota, M. and M. Kotabe (1997), 'A Marketing Perspective of the US International Trade Commission's Antidumping Actions: An Empirical Inquiry', *Journal of World Business*, Vol. 32, Summer 1997, pp. 169–87.

Dam, K.W. (1970), *The GATT: Law and International Economic Organization*, University of Chicago Press, Chicago.

—— (2001), *The Rules of the Global Game*, University of Chicago Press, Chicago.

Deardorff, A.V. (1989), 'Economic Perspectives on Dumping Law', in J.H. Jackson and E.A. Vermulst (eds), *Anti-Dumping Law and Practice: A Comparative Study*, The University of Michigan Press, Ann Arbor, pp. 23–39.

DeLong, B. and S. Dowrick (2003), 'Globalization and Convergence', in M. Bordo, A.M. Taylor, and J. Williamson (eds), *Globalization in Historical Perspective*, Chicago University Press, Chicago.

DeVault, J.M. (1993), 'Economics and the International Trade Commission', *Southern Economic Journal*, Vol. 60, pp. 463–78.

—— (1996), 'The Welfare Effects of US Anti-dumping Duties', *Open Economics Review*, Vol. 7, No. 1, pp. 19–33.

Diamond, R. (1989), 'Economic Foundations of Countervailing Duty Law', *Virginia Journal of International Law*, Vol. 29, pp. 767–812.

Didier, P. (2001), 'The WTO Anti-Dumping Code and EC Practice: Issues for Review in Trade Negotiations', *Journal of World Trade*, Vol. 35, No. 1, pp. 33–54.

Dijk, R.M. van (1997), 'Antidumping in Mexico: Curtailment of Unfair Trade Practices or Renewed Protectionism?', M.Sc. Thesis, Erasmus University, Rotterdam.

Dowrick, S. and J. Golley (2000), 'Trade Openers and Growth: Who Benefits', *Oxford Review of Economic Policy*, Vol. 20, No. 1, pp. 38–56.

Durling, J.P. (2003), 'Deference but only When Due: WTO Review of AD Measures', *Journal of International Economic Law*, Vol. 6, No. 1, pp. 125–53.

Durling J.P. and T.J. Prusa (2004), 'The Trade Effects Associated with an Antidumping Epidemic: The Hot-Rolled Steel Market 1996–2001', *Paper Presented at the University of Nottingham Conference on the 100th Anniversary of Anti-dumping*, 25–26 June, 2004.

Dutta, S. (2004), 'Brief Analysis of Proposals on Facts Available', *Paper Presented at the National Seminar Organized by the Ministry of Commerce in Delhi*, 21–22 September 2004.

Dutz, M. (1998), 'Economic Impact of Canadian Anti-dumping Law', in R.J. Lawrence (ed.), *Brookings Trade Forum 1998*, Brookings Institution Press, Washington, D.C.

Easterbrook, F. (1981), 'Predatory Strategies and Counterstrategies', *University of Chicago Law Review*, Vol. 48, pp. 263–337.

Easterly, W. (2001), 'The Effect of International Monetary Fund and World Bank Programs on Poverty', *Policy Research Working Paper Series 2517*, The World Bank.

Eichengreen, B. and H. James (2001), 'Monetary and Financial Reform in Two Eras of Globalization', *Paper Prepared for the NBER Conference on the History of Globalization*, Santa Barbara, 4–6 May 2001.

Ethier, W.J. (1982), 'Dumping', *Journal of Political Economy*, Vol. 90, No. 31, pp. 487–506.

Eymann, A. and L. Schuknecht (1993), 'Antidumping Enforcement in the European Community', in J. Michael Finger (ed.), *Antidumping: How it Works and Who Gets Hurt*, University of Michigan Press, Ann Arbor.

Feigenbaum, S. and T.D. Willet (1985), 'Domestic Versus International Influences on Protectionist Pressures in the United States', in Sven W. Arndt, Richard J. Sweezy, and Thomas D. Willets (eds), *Exchange Rates, Trades, and the U.S. Economy*, American Enterprise Institute and Ballinger Publishing Company, Cambridge, MA, pp. 181–90.

Feinberg, R.M. and K.M. Rexnold (2005), 'Tariff Liberalization and Increased Administrative Protection: Is There a Quid Pro Quo?', *American University Working Paper No. 2005–7*.

Feinberg, R.M. (1989), 'Exchange Rates and Unfair Trade', *Review of Economic and Statistics*, 71, pp. 704–7.

—— (2005), 'U.S. Antidumping Enforcement and Macroeconomic Indicators Revisited: Do Petitioners Learn?', *Review of World Economics*, Vol. 141, No. 4, pp. 612–22.

Feinberg, R.M. and B.T. Hirsch (1989), 'Industry Rent Seeking and the Filing of "Unfair Trade" Complaints', *International Journal of Industrial Organization*, Vol. 7, No. 3, pp. 325–40.

Finger, J. (1998), 'GATT Experience with Safeguards: Making Economic and Political Sense out of the Possibilities that the GATT Allows to Restrict Imports', *Policy Research Working Paper 2000*, World Bank, Development Research Group, Washington, D.C., October.

Finger, J.M. (1981), 'The Industry-Country Incidence of "Less than Fair Value" Cases in US Import Trade', *Quarterly Review of Economics and Business*, Vol. 21, pp. 260–79.

—— (1991), 'The Origins and Evolution of Antidumping Regulation', *World Bank Working Paper WPS 783*, 23 October 1991.

—— (1992), 'Dumping and Antidumping: The Rhetoric and the Reality of Protection in Industrialized Countries', *The World Bank Research Observer*, Vol. 7, No. 2, pp. 121–43.

—— (1993), *Antidumping: How It Works and Who Gets Hurt*, University of Michigan Press, Ann Arbor, p. 56.

Finger, J.M. (2002), 'Safeguards: Making Sense of GATT? WTO Provisions Allowing for Import Restriction', in B. Hoekman, A. Mattoo, and P. English (eds), *Development, Trade and the WTO: A Handbook*, World Bank, Washington, D.C.

Finger, J.M., H.K. Hall, and R.D. Nelson (1982), 'The Political Economy of Administered Protection', *American Economic Review*, Vol. 72, No. 3, pp. 452–66.

Finger, J.M., N.G. Francis, and S. Wangchuk (2001), 'Antidumping as Safeguard Policy', *Working Paper No. 2730*, World Bank, Washington, D.C.

Finger, M. and A. Zlate (2003), 'WTO Rules That Allow New Trade Restrictions: The Public Interest Is a Bastard Child', *Paper Prepared for the U.N. Millennium Project Task Force on Trade Coordinated by E. Zedillo and P. Messerlin*, 16 April 2003.

Fisher, R.O. and J.M. Prusa (1999), 'Contingent Protection of Better Insurance', *NBER Working Paper No. 6933.*

Footer, M. (2001), 'Developing Country Practice in the Matter of WTO Dispute Settlement', *Journal of World Trade*, Vol. 35, No. 1, pp. 55–98.

Francois, J. and G. Niels (2004), 'Political Influence in a New Anti-dumping Regime: Evidence from Mexico', *C.E.P.R. Discussion Paper 4297.*

Fritz, T. (May 2005), 'Special and Differential Treatment for Developing Countries', *Global Issue Papers, No. 18*, Heinrich-Boll Stiftung and Germanwatch, Berlin.

FTC (1994), 'Antidumping and Competition Policy, Chapter 2: Census and Analysis of Antidumping Actions in the United States', *Working Party No. 1 on Competition and International Trade*, September, *http:// www.ftc.gov/bc/international/ussubs.htm#1994.*

Gallaway M.P., B.A. Blonigen, and J.E. Flynn (1999), 'Welfare Costs of the US Antidumping and Countervailing Duty Laws', *Journal of International Economics*, Vol. 49, pp. 211–2.

Garcia (2004), 'Beyond Special and Differential Treatment', *Boston College International and Comparative Law Review,* Vol. 27, pp. 291–317.

GATT (1954), *Basic Instruments and Documents (BISD)*, 3rd Supplement, Geneva.

Goel, N. (2004) 'Special and Differential Treatment in the Anti Dumping Agreement Article 15: Specific Proposals for Review', *Paper Presented at the National Seminar Organized by the Ministry of Commerce in Delhi*, 21–22 September.

Grant G. (2006), 'The WTO—Ten Years On: Trade and Development', *Tralac (Trade Law Centre for South Africa) Working Paper WP 5/May.*

Group on Rules on Anti-dumping measures TN/RL/W/1028 June 2002, negotiating group on rules.

Guash, J.L. and S. Rajapatirana (1998), 'Total Strangers or Soul Mates? Antidumping and Competition Policies in Latin America and the Caribbean', *The World Bank Policy Research Working Paper Series 1958.*

Gupta, P. and A. Panagariya (2006), 'Injury Investigation in Anti-dumping and the Super-Additivity Effect: A Theoretical Explanation', *Review of World Economy,* Vol. 142, No. 1, pp. 151–61.

Haberler, G. (1936), *The Theory of International Trade with its Applications to Commercial Policy,* translated by A. Stonier and F. Berham, Willian Hodge, London.

Hansen, J.D. and J.U.M. Nielsen (2006), 'Economic Integration and Quality Standards in a Duopoly Model with Horizontal and Vertical Product Differentiation, *Journal of Economic Integration,* Vol. 21, No. 4, pp. 837–60.

Hansen, W.L. (1990), 'International Trade Commission and the Policies of Protectionism', *American Political Science Review,* Vol. 84, pp. 21–46.

Hansen, W.L. and T.J. Prusa (1996), 'Cumulation and ITC Decision Making: The Sum of the Parts is Greater than the Whole', *Economic Inquiry,* Vol. 34, No. 4, pp. 746–69.

Hansen, W.L. and T.J. Prusa (1997), 'Economics and Politics: An Empirical Analysis of ITC Decision-Making', *Review of International Economics,* Vol. 5, No. 2, pp. 230–45.

Hartigan, J.C. (2000), 'An Antidumping Law Can Be Pro-Competitive', *Pacific Economic Review,* Vol. 5, pp. 5–14.

Herander, M.G. and J.B. Schwartz (1984), 'An Empirical Test of the Impact of the Threat of US Trade Policy: The Case of Antidumping Duties', *Southern Economic Journal,* Vol. 51, pp. 59–79.

Hindley, B. (1991), 'The Economics of Dumping and Anti-Dumping Action: Is There a Baby in the Bath Tub', in P.K.M. Tharakan (ed.), *Policy Implication of Anti-dumping Measures,* North Holland Elsevier Science, Amsterdam, pp. 25–43.

Hindley, B. and P.A. Messerlin (1996), 'Antidumping Industrial Policy: Legalized Protectionism', *The WTO and What to Do About It,* American Enterprise Institute Press Washington, D.C.

Hochman, G. (2004), 'The Pros and Cons of the Use of Safeguard Regimes in Trade Agreements', *Paper Presented in 'Special Seminar' Series at Columbia University,* 12 April.

_____ (2006), 'Trade Negotiations, Domestic Policies, and the Choice of Safeguard Regimes', *Papers Presented at the European Economic Association (EEA) Conference,* University of Mainz, Amsterdam, 27 August.

Hoda, A. (1987), *Developing Countries in the International Trading System,* Allied Publishers, New Delhi.

Hoekman, B. (1998), 'Free Trade and Deep Integration: Antidumping and Antitrust in Regional Agreements', *World Bank and CEPR*.

——— (2002), 'Strengthening the Global Trade Architecture for Development: The Post-Doha Agenda', *World Trade Review*, Vol. 1, No. 1, pp. 23–45.

——— (2005), 'Operationalizing the Concept of Policy Space in the WTO: Beyond Special and Differential Treatment', *Journal of International Economic Law*, Vol. 8, No. 2, pp. 405–24.

Hoekman, B. and C. Ozden (2005), 'Trade Preferences and Differential Treatment of Developing Countries: A Selective Survey', *Policy Research Working Paper 3566*, World Bank.

Hoekman, B. and P. Mavroidis (1994), 'Competition, Competition Policy and the GATT', with Petros C. Mavroidis, *The World Economy*, Vol. 17, pp. 121–50.

——— (1996), 'Dumping, Antidumping and Antitrust', *Journal of World Trade*, Vol. 30, No. 1, pp. 27–52.

Hoekman, B.M. and M.P. Leidy (1989), 'Dumping, Antidumping and Emergency Protection', *Journal of World Trade*, Vol. 23, No. 5, pp. 27–44.

Holden, M. (1998), 'Anti-Dumping: A Reaction to Trade Liberalisation or Anti-Comeptitivity?', *South African Journal of Economics*, Vol. 70, No. 5, pp. 912–1011.

Holmes, P. and J. Kempton (1997), 'Study on the Economic and Industrial Aspects of Anti-Dumping Policy', *Working Paper No. 22*, Sussex European Institute, University of Sussex.

Horlick, G.N. and G.D. Oliver (1989), 'Antidumping and countervailing duty law provisions of the Omnibus Trade and Competitiveness Act of 1988', *Journal of World Trade*, Vol. 23, No. 3, pp. 5–49.

Horlicks, G.N. and P.A. Clarke (1994), 'The 1994 WTO subsidies Agreement', *World Competition*, Vols 17 and 41, No. 4, 41–54.

Hsu, L. (1998), 'The New Singapore Law on Anti-dumping and Countervailing Duties', *Journal of World Trade*, Vol. 32, No. 1, pp. 121–45.

Hufbauer, G.C. (1999), 'Antidumping: A Look At U.S. Experience—Lessons For Indonesia', *Institute for International Economics For the Ministry of Industry and Trade Republic of Indonesia*, 20 August 1999.

Hutton, S.J. and M.J. Trebilcock (1990), 'An Empirical Study of the Application of Canadian Anti-Dumping Laws: A Search for Normative Rationales', *Journal of World Trade*, Vol. 24, No. 3, pp. 123–46.

India and the WTO (2000), *A Monthly Newsletter of the Ministry of Commerce and Industry*, Vol. 2, No. 1, January 2000.

Irwing, D.A. (1995), *Antidumping Policies and International Trade in Semiconductors*, Graduate School of Business of Chicago, Mimeo.

Irwing, D.A. (1998), 'The Semocinductor Industry', in R.Z. Lawrence (ed.), *Brookings Trade Forum*, The Brookings Institution Press, Washington, D.C., pp. 173–200.

_____ (2005), 'The Rise of U.S. Antidumping Actions in Historical Perspective', *The World Economy*, Vol. 28, No. 5, pp. 651–68.

Jackson, J.H. and E.A. Vermulst (eds) (1989), *Antidumping Law and Practice: A Comparative Study*, University of Michigan Press, Ann Arbor, MI.

Joskow, P.L. and A.K. Klevorick (1979), 'A Framework for Analyzing Predatory Pricing Policy', *Yale Law Journal*, Vol. 89, pp. 213–70.

Kaplan, S. (1991), 'Inquiry and Causation in USITC Anti-dumping Determinations: Five Recent Approaches', in P.K.M. Tharakan (ed.), *Policy Implication of Anti-dumping Measures, Amsterdam*, North Holland, Oxford, Tokyo, pp. 143–73.

Karsenty, G. and S. Laird (1987), 'The GSP, Policy Options, and the New Round', *Weltwirtschaftliches Archiv*, Vol. 123, No. 3, pp. 262–95.

Katrak, H. (1977), 'Multinational Monopolies and Commercial Policy', Oxford Economic Papers, Vol. 29, pp. 283–91.

Kim, H.J. (1996), 'The Korean Anti-Dumping System', *Journal of World Trade*, Vol. 30, No. 2, pp. 101–33.

Kiyono, K. (1995), 'Anti-Dumping Regulation under Strategic Interdependence', *The Economic Review*, Vol. 46, No. 1.

Knetter, M.M. and T.J. Prusa (2003), 'Macroeconomic Factors and Antidumping Filings: Evidence from Four Countries', *Journal of International Economics*, Vol. 61, No. 1, pp. 1–17.

Knoll, M.S. (1991), 'Dump our Anti-dumping Law', *Cato Institute Foreign Policy Briefing Papers, Series No. 11*, 25 July.

Krishna, R. (1997), 'Antidumping in Law and Practice', *World Bank Working Paper 1823*, World Bank.

_____ (1998), 'Antidumping in Law and Practice', *World Bank Policy Research Working Paper No. 1823*, World Bank, Washington, D.C.

Krupp, C. (1994), 'Antidumping Cases in The US Chemical Industry: A Panel Data Approach', *Journal of Industrial Economics*, Vol. 42, pp. 299–311.

Kufuor, K.O. (1998), 'The Developing Countries and the Shaping of GATT/ WTO Anti-dumping Law', *Journal of World Trade*, Vol. 32, No. 6, pp. 167–96.

Lawrence, R. (1995), 'US Will Lodge WTO Complaint Against Japan', *Journal of Commerce*, 11 May 1995.

Leclerc, J.M. (1999), 'Reforming Anti-dumping Law: Balancing the Interests of Consumers and Domestic Industries', *McGill Law Journal*, Vol. 44, No. 1, pp. 111–40.

276   References

Lee, Y.S. (2003), *Safeguard Measures in World Trade: The Legal Analysis*, Kluwer Law International 2003, The Nether bonds.

Leebron (1997), 'Implementation of the Uruguay Round Results in the US', in J.H. Jackson and A.O. Sykes (eds), *Implementing the Uruguay Round,* Oxford Clendon Press, Oxford, pp. 175–242.

Leidy, M.P. (1997), 'Macroeconomic Conditions and Pressures for Protection under Antidumping and Countervailing Duty Laws: Empirical Evidence from the United States', *IMF Working Paper 44*, Vol. 1, March.

Lichtenberg, F. and H. Tan (1994), 'An Industry-Level Analysis of Import Relief Petitions Filed by US Manufacturers,1958–1985', in H. Tan and H. Shimada (eds), *Troubled Industries in the United States and Japan,* St. Martin's Press, New York, pp. 161–88.

Lindsey, B. (2000), 'The US Anti-dumping Law: Rhetoric versus Reality', *Journal of World Trade*, Vol. 34, No. 1, pp. 1–38.

Lindsey, B. and D. Ikenson (2002a), 'Anti-dumping 101: The Devilish Details of 'Unfair Trade Law', *Cato Trade Policy Analysis No. 20*, 26 November.

Lindsey, B. and D. Ikenson (2002b), 'Reforming the Antidumping Agreement: A Road Map for WTO Negotiations', *Cato Trade Policy Analysis No. 21,* 11 December.

Lott Jr., J.R. (1999), *Are Predatory Commitmebts Credible? Who should the Courts Believe*, University of Chicago Press, Chicago.

Low, P. (1993), *Trading Free: The GATT and US Trade Policy*, The Twentieth Century Fund Press, New York.

Magee, S., W. Brock, and L. Young (1989), *Black Hole Tariffs and Endogenous Policy Theory and Policy*, Cambridge University Press, Cambridge.

Mai, Y. (2002), 'An Analysis of EU Anti-dumping Cases Against China', *Asia-Pacific Development Journal*, Vol. 9, No. 2, pp. 131–50.

Marvel, H.P. (1995), 'Edward John Ray Countervailing Duties', *Economic Journal*, Vol. 105, No. 433 November, pp. 1576–93.

Marvel, H.P. and E.J. Ray (1995), 'Countervailing Duties', *Economic Journal*, Vol. 105, No, 433, pp. 1576–96.

Mastel, G. (1998), *Antidumping Laws and the US Economy*, ME Sharpe, Armonk, NY.

Mavroidis, P.C. (2005), 'The General Agreement on Tariffs and Trade: A Commentary Series', *Oxford Commentaries on International Law*, Vol. V, No. 1, Oxford University Press, Oxford.

Mayda, A.M. and D. Rodrik (2001), 'Why are some people and countries more Protectionist than others', *NBER Working Paper 8461*, September.

Mayer, W. (1998), 'Trade Policy Platforms of Competing Parties: What makes them Different?' *Review of International Economics*, Vol. 6, No. 2, pp. 185–203.

McGee, J. (1958), 'Predatory Price Cutting: The Standard Oil (N.J.) Case', *Journal of Law and Economics*, Vol. 1, pp. 137–69.

McPhee, C.R. (1989), 'A Synthesis of the GSP Study Programme', *Report Prepared for the United Nations Conference on Trade and Development*, Mimeo.

Messerlin P.A. (1986), 'The European Iron and Steel Industry and the World Crisis', in Meny Yves and Vincent Wright (eds), *The Polictics of Steel: Western Europe and the Steel Industry in the Crisis Years*, European University Institute, Series C, Political and Social Sciences, Walter de Cruyter, Berlin, New York.

_____ (1991), 'Antidumping in the Uruguay Round: No more "Clever" Provisions, Please', *The Uruguay Round: Unresolved Issues and Prospects*, Paper Prepared for the Korea Institute for International Economic Policy Conference, Seoul, March.

_____ (1993), 'The EC and Central Europe: The Missed Rendez-Vous of 1992?', *Economics of Transition*, Vol. 1, No.1, pp. 89–109.

_____ (1995), 'Trade Policy vs Competition Policy', *Revue Economique*, Vol. 46, No. 3, pp. 717–26.

Messerlin, P.A. and P.K.M. Tharakan (1999), 'The Question of Contingent Protection', *The World Economy*, Vol. 22, No. 9, pp. 1251–70.

_____ (1996), 'Competition Policy and Antidumping Reform: An Exercise in Transition', in Jeffrey J. Schott (ed.), *The World Trading System: Challenges Ahead,* Institute for International Economics, Washington, D.C., pp. 219–46.

Messerlin, P.A. and Y. Noguchi (1993), 'Anti-dumping Policies in Electronic Products', in R.Z. Lawrence (ed.), *Brookings Trade Forum*, The Brookings Institution Press, Washington, D.C., pp. 147–72.

METI (2005), 'Report on the WTO Inconsistency of Trade Policies by Major Trading Partners', Part II, *Committee Report by Ministry of Economy*, Trade and Industry, Japan, Chapter 7, pp. 293–312.

Michalopoulos, C. (2000), 'Special and Differential Treatment for Developing Countries in GATT and the WTO', *Policy Research Working Paper No. 2388*, The World Bank, Washington, D.C.

Miranda, J., R.A. Torres, and M. Ruiz.(1998), 'The International Use of Antidumping: 1987–1997', *Journal of World Trade*, Vol. 32, No. 5, pp. 5–71.

Moore, M.O. (1992), 'Rules or Politics? An Empirical Analysis of ITC Anti-dumping Decisions', *Economic Enquiry*, Vol. 30, No. 3, pp. 449–66.

_____ (2005), 'VERs and Price Undertakings under the WTO', *Review of International Economics,* Vol. 13, No. 2, pp. 298–310.

Moore, M.O. (2006), 'U.S. Facts-available Antidumping Decisions: An Empirical Analysis', *European Journal of Political Economy*, Vol. 22/3, September, p. 639.

Murray, T. and D.J. Rousslang (1989), 'A Method Estimating Injury Caused by Unfair Trade Practices', *International Review of Law and Economics*, Vol. 9, pp. 149–64.

NBT (2004), 'The Agreement on Safeguards: Use of the Instrument, Problem Areas, and Proposals for Change', *Report by National Board of Trade*, Sweden, November 2004.

Nedumpara, J. (2003), 'In Search of the Missing Link in the Examination of Injury and Causality Issues in Anti-dumping and Safeguard Investigations', *Paper Presented at the Department of Commerce on 13 December 2003*.

———— (2004), 'Swift Dispute Control Mechanism to Deal with Unjustified Initiations in Respect of Antidumping and Countervailing Duty Investigation: An Examination of EC's Proposal', *Paper Presented at the National Seminar on Negotiations on WTO Rules*, 21–22 September, New Delhi: A Draft Version.

Neils, G. and A. Kate (1997), 'Trusting Antitrust to Dump Antidumping, Abolishing Antidumping in Free Trade Agreements Without Replacing it with Competition Law', *Journal of World Trade*, Vol. 31, No. 6, pp. 29–43.

Nelson, D. (2006), 'The Political Economy of Antidumping: A Survey', *European Journal of Political Economy*, Vol. 22/3, September, p. 554.

Neufeld I.N. (2001), 'Anti-dumping and Countervailing Procdures: Use or Abuse Implication for Developing Countries', *Policy Issue in International Trade and Commodities Study Series 9*, UNCRAD/ITCD/TAB/10.

Nicolaides, P. and R. van Wijngaarden (1993), 'Reform of Anti-Dumping Regulations—The Case of the EC', *Journal of World Trade,* Vol. 27, No. 3, June, pp. 31–53.

Nivola (1993), *Regulating Unfair Trade*, The Brookings Institution Press, Washington, D.C., p. 30.

O'Rourke, K.H. and R. Sinnott (2001), 'What Determines Attitudes Towards Protection? Some Cross-Country Evidence', in Susan M. Collins and Dani Rodrik (eds), *Brookings Trade Forum 2001,* Brookings Institute Press, Washington, D.C., pp. 157–206.

OCED (1994), 'Competition Policy: 1994 Workshop with the Dynamic Non-member Economics', *OECD Document Number: OECD/GD/(96) 59*.

———— (1996), *Antitrust and Market Access: The Scope and Coverage of Competition Laws and Implications for Trade*, Organization for Economic Co-operation and Development, Paris.

Oleksiy, I. and A. Shcherbakov (2001), 'The Causes of Increase in Antidumping against Transition Economies', *00-466E, EERC*, Economic Education and Research Consortium, Research Network, Russia and CIS.

Ordover, J. (1998), 'Predatory Pricing', in P., Newman (ed.), *The New Palgrave Dictionary of Economics and the Law*, Vol. 3, Macmillan, London and New York.

Ozden, C. and B. Hoekman (2005), 'Trade Preferences and Differential Treatment of Developing Countries: a Selective Survey', *Policy Research Working Paper Series 3566*, The World Bank.

Palmeter, D. (1996), 'A Commentary on the WTO Anti-Dumping Code', *Journal of World Trade*, Vol. 30, No. 4, pp. 43–69.

Palmeter, N.D. (1991), 'The Anti Dumping Law: A Legal and Administrative Non Tariff Barrier', in R. Boltuck and R.E. Litan (eds), *Down in the Dumps: Administration of the Unfair Trade Laws*, Brookings, Washington, D.C., pp. 64–94.

Panagariya A. (Online), 'Core WTO Agreements: Trade in Goods and Services and Intellectual Property', *http://66.102.7.104/search?q=cache:rNoV48BKThEJ:www.columbia.edu/~ap2231/Policy%2520Papers/wto-overview.doc+part+IV+and+MFN+exemption&hl=en&ct=clnk&cd=8&client=firefox-a*

_____ (1999), 'Anti-dumping: Let Us Not Shoot Ourselves in the Foot', *Economic Times,* 30 June 1999.

_____ (2002), 'Developing Countries at Doha: A Political Economy Analysis', *The World Economy*, Vol. 25, No. 9, pp. 1205–33.

Parthasarthy, R. (2004), 'Reviews: Issues At-a-Glance', Paper Presented at the National Seminar Organized by the Ministry of Commerce in Delhi, 21–22 September 2004.

Peltzman, S. (1991), 'The Handbook of Industrial Organization: A Review Article', *Journal of Political Economy*, February, pp. 201–17.

Plowman, D.H. (1993), *Protectionism and Labour Regulation in A New Pounce for Law and Order: The Proceedings of the XIIIth conference of the H.R. Nichous Society at the Terrace Adelaide Hotel 13th–14th November, 1992*, Vol. 13, No. 4, Chapter 5, the HR Nichous Society, Inc.

Prasad, E.S., K. Rogoff, S.J. Wei, and M.R. Kose (2003), 'Effects of Financial Globalization on Developing Centuries: Some Empirical Evidence', *Occasional Paper 220*, International Monetary Fund, October.

Prusa, T.J. (1992), 'Why Are So Many Anti-dumping Petitions Withdrawn?', *Journal of International Economics,* Vol. 33, Nos 1–2, pp. 1–20.

_____ (1997), 'The Trade Effects of US Anti-Dumping Actions', in R.C. Feenstra (ed.), *The Effects of US Trade Protection and Promotion Policies*, University of Chicago Press, Chicago, pp. 191–214.

Prusa, T.J. (1998), 'Cumulation and Anti-dumping: A Challenge to Competition',
    World Economy, Vol. 21, No. 8, pp. 1021–33.

_____ (2001), 'On the Spread and Impact of Antidumping', *Canadian Journal of
    Economics*, Vol. 34, No. 3, pp. 591–611.

Prusa, T.J. and S. Skeath (2002), 'The Economic and Strategic Motives for
    Antidumping Filings', *Weltwirtshftliches Archiv*, Vol. 138, No. 3, pp. 389–
    415.

Reinhardt, E. (2001), 'Adjudication without Enforcement in GATT Disputes',
    Journal of Conflict Resolution, Vol. 45, No. 2, pp. 174–95.

Rodrik, D. (1995), 'Political Economy of Trade Policy', in G. Grossman and
    K. Rogoff (eds), *Handbook of International Economics*, North Holland,
    Amsterdam, pp. 1457–94.

Roitinger, A. (2003), 'Preserving Trade Policy Flexibility in Antidumping Reform',
    Aussenwirtschaft, Vol. 58, No. 3, pp. 353–81.

Sabry, F. (2000), 'An Analysis of the Decision to File, the Dumping Estimates,
    and the Outcome of Antidumping Petitions', *International Trade Journal*,
    Vol. 14, pp. 109–45.

Sadni-Jallab, M., R. Sandretto, and M.B.P. Gbakou (2006), 'Antidumping
    Procedures and Macroeconomic Factors: A Comparison Between the
    United States and the European Union', *Global Economy Journey*, Vol. 6,
    No. 3.

Sagara, N. (2002), 'Provisions for Trade Remedy Measures (Anti-dumping,
    Countervailing and Safeguard Measures) in Preferential Trade
    Agreements', *RIETI Discussion Paper Series 02-E-13*, September.

Salvatore, D. (1987), 'Import Penetration, Exchange Rates and Protectionism in
    the United States', *Journal of Policy Modeling*, Vol. 9, No. 1, pp. 125–41.

Sauvé, P. and A. Zampetti (1995), *Onwards to Singapore: The International
    Contestability of Markets and The New Trade Agenda*, OECD Trade
    Directorate, Paris.

Schöne, R. (1996), *Alternatives to Antidumping from an Antitrust Perspective*,
    University of St. Gallen Doctoral Dissertation.

Schott, J.J. (1994), *The Uruguay Round: An Assessment*, Institute for International
    Economics, Washington, D.C.

Shafaeddin, S.M. (2005), 'Trade Liberalisation and Economic Reforms in
    Developing countries: Structiral Change or De-indistrialisation?',
    UNCTAD Discussion Paper No. 179.

Shin, H.J. (1992), *Census and Analysis of Anti-dumping Cases in the US
    (Monograph)*, Princeton University, Princeton.

_____ (1998), 'Possible Instances of Predatory Pricing in Recent U.S. Anti-dumping
    Cases', in R.Z. Lawrence (ed.), *Brookings Trade Forum 1998*, Brookings
    Institution, Washington, D.C., pp. 81–97.

Staiger, R.W. and F.A. Wolak (1989), 'Strategic Use of Anti-dumping Law to Enforce Tacit International Collusion', *Working Paper No. 3016*, National Bureau of Economic Research, Washington, D.C.

_____ (1994), 'Measuring Industry Specific Protection Anti-dumping in the United States', *Brookings Paper and Economic Activity: Microeconomics*, Vol. 1, pp. 51–118.

Stanbrook, Clive and Philip Bentley (1996), *Dumping and Subsidies: The Law and Procedures Governing the Imposition of Antidumping and Countervailing Duties in the European Community*, 3rd ed., Kluwer Law International, London.

Stewart, T.P., S.G. Markel, and M.T. Kerwin (1993), 'Anti-Dumping', in T.B. Stewart (ed.), *The GATT Uruguay Round: A Negotiating History*, (1986–1992), Vol. 11, Kluwar Law & Taxation Publishers, pp. 1383, 1391.

Stiglitz, J.E. (1997), 'Dumping on Free Trade: The US Import Trade Laws', *Southern Economic Journal*, Vol. 64, pp. 402–24.

Stiglitz, J.E. and A. Charlton (2004), 'The Development Round of Trade Negotiations in the Aftermath of Cancun: A Report for the Commonwealth Secretariat', *Initiative for Policy Dialogue*, Columbia University, New York.

Svedberg, P. (1979), 'Optimal Tariff Policy on Imports from Multinationals', *Economic Record*, Vol. 55, pp. 64–7.

Sykes, A.O. (1989), 'Countervailing Duty Law: An Economic Perspective', *Columbia Law Review*, Vol. 89, No. 2, March, pp. 199–263.

_____ (1998), 'Antidumping and Antitrust: What Problems Does Each Address?', in R.Z. Lawrence (ed.), *Brookings Trade Forum 1998*, Brookings Institution Press, Washington, D.C.

_____ (1991), 'Protectionism as a Safeguard: A Positive Analysis of the GATT "Escape Clause" with Normative Speculation', *University of Chicago Law Review*, Vol. 58, No. 255.

_____ (1999), *International Trade*, School of Law, University of Chicago, Chicago.

_____ (2003), 'The Safeguards Mess: A Critique of WTO Jurisprudence', *World Trade Review*, Vol. 2, No. 3, pp. 261–95.

_____ (2005), 'Trade Remedy Laws', *John Olin Law & Economics Working Paper 240(2D series)*, The Law School, The University of Chicago, April.

Takacs, W. (1981), 'Pressures for Protection: An Empirical Analysis', *Economic Inquiry*, Vol. 19, October, pp. 687–93.

Tarr, D.G. and M.E. Morkre (1984), 'Aggregate Cost to the United States of Tariffs and Quotas on Imports', *A Federal Trade Commission (FTC) Study*.

Tavares, J., C. Macario, and K. Steinfatt (2001), 'Anti-dumping in the Americas', *Journal of World Trade*, Vol. 35, No. 4, August.

Tavares, de A. Jr. Jose (1995), 'The Political Economy of Protection After the Uruguay Round', *CEPAL Review* 55, Santiago, Chile.

Tharakan P.K.M. (ed.) (1991), *Policy Implications of Antidumping Measures*, North Holland, Amsterdam, Oxford, Tokyo.

____ (1994), 'Anti-dumping Policy and Practice of the European Union: An overview', *Economisch en sociaal tijdschrift*, Vol. 48, No. 4, pp. 557–75.

____ (1995), 'Political Economy and Contingent Protection', *Economic Journal*, Vol. 105, No. 433, pp. 1550–64.

____ (1999), 'Is Anti-Dumping here to Stay?', *The World Economy*, Vol. 22, 179–206.

____ (2000), 'Predatory Pricing and Anti-dumping', in G. Norman and J.F. Thisse (eds), *Market Structure and Competition Policy*, Cambridge University Press, London, pp. 71–95.

Tharakan, P.K.M. and J. Waelbroeck (1994), 'Determinants of Anti-dumping and Countervailing Duty Decisions in the European Communities', in M. Dewatripont and V. Ginsburgh (eds), *European Economic Integration: A Challenge in the Changing World*, North Holland, Amsterdam, London, and Tokyo, pp. 181–99.

Tharakan, P.K.M., D. Greenaway, and B. Kersten (2006), 'Anti-dumping and Excess Injury Margins in the European Union: A Counterfactual Analysis', *European Journal of Political Economy*, Vol. 22/3, September, p. 653.

Tharakan, P.K.M., D. Greenaway, and J. Tharakan (1998), 'Cumulation and Injury Determination of the European Community in Anti-dumping Cases', *Weltwirtschaftliches Archiv*, Vol. 134, No. 2, pp. 320–39.

Tharakan, P.K.M., E. Vermulst, and J. Tharakan (1998), 'Interface Between Anti-Dumping Policy and Competition Policy: A Case Study', *The World Economy*, Vol. 21, No. 8, pp. 1035–60.

TN/RL/W/1 (2002), 'Negotiating Group on Rules—Improved Disciplines under the Agreement on Subsidies and Countervailing Measures and the Anti-Dumping Agreement', Communication from Canada, 15 April.

TN/RL/W/6 (2004), 'Negotiating Group on Rules—Anti-Dumping: Illustrative Major Issues', Paper from Brazil; Chile, Colombia, Costa Rica, Hong Kong, China, Israel, Japan; [...]tzerland, Thailand and Turkey', 26 April.

TN/RL/W/7 (2002), 'Negotiating Group on Rules—Implementation-Related Issues', Paper by Brazil, 26 April.

TN/RL/W/10, 'Negotiating Group on Rules—Second Contribution to Discussion of the Negotiating Group on Rules on Anti-dumping Measures', Paper by Brazil; Chile; Colombia[...]re; Switzerland; and Thailand.

TN/RL/W/13 (2002), 'Negotiating Group on Rules—Submission from the European Communities Concerning the Agreement on Implementation of Article VI of GATT 1994 (Anti-Dumping Agreement)', 8 July.

TN/RL/W/26 (2002), 'Negotiating Group on Rules', Second Submission of India—(Anti-Dumping Agreement), 17 October.

TN/RL/W/27 (2002), 'United States to the WTO Negotiating Group on Rules', 22 October.

TN/RL/W/29 (2002), 'Negotiating Group on Rules—Third Contribution to Discussion of the Negotiating Group on Rules on Anti-Dumping Measures', Paper from Brazil; Chile; Colombi[.../]zerland; Thailand; and Turkey, 15 January.

TN/RL/W/44 (2003), 'Negotiating Group on Rules—Treatment of Confidential and Non-Confidential Information under Article 6.5 of the WTO Anti-Dumping Agreement', Submission by Australia, 24 January.

TN/RL/W/66 (2003), 'Negotiating Group on Rules—Proposal of the People's Republic of China on the Negotiation on Anti-Dumping', 6 March.

TN/RL/W/67 (2003), 'Negotiating Group on Rules—Negotiations on Anti-Dumping and Subsidies', Reflection Paper of the European Communities on a Swift Control Mechanism for Initiations, 7 March.

TN/RL/W/72 (2003), 'Negotiating Group on Rules—Identification of Certain Major Issues under the Anti-Dumping and Subsidies Agreements', Submission by the United States, 19 March.

TN/RL/W/81 (2003), 'Negotiating Group on Rules—Communication from Argentina', Clarifying and Improving Disciplines under the Agreement on Implementation of Article VI of the 1994 (Anti-dumping Agreement), 23 April.

TN/RL/W/86 (2003), 'Negotiating Group on Rules—General Contribution to the Discussion of the Negotiating Group on Rules on the Anti-dumping Agreement', Submission from Australia, 30 April.

TN/RL/W91 (2003), 'Negotiating Group on Rules—Like Product within the Meaning of the WTO Anti-dumping Agreement—Submission by Australia', 1 May.

TN/RL/W/97 (2003), 'Negotiating Group on Rules—Submission from Canada Respecting the Agreement on Implementation of Article VI of the GATT 1994 (the Anti-Dumping Agreement)', 28 January.

TN/RL/W/111 (2003), 'Negotiating Group on Rules—Korea's View on the Improvement of the Sunset System', Submission of the Republic of Korea, 27 May.

TN/RL/W/113 (2003), 'Negotiating Group on Rules—Proposal on Prohibition of Zeroing', Paper from Brazil; Chile; Columbia; Costa Rica; Hong Kong, China; Israel; Japan; Korea; Me[.../]pore; Switzerland and Thailand', 6 July.

TN/RL/W/118 (2003), 'Negotiating Group on Rules—Proposal on Price Undertakings', Paper from Brazil; Chile; Colombia; Costa Rica;

Hong Kong, China; Japan; Korea; Norway; the Se/...]atsu; Switzerland and Thailand, 12 June.

TN/RL/W/130 (2003), 'Negotiating Group on Rules—Further Issues Identified under the Anti-Dumping and Subsidies Agreements for Discussion by the Negotiating Group on Rules—Co/...]ication from the United States', 20 June.

TN/RL/W/146 (2004), 'Negotiating Group on Rules—Proposal on Issues related to Affiliated Parties', Paper from Brazil; Colombia; Costa Rica; Hong Kong, China; Japan; Korea;/...]n and Matsu; and Thailand 11 March.

TN/RL/W/150 (2004), 'Negotiating Group on Rules—Proposals on Determination of Normal Value', Paper from Chile; Colombia; Costa Rica; Hong Kong, China; Japan; Korea, Republic o/...]Kinmen and Matsu; and Thailand, 16 April.

TN/RL/W/156 (2004), 'Negotiating Group on Rules—New Shipper Reviews (ADA Article 9.5)', Communication from the United States, 4 June.

TN/RL/W/158 'Negotiating Group on Rules—Proposals on Fair Comparison, Paper from Chile; Colombia; Costa Rica; Hong Kong; China; Japan; Korea; Republic of Norway; S[...]inmen and Matsu; and Thailand, 28 May (The Friends of the Anti-dumping Negotiations).

TN/RL/W/174 (2005), 'Negotiating Group on Rules—Public Interest', Paper from Chile, Costa Rica, Hong Kong, China; Israel, Japan, Korea, Rep. of; Norway, Switzerland, the Separ/...] Kinmen and Matsu and Thailand', 29 April.

TN/RL/W/194 (2005), 'Negotiating Group on Rules—Further Explanation of the Public Interest Proposal', Paper from Hong Kong, China', 17 November.

TN/RL/W/205 (2006), 'Negotiating Group on Rules—Circumvention', Paper from Hong Kong, China, 21 April.

TN/RL/W/205/Rev.1 (2006), 'Negotiating Group on Rules—Circumvention', Paper from Chile and Hong Kong, China—Revision, 27 April.

Tortora, M. (2003), 'Special and Differential Treatment and Development Issues in the Multilateral Trade Negotiations: The Skeleton in the Closet', *WEB/CDP/BKGD/16*, UNCTAD, Geneva.

Trebilcock M.J. and R. Howse (1995), *The Regulation of International Trade*, Routledge, London.

___ (1999), *The Regulation of International Trade*, Second Edition, Routledge, London.

Trebilcock, M.J. and J. Quinn (1979), 'The Canadian Anti-Dumping Act: A Reaction to Professor Slayton', *Canadian-US Law Journal*, Vol. 2, p. 101.

Tyson, L.D. (1992), 'Who's Bashing Whom: Trade Conflict in High-Technology Industries', Institute for International Economics, Washington, D.C.

UNCTAD (1999), African Development in a Comparative Perspective, published for an on behalf of the United Nations, *Sales No. GV.E. 99.0.21*, New York and Geneva.

_____ (2000), Impact of Anti-Dumping and Countervailing Duty Actions, *UNCTAD Paper No. TD/B/COM.1/EM.14/2*.

_____ (2003), 'Subsided in Countervailing Measures', *Module Volume 3.7* in the Course on *Dispute Settlement in International Trade, Investment and Intellectual Property*, UNCTAD/EDM/MISC 232/Add. 15, United National New York and Geneva, 2003.

_____ (2004), 'The Least Developed Countries Report 2004—Linking International Trade with Poverty Reduction', UN, New York, and Geneva.

US (2002), 'Basic Concepts and Principles of the Trade Remedy Rules', Communication from the USITC website *http://usitc.gov/7ops/ad_cvd_orders.htm*

USITC (1995), 'The Economic Effects of Antidumping and Countervailing Duty Orders and Suspension Agreements', USITC, Washington, D.C.

Venables, A. (1991), 'Trade Policy Under Imperfect Competition: A Numerical Assessment', in P. Krugman and M.A. Smith (eds), *Empirical Assessment of Strategic Trade Policy*, Chicago University Press, Chicago.

Vermulst, E. (1987), *Anti-dumping Law and Practice in the United States and the European Community*, North Holland, Amsterdam.

_____ (1997), 'Adopting and Implementing Anti-dumping Laws: Some Suggestions for Developing Countries', *Journal of World Trade*, Vol. 31, No. 2, pp. 5–24.

_____ (1999), 'Competition and Anti-dumping: Continued Peaceful Co-existence?', *http://www.feem.it/web/activ/wp/abs99/67-99.pd*

_____ (2000), 'Anti-dumping and Countervailing Duties' *Positive Agenda and Future Trade Negotiations*, United Nations Conference of Trade and Developments, United Nations, Geneva and New York.

_____ (2005), 'The 10 Major Problems with the Anti-dumping Instrument in the European Community', *Journal of World Trade*, Vol. 39, No. 1, pp. 105–13.

_____ (2000), 'EC Countervailing duty law and Practice revisited', *Legal Issues of Economic Intergration*, Vol. 27, No. 3, pp. 217–38.

Vermulst, E. and B. Driessen (1997), 'New Battle Lines in the Anti-Dumping War, Recent movements on the European Front', *Journal of World Trade*, Vol. 31, No. 3, pp. 513–158.

Vermulst, E. and P. Waer (1991), 'The Calculation of Injury Margins in EC Anti-Dumping Proceedings', *Journal of World Trade*, Vol. 25, No. 6, pp. 5–42.

Viner, J. (1923), *Dumping: A Problem in International Trade*, University of Chicago Press, Chicago, IL.

Waincymer, J. (2001), 'An Australian and USA Free Trade Agreement: Opportunities and Challenges: Implications for Anti-Dumping and Countervailing', *Paper Presented at Hyatt Hotel*, Canberra, 21 June 2001.

Wang, J. (1999), 'A Critique of the Application to China of the Non-market Economy Rules of Antidumping Legislation and Practice of the European Union', *Journal of World Trade*, Vol. 33, No. 3, June, pp. 117–45.

Whalley, J. (1999), 'Special and Differential Treatment in the Millennium Round', *Working Paper No. 30/99*, Centre for the Study on Globalisation and Regionalisation, University of Warwick, May.

Willig, R.D. (1998), 'Economic Effects of Antidumping Policy', in R.Z. Lawrence (ed.), *Brookings Trade Forum*, Brookings Institution Press, Washington, D.C.

Wooton I. and M. Zanardi (2002), 'Trade and Competition Policy: Anti-Dumping versus Anti-Trust', Discussion Paper in Economics, Number 02–06, University of Glasgow; Also Published in K.E. Choi and J.C. Hartigam (eds) (2004), *Handbook of International Trade*, Economic and Legal Analyses of Trade Policy and Institutions Blackwell Handbooks in Economics, Blackwell Publishing Malden, USA, pp. 383–402.

World Bank (2000), 'World Development Indicators', World Bank

——— (2002), Available at *http://www1.worldbank.org/wbiep/trade/*

WTO (1998), 'Observations on the Distinction Between Competition Laws and Anti-Dumping Rules', submitted by the US, *WT/WGTCP/W/88*, Geneva, p. 7.

——— (1999), *Background Document: High Level Symbolism on Trade and Development: 17–18 March, 1999*, World Trade Organization Secretariat—Development Division, Geneva.

——— (2001), 'The Generalised System of Preferences: A Preliminary Analysis of the GSP Schemes in the Quad', *WT/COMTD/W/93*, 5 October.

——— (2002), 'Information on the Utilisation of Special and Differential Treatment Provisions', Note by the Secretariat Committee on Trade and Development, WTO, Geneva, *WT/COM/TE/W/77/Rev. 1/Add. 4.*

——— (2003), 'Negotiating Group on Rules: Note by the Chairman', *TN/RL/W/ 143,* Geneva, Switzerland, 22 August 2003.

——— (2005), *International Trade Statistics 2005*, World Trade Organization, Geneva.

Yano, K. (1999), 'Thirty Years of Being A Respondent in Antidumping Proceedings', *Journal of World Trade*, Vol. 33, pp. 31–47.

Youssef, H. (1999), 'Special and Differential Treatment for Developing Countries in the WTO', Working Paper No. 2, South Centre, Geneva.

Zanardi, M. (2000), 'Antidumping Law as a Collusive Device,' Boston College Working Paper 487, Boston, MA.

_____ (2004), 'Antidumping: What are the Numbers to Discuss at Doha?', *The World Economy*, Vol. 27, No. 3, pp. 403–33.

_____ (2006), 'Antidumping: A problem in international trade', *European Journal of Political Economy*, Vol. 22/3, September, p. 591.

Index

'factor of production method', in the
US 75–6
'facts available' rules 73, 74, 210–1
fair comparison 212
  allowance for duty drawback
  213–14
  burden of proof 214
  calculation of export prices 214
Fielding, W.S. 52
Fisheries subsidies, WTO disciplines
  on 7
foreign direct investment (FDI),
  countries with, and domestic
  producers 84
free trade agreements (FTA) 167,
  190, 225
'The Friends of Anti-dumping' (FANs)
  64, 65, 200, 204, 211
  on 'model matching' for like
  products 203

game theory 162
General Agreement on Tariffs and
  Trade (GATT), 1947 3, 13
  Article of 1 of 59
  Article 6 of 13–20, 53–4, 55, 64,
  75
  Article 16 of 53
  Article 18 of 56, 246
  Article 36 of 56
  Article 37 of 56, 57, 103
  Article 38 of 56
  'Enabling Clause' in 59
  formation of 52–4
  S& D treatment in the 230
  and reduction in trade barriers
  263
  on trade subsidies 20–4, 32
  Working Party, 1970 59
Generalized System of Preferences
  (GSP) 110, 247, 250

'generally accepted accounting
  principles' (GAAP) 70
Geneva Round 55
GIMELEC judgement 85
Global anti-dumping database 219
globalization 1, 39, 52, 200
Grain Corn inquiry 242
'grey-area measure' 35, 36
Guatemala-Mexico case, of Grey
  Portland Cement case 223

Haberler panel 56
'hard reform proposal', on reform of
  Anti-dumping Agreement 184,
  185–200
Havana Charter 53, 246
Hoekman-Mavroidis proposal, two-tier
  approach 195–6
Hong Kong Ministerial Declaration 7
Hot-rolled Steel Plates case, Japan 85,
  89
Hot-Rolled Steel Production
  originating case, India 66, 85
import, restriction 197, 198
  share, de minimis 256–7
  substitution trade policies 21, 23,
  61
  surge, impact on anti-dumping
  filings 178

India, anti-dumping cases against, by
  US and EU, and impact on trade
  127–9
  anti-dumping initiation by
  118–19, 127, 128–9
  anti-dumping investigations against
  87, 88
  dumping margin for companies in
  255
industrial policies, leading to dumping
  153

suggestions for strengthening
254–63
'Special Import Measures Act' (SIMA)
Canada   237, 238, 242
Stainless Steel Wire Rod case, India
81
Steel Plate case, India   74
Steel Ropes and Cables case   66
Steel Wires case, India   100
strategic behaviour, kinds of   163
'strategic dumping'   156, 157, 159,
162–3, 167, 187
two-tier approach to   193,
194–5
'strategic Trade Theory' framework
162
structural adjustment   198
subsidies, in trade   20–1, 30, 32, 40
actionable   22
export   21, 23
import substitution   21, 23
non-actionable   22
prohibited   21
'specific'   21
Subsidies Code   21
Sunset Clause   63
'Sunset Review', of anti-dumping
orders, Uruguay Round   102
in US   123
Reviews   224–6
'super-additivity effect'   91
supranational institutional
arrangement, creation of   190–1
'surrogate method'   75–6
Swift Dispute Control Mechanism, of
EC   223
Synthetic Fibre Polyester case, India
80
Synthetic Fibre Ropes case, India
94–5

Taiwan, anti-dumping law in, 1984
112
'target dumping' cases   83
targeted countries, of anti-dumping
cases   133–6
tariff(s)   115–16, 172–3, 179
concessions   53, 54
elimination of   13
escalation of   2
peak   2
TBT   261
Textile Monitoring Body (TMB)   108
Third World nations   1
Tokyo Code   60, 61, 72, 93
Tokyo Round, (1973–9)   15, 55,
59–61, 70, 246–8
Agreement   63, 103
Declaration 1973   230
on price undertakings   98
reforms on injury analysis   253
on special and differential
treatment   103
on standards for causal link   93
trade, agreements, WTO provisions'
application for regional   7
barriers, by developed countries
2
deflection, and developing
countries   127, 131
distorting subsidies   154
impediments   3
liberalization   1, 2, 148, 168, 172
and benefits to developing
countries   179, 181, 253
policies   1, 188
flexibility in   197, 198
and sustainable development   2
weighted measures, by developed
and developing countries   125,
127